The Economics of Singularities of Science Elucidated with Buddhist Thoughts

S. Niggol Seo

The Economics of Singularities of Science Elucidated with Buddhist Thoughts

palgrave
macmillan

S. Niggol Seo
Lamajel Ling
Chiang Mai, Thailand

ISBN 978-3-031-69117-1 ISBN 978-3-031-69118-8 (eBook)
https://doi.org/10.1007/978-3-031-69118-8

This Palgrave Macmillan imprint is published by the registered company Springer Nature Switzerland AG.
The registered company address is: Gewerbestrasse 11, 6330 Cham, Switzerland

To Lumo Tso (ཀླུ་མོ་མཚོ།) who will be born near Tsongkha Valley in Amdo on November 19, 1989, and who will appear to me as Snake Girl Lake with many auspicious signs.

Gaden Je

Preface

The optimism about what science can achieve for humanity is as high as it has ever been while the fear about what science can cause on humanity is also as high as it has ever been. This book is about the crossroads of the two attitudes reflected upon through the ancient but perfect wisdom laid out by the Buddha, the omniscient one, and especially Lama Tsongkhapa, the Buddha in the Land of Snows (Fig. P.1). For that, this book is entitled The Economics of Singularities of Science Elucidated with Buddhist Thoughts.

This book clarifies the five science disciplines that are at the frontiers of science, each of which is full of exciting novel experiments, and broadly encompass the entire range of science. The five are the physics of relativity, quantum mechanics, mRNA virology, stem cell research, and neuroscience. From the five disciplines, this book explains the five experiments at the frontiers: the Large Hadron Collider (LHC) experiment, the Artificial Intelligence (AI) development, an mRNA virus generation, a stem-cell-based cloning and organ regeneration, and a consciousness generation from pure matter, respectively.

From each of the five experiments, this book puts forth a truly catastrophic consequence, which is called a singularity in this book, based on the respective scientists' works. The five singularities are the LHC strangelet catastrophe from the field of physics, the AI robot supremacy from the field of quantum mechanics, a fatal worldwide pandemic from the mRNA virology research, a human cloning catastrophe from the stem cell research, and a consciousness-generation catastrophe from the neuroscience.

Fig. P.1 Je Rinpoche (1357–1419), sixteenth century

The economics of singularities does not exist yet. However, in the recent decade, some economists presented a novel theory regarding a policy decision on a truly catastrophic event at the scale of "terminating all the planetary civilizations as we know them." This analysis was focused on the probability distribution of such an event which is referred to as a fat-tail distribution. The upshot of their conclusion is that the planet's community should prevent such an event at all cost, that is, regardless of the cost. This policy is known to economists as a precautionary principle.

Should then all these exciting scientific experiments be put to a stop, following the advice of the fat-tail economics or the precautionary principle? Nobody, as far as the present author is aware, has called for such a drastic political intervention regarding any of these scientific experiments. Even the critics of these experiments who are scientists themselves did not argue that far.

In this book, the present author tackles these major scientific experiments and singularities with the 2657-year-old Buddhist thought system. As the book will reveal to readers, this ancient philosophy provides a far more flexible and reasoning approach to explicating what is advancing in these experiments and what is at stake. As readers will certainly get to eventually, these experiments are an anthropogenic effort to get to the most puzzling questions of humankind since its coming into being. That is, the questions of life and death, of diseases and suffering, of how a human being is able to perceive and think, of where the limit of the universe or the beginning of the universe is. These questions are also what has perplexed the Western philosophers for a long time, including Descartes, Spinoza, and Schopenhauer.

Although, as this book will elaborate, all of these questions were and have been analyzed acutely by Buddhist philosophers including Buddha Shakyamuni and Je Rinpoche, they were never brought into the sphere of such intense material pursuits as being unfolded in the science today. In Buddhism, these questions were all matters of mind. In science, these questions are purely matters of pure matter. Resorting to the enlightened view of the Buddha, Buddhists were able to approach and explore these matters with little obsession.

I am sure that the preceding paragraph will be immensely perplexing to many readers of this book including scientists, economists, philosophers, and some Buddhists as well. This book will clarify the Buddhist perspectives on the full range of the matters of scientific importance to contemporary scientists and economists. Ultimately, it is hoped that this book will clear away the doubts and bewilderments from the readers' hearts.

To give you a glimpse, the Buddhist principle or the Buddhist door for the readers to reach there is the tenet of Mind-only. The Buddha, the Omniscient One, declares that "all things, physical and mental, are mind-only." I ran into this phrase at the age of 10. Since then, it had always bothered me: what does that mean? I may have given hundreds of interpretations to that pithy phrase over the next 40 years, all of which seemed to fail to truly explain the true meaning of the phrase. When I heard the exposition by Lama Tsongkhapa (Fig. P.1), who is renowned as Manjushri, the Buddha of Wisdom to Tibetans, I finally realized the true meaning of it. That was at the age of 50.

I give the true meaning of it to the scientist and economist friends through this book. If you are still curious about why this phrase matters that much in this book, which is quite natural, consider how neuroscientists are so enthused in the idea of creating the mind; how AI robots cannot be superior to humans as long as they do not possess "mental functions"; how a human cloning cannot be successful at all without uncovering the mind-body associations; how the universe's end or beginning cannot be understood without first understanding how the mind began. I am just giving you a glimpse here at the door, which is rather remotely located at this point, to the realm of Buddhist thoughts.

Reading through this book, readers will be able to see inside that door snow mountains in high peaks, grasslands scattered with wild flowers, lands and lakes touching an azure sky with white clouds, red hawks, mountain passes, meandering rivers which are endless, turquoise lakes, palaces of splendor, gold and silver monasteries, bustling cities with busy people, grand wish prayer festivals, and markets with precious jewels. You may meet a sixteen-year-old bald-headed boy on a pass road. If you would ask him about all of these, he may tell you, smiling and carefree, that it is okay for you to go on as long as you know where you are going.

In closing, I would like to express my gratitude to late Harvard economist Martin Weitzman from whose research in 2007 the present author gained the first view as an economist into the frontier science experiments and Yale economist Robert Shiller for his analysis on great crashes of markets. I am thankful to Wyndham H. Pain, the commissioning editor of this book, who expressed his interest in publishing the present author's work on AI singularities. As they foresaw it, this subject will become an elegant area of economics soon, I am certain. Lastly, I am thankful to the editorial and production teams at Palgrave Macmillan whose efforts have made this book even better.

Lamajel Ling, Thailand
June 2024

Gaden Je

Contents

About the Author

S. Niggol Seo [Also referred to as *Gaden Je* in the book] is a natural resource economist who specializes in the study of global warming and globally shared goods. He was born in a remote rural village in South Korea in the lunar month of February in 1972. After obtaining a Ph.D. Degree in Environmental and Natural Resource Economics from Yale University in May 2006, he held professor positions in the UK, Spain, and Australia from 2006 to 2015. Since 2003, he worked on various World Bank projects on climate change in Africa, Latin America, and Asia. He received an Outstanding Applied Economic Perspectives and Policy Article Award from the Agricultural and Applied Economics Association (AAEA) in Pittsburgh in June 2011. He has written 14 books on climate change, pandemics, globally shared goods, and recently Buddhism. He is the editor-in-chief of the *Handbook of Behavioral Economics and Climate Change* published by Edward Elgar in 2022. He is the author of the most recent books *Buddha, Wisdom and Economics* published in January 2024 and *Protecting Nature with Buddha's Wisdom* published in July 2024.

S. Niggol Seo founded the Lamajel Ling on the winter solstice of 2022. He is also referred to as *Gaden Je* in this book.

List of Figures

List of Tables

CHAPTER 1

An Introduction to Singularities of Science and Economics with Buddhist Thoughts

1 Introduction

Since the turn of the twentieth century, science has made notable advances in many areas of importance to human life and the planet. From the early engineering revolutions such as the light bulb by Edison and the Alternating Current (AC) motor by Tesla to the theoretical innovations such as Einstein's 1905 papers, the science and engineering endeavors since then have turned out to be meaningful in many areas of people's life over the course of time (USEIA 2024; Einstein 1905a, 1905b, 1905c).

By the turn of the twenty-first century, there arose scientists who questioned frontier science experiments and elaborated the truly catastrophic possibilities that such experiments could bring. The concerns that they express are not a high-risk event, nor a really high-risk event, but an event that is so utterly destructive and irrecoverable for good. This risk is expressed through such expressions as "the end of all planetary civilizations" or "the end of the present universe" or "the last achievement of humankind" by varied groups of scientists (Turco et al. 1983; Jaffe et al. 2000; Posner 2004; Kurzweil 2005; Peskin 2008; Mills et al. 2008; Weitzman 2009; Hawking et al. 2014; NYT 2023b). In a more formal way, this risk is expressed in mathematics as a singularity, whose term originated from the theoretical mathematics and was made popular in the ecological sciences (Poincaré 1880–1890; Thom 1972, 1975). By the early

S. N. Seo, *The Economics of Singularities of Science Elucidated with Buddhist Thoughts*,
https://doi.org/10.1007/978-3-031-69118-8_1

twenty-first century, this term was used by some scientists to refer to an existential threat posed by Artificial Intelligence (AI) (Kurzweil 2005; Hawking et al. 2014).

Put in simple terms, singularity refers to the point of time beyond which the world as we know it no longer exists or the point of time beyond which the world as we know it turns into a completely different one unrecognizable from the current world. As soon as the singularity point is crossed, there is no coming back to the previous state, that is, irreversible (Zeeman 1977; Seo 2018).

What are these catastrophes that scare the alarmist scientists, who are nonetheless highly rational, so much? They are worried about a specific science experiment or another at the forefront of science, all of which are among the largest-scale science experiments ever conducted by humankind. To give perhaps the best-known example to the public, the development of artificial intelligence (AI) robots is one of them. The robots are in one way like the humanoid robots such as the Pepper developed by SoftBank or the Optimus developed by Tesla (SoftBank 2019; Tesla 2023). They can overwhelm a human's physical capacities, even including speaking many languages. The robots are in another way a purely information machine such as the ChatGPT robot (OpenAI 2023). The Chatbots can give the answers to any question you might have as fast as one can imagine. They too can overwhelm a human's capacities of learning and thinking (Wadhwa 2022; NYT 2023a).

Can the robots really overwhelm humanity to induce a truly catastrophic event? According to the longtime AI and robot scientists, they believe so and further than that they believe that such a future is imminent. "The singularity is near" is what a Google scientist pronounced back in 2005 (Kurzweil 2005). That the end of humanity as we know it by a super-intelligent robot will occur within a decade is what the eminent AI scientists at UC Berkeley, MIT, and Stephen Hawking proclaimed back in 2014 (Hawking et al. 2014). If you think that their doomsday predictions are baseless, just have a peek at today's world in which the Russia-Ukraine war and the Israel-Hamas war are both being dominated by the robots, called the Lethal Autonomous Weapons (LAWS) by the international community.

On the other hand, the optimism about what science can do for humankind appears to have never been higher than today. The scientific research and engineering outcomes are often translated into medical sciences, disease treatments, and health care, which directly affect the lives of people, especially their health and long life (Alison et al. 2002; Pardi et al. 2018). Such optimism can be glimpsed through the changes in the life expectancy of people at birth during the past 70 years, which are drawn in Fig. 1.1. The figure depicts the change in the life expectancy of people at birth from 1950 to 2022 relying on the United Nations Population Prospects data (UN Population Division 2022). The drops in 2020–2022 at the right end of the graph are due to COVID-19 deaths (Seo 2022a).

There is a remarkable increase in the life expectancy of people through the past seven decades since World War II, which can be verified in the respective trend of South Korea, Thailand, and India. The life expectancy of Thai people was about 42 years in 1950, which has steadily increased to reach 80 years in 2020. The similar has occurred in India and South Korea. In North America and Europe, the life expectancy has increased from around 65 years to 80 years during this period.

The fear of science-driven catastrophes is as high as it has ever been, while the optimism about scientific achievements is as high as it has ever been at the time of this writing. From the social milieu such as this, the

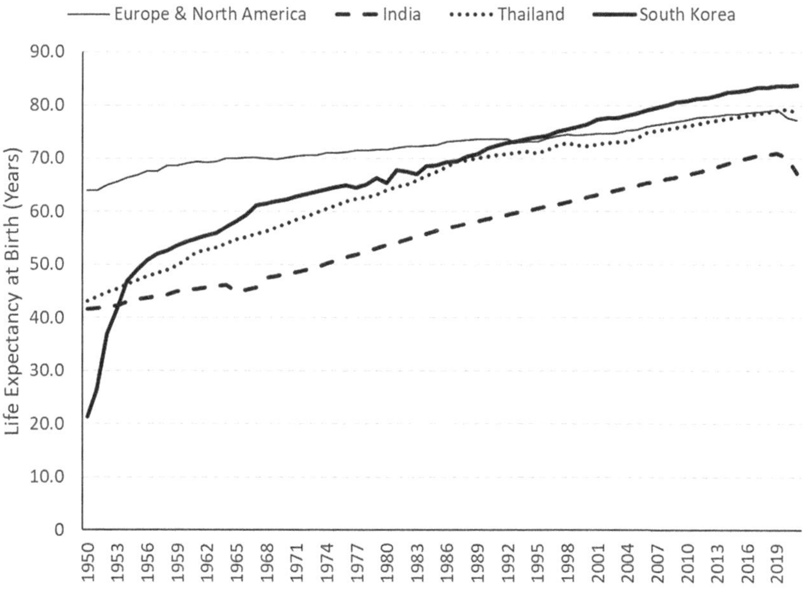

Fig. 1.1 Life expectancy at birth during the past 70 years

present author will provide a succinct but comprehensive review of the five science disciplines, to be enumerated shortly, and the singularities that can be associated with each of these disciplines. This book will also offer an exposition of the economic analyses relevant to addressing these events.

At the heart of the book, however, lies a critical investigation of the contemporary science endeavors through the mirror of a detailed analysis of the five singularity events which are one salient aspect of contemporary science (Newton 1687; Darwin 1859). This critical investigation is conducted through the viewpoints of the ancient thought system which has survived and thrived till this day since its first appearance 2667 years ago set forth by Buddha Shakyamuni (Sutra on Setting the Wheel of Dharma in Motion).[1]

From one point of view, some readers will feel that this book offers a titanic clash between modernism and the ancient but sacred tradition. As you will realize throughout this book, that is indeed the case. However, this book will tell you without any uncertainty that Buddhism is not against science, nor science is against Buddhist thoughts. Both traditions share much common ground and further may be understood to be complementary in many situations, for example, both traditions' reliance on rationality and logic (Nagarjuna's Reasoning Sixty, Dharmakirti's Valid Cognition, Lama Tsongkhapa's Ocean of Reasoning).[2]

At the personal level, this book is a summary and synthesis of my thoughts through the five disciplines of science since I first heard the Buddhist wisdom "All things are mind-only" at the age of 10 (Ten Grounds Sutra). A detailed account of this early experience is given in Chap. 9. Since then, I have always wondered what that phrase means. It has bothered me throughout my life. This is the culmination of the personal pursuits for the past 40 years to understand that crisp but powerful phrase.

The present author was able to clearly without doubt understand the meaning of that phrase at the age of 50 through the encounters with the marvelous writings of Lama Tsongkhapa who is known to be the Buddha of the Land of Snows [Gang-chen in Tibetan] or the Vajradhara Buddha

[1] The Buddhist Pali Canon, Tibetan Kangyur and Tengyur, and the Chinese Dazangjing are compiled separately as Appendix at the end of the book.

[2] Throughout the book, the Buddhist commentaries are cited by an author name and a two-letter short name of the text.

to the Tibetans (Panchen Lama's Ritual, Thubten Jinpa 2019).[3] This book relies on the wisdom of emptiness elucidated by Je Lama, the gentle protector [Jam-goen Lama in Tibetan] (Lama Tsongkhapa's True Eloquence, Ocean of Reasoning, Stages of the Path).

2 Scientists' Pursuits

Science refers to the study of matter in a rational manner. Put slightly differently, science is the rational study of the physical world. The most fundamental disciplines of science are physics, biology, chemistry, and medical sciences, where medical sciences overlap biology to a substantial extent. Science is often defined to include engineering which is the study of how to make all sorts of things work. A broader definition of science is the STEM (Sciences, Technology, Engineering, and Medicine), which is a widely used term in education (National Academies 2024).

To encompass the entire spectrum of scientific inquiries, this book examines the five disciplines of science which have captivated the public in the recent decades. The first is the relativity theory of physics. The second is quantum physics and mechanics. The third is mRNA virology and vaccinology. The fourth is stem cell research. The fifth is brain science or neuroscience of consciousness.

The theory of relativity is the modern physics theory put forth by Einstein in the early decades of the twentieth century (Einstein 1905a, 1905b, 1905c). Einstein assumes that the speed of light is fixed and everything else can be explained relative to the light, from which he went on to put forth special relativity and general relativity (Einstein 1915a, 1915b). Relativity physics explains the beginning of the universe as a Big Bang (Lemaitre 1931; Hubble 1929). The Large Hadron Collider (LHC) experiments by the European Organization of Nuclear Research (CERN) is a frontier global collaborative physics experiment aimed at proving the Big Bang theory and, more broadly, relativity physics (CERN 2023). The LHC is a giant ring of superconducting magnets whose circumference is 27 km, built at the France-Switzerland border. Inside the LHC, particles run at the speed of light and are made to collide, replicating the state of the universe after the Big Bang. Through this experiment, physicists hope to find the secret of the universe, sometimes referred to as the God particle

[3] The Tibetan letters of these Tibetan words are compiled in the Appendix: Essential Words of Tibetan Buddhism.

(Dar et al. 1999; Jaffe et al. 2000). The discovery of the Higgs Boson, namely, the God particle, in 2013 resulted in the Nobel Prize in Physics in that year (Nobel Prize 2013).

Quantum physics and mechanics is another theory of physics, which is indeed a competing theory of physics or an alternative theory of physics against relativity physics. Early pioneers included Niels Bohr, Heisenberg, and Schrodinger, while Einstein notably opposed it (Heisenberg 1930; Schrodinger 1935; Einstein et al. 2015). Quantum physics is the study of behaviors of matter at the smallest possible level, such as electrons, photons, and quanta (Feynman et al. 2010; Caltech Exchange 2022). It is in contrast to relativity physics which is the study of the biggest things in human life, that is, the planets, the Sun, and the universe. Notwithstanding, quantum physics is also applicable to the biggest things and events such as the universe. What quantum physics truly is is explained by its protagonists through quantum principles such as the wave-particle duality, superposition, uncertainty principle, and entanglement (Carroll 2020; Al-Khalili 2020).

Quantum physics is often associated with artificial intelligence (AI) and AI robots. This is because many experts believe that quantum technology, resorting to such principles as entanglement, will make the computing system exceedingly faster. A successful quantum computer, if successful, will dramatically change the fate of the AI and AI robots. It will also dramatically alter the possibility of neuroscience, which aims to generate consciousness from pure matter (Ananthaswamy 2021; Wadhwa 2022; Forbes 2023). What these predictions foretell is the possibility of AI far exceeding the biological intelligence of a human being (Hawking et al. 2014).

The third is genetics and microbiology, more specifically mRNA (messenger Ribonucleic Acid) virology and vaccinology. Genetics is the study of life through the concept of genes. In genetics, a sentient being is simply a composite of genes such as DNA (Deoxyribonucleic Acid) and RNA (Pierce 2019). A particular application of it is in the field of virology and vaccinology especially through mRNA viruses and vaccines (Kariko et al. 2011; Pardi et al. 2018). This field is intricately related with humankind's fights against notorious diseases that have plagued it for so long (Potter 2001).

Illness owing to various diseases is one of the four fundamental sufferings explicated by Buddha Shakyamuni through numerous teachings such as the "Observations at the Four Gates" and the very first teaching given at Deer Park, Sarnath, after his full enlightenment (Buddha Carita,

Abhiniṣkramaṇa Sutra). So, virologists' works to eliminate long-feared diseases would be of interest to Buddhist philosophers (Medicine Buddha Sutra).

This area of science gained prominence among common people through the COVID-19 (Corona Virus Disease) pandemic during 2020 to 2023, which was caused by the mRNA virus named the SARS-CoV-2 virus (Weiss 2020). Although it might have been the most efficient virus in transmissibility to humans in history, it has not turned out to be most fatal in terms of the number of deaths during the four-year period (Potter 2001; Seo 2022a). This is largely attributed to the success of the mRNA vaccines developed in record time by the world's big pharmaceutical companies based on mRNA virologists' works (Kariko et al. 2011; Pardi et al. 2018). This work has received the Nobel Prize in Physiology or Medicine in 2023 (Nobel Prize 2023).

The fourth discipline also belongs to microbiology and cell biology, specifically, stem cell research. Microbiology is the study of life at the microorganism level while cell biology is the study of life at the cell level (Alberts et al. 2019). In brief, the stem cell is the root cell from which daughter cells can be grown (Alison et al. 2002). As such, stem cell research has become a prominent medical science area because it can grow in a laboratory the damaged bodily organs such as liver, kidney, nerve, and heart. This field of medicine is known as regenerative medicine (Atala et al. 2019).

Stem cell research is of two types depending upon where the stem cell is obtained. One is the embryonic stem cell which is obtained from the mothers' embryos (Thomson et al. 1998). The other is the non-embryonic stem cell such as the stem cells obtained from bone marrows, discarded umbilical cords after the baby's birth, or reprogrammed stem cells (Takahashi and Yamanaka 2006; Nobel Prize 2012). The embryonic stem cell is, however, far better for regenerative medicine since it is pluripotent (Atala et al. 2019).

Like mRNA virology, stem cell research offers a big hope for the ill who are suffering from defective inner organs such as liver, lung, kidney, intestines, etc. Further, it is a primary technology applied for cloning animals from their stem cells. From the first sheep Dolly cloning, many animals were cloned successfully since then, for example, dogs, cats, cows, horses, deer, goats, frogs, etc. (Campbell et al. 1996; NHGRI 2020).

The fifth area of science is neuroscience, which can be also called brain science. Neuroscience is the study of brains as pure matter, including the brain of a human being. It examines the physical characteristics of the brain but also the functions of the brain which constitute the mental activities of a person or an animal (Singer 1999; Purves et al. 2011).

Neuroscientists strive to answer all the daunting questions that Buddhists and Western philosophers have tried to answer for millennia with regard to mental functions, minds, and consciousness (Descartes 1637; Spinoza 1677; Schopenhauer 1818): how does a human think? How does a human feel? Where does the consciousness originate? How does a human control negative feelings and thoughts? How the world is perceived to exist? (Varela et al. 1992; Hayward and Varela 1992)

The basis of neuroscience is a neuron, of which there are 100 billion in number in an adult brain. From the neuronal connections, of which there are 60 trillion, scientists strive to explain all these questions about consciousness and mental activities (Pakkenberg and Gundersen 1997; Singer 1999). From such a basis, they also began a journey to produce a human consciousness. They contend that a human consciousness can arise in a laboratory from pure matter like, say, a clump of dirt (Tegmark 2015).

The five fields of endeavors of science thus described encompass the full range of modern science. All of these disciplines and experiments are forging ahead with great force with a variety of novel and intriguing research agendas on the table, some of which were explained above in this section. The present author will give a detailed exposition of each of the five disciplines in this book from Chaps. 4–8.

3 Singularities Science

This book tackles the five disciplines of science thus described. But the entirety of the five disciplines of science is beyond the scope of this single book. This book, notwithstanding, is able to string all the five disciplines of science together through a single concept of science: singularities. Relying on this innovative approach, this book is able to present the entire spectrum of science to readers in a single book.

A singularity is a mathematical term originally coming from the bifurcation theory of mathematics (Poincare 1880). It was then utilized as the core concept in the catastrophe theory in the latter half of the twentieth century which became very popular beyond mathematics and science (Thom 1972, 1975). The catastrophe theory was put forth by an ecological analysis in which a catastrophe is defined as an event or a point in time beyond which the biological/ecological system as people know it is destroyed for good (Zeeman 1977; Gilmore 1981).

The popularity of the terms singularity and catastrophe was at its peak during the 1980s and the early 1990s, after which it declined swiftly. In the early twenty-first century, it resurfaced in a big way alongside the proliferation of catastrophe theories and alarmist theories at that time (Kurzweil 2005). One of the areas where catastrophe theories flourished, which became prominent in the public discourses of the century, was global warming (Lenton et al. 2008; Weitzman 2009; Seo 2018, 2021).

This book analyzes the five science-driven singularities that were saliently put forth during the twenty-first century by numerous concerned experts, one for each of the five science disciplines described in the preceding section. They are the Large Hadron Collider (LHC) strangelet singularity from relativity physics; the AI and super-intelligent robot singularity relating to quantum physics; an mRNA virus singularity from virology and medicine; a human cloning and organ regeneration singularity through stem cell research; and a consciousness-generation singularity from neuroscience.

Let me give a brief introduction to each. The LHC experiment is a signature experiment of the twenty-first century from the discipline of physics, in particular relativity physics (CERN 2023). The singularity put forth by concerned scientists is as big as it can get. The formation of a dark matter, called a strangelet, from the LHC experiment accident will form a black hole, which then would, as predicted by some scientists, destroy not only the planet or the solar system, but the entire universe as we know it (Dar et al. 1999; Jaffe et al. 2000). Their predictions are not supported by all scientists (Ellis et al. 2008; Peskin 2008; Plaga 2009).

Such is the defining characteristic of a singularity event as defined by mathematics. In other words, the LHC-strangelet catastrophe is the clearest example of what the mathematical singularity looks like. It abruptly turns the current universe into a new state of the universe from which there is no returning, that is, irrecoverable for good (Thom 1972, 1975; Zeeman 1977).

Second, the AI and super-intelligent robot singularity is a familiar scenario to the general public, owing to the constant media coverage and numerous Hollywood films about it. This singularity may be realized from quantum physics and mechanics, in particular, the advances in quantum computing (Wadhwa 2022; Forbes 2023). The AI singularity is defined by scientists as the point in time in which the AI or robot intelligence equals the human intelligence (Kurzweil 2005; Hawking et al. 2014). There is no turning back from the robot supremacy after that point. The robots will only get better (NYT 2023a, 2023b).

The AI robots are developed in two tracks. One is the humanoid track such as SoftBank's the Pepper and the Tesla's Optimus (SoftBank 2019; Tesla 2023). The other is the AI information faceless robot such as the OpenAI's ChatGPT, more commonly called the Chatbot (OpenAI 2023). Each track can be described as leading to a singularity event.

Third, the mRNA virus singularity is perhaps the least known to the public yet. This singularity originates from mRNA genetics and virology. The possibility of an mRNA virology singularity was indicated through the COVID-19 pandemic's origin which still remains unresolved (WHO 2021; Seo 2022a). Critics point to the possibility that the SARS-COV-2 virus escaped from the Wuhan laboratory of virology where the partially US-funded Coronavirus research was underway. The type of research was, critiques argued, the gain-of-function research which is the research that artificially increases the virulence of the existing virus in order to develop an effective defense against it a priori (Wade 2024; USDOI 2024).

Owing to the exceptional or even unprecedented rate of transmission of the virus during 2020–2022 period, many prominent virologists stated that the virus cannot have originated from animals, that is, of a natural origin (Reuters 2021). The most prominent was Dr. Robert Redford who was the Director of the Centers for Disease Control and Prevention (CDC) at the time of the pandemic outbreak.

Ironically, the mRNA research was the one that ended the worldwide pandemic through its contributions to developing the mRNA vaccines (Kariko et al. 2011; Pardi et al. 2018; Azar 2020). Had it not been for the mRNA vaccines which had not existed until that time, the COVID-19 pandemic could have been truly catastrophic to humankind, perhaps, far exceeding the 1919 influenza pandemic's great tragedy (Potter 2001).

Fourth, a stem cell research singularity may emerge from the possibility of a human cloning or the possibility of replacing all inner organs of a human being (NIH 2009). The possibility of a human cloning is demonstrated frequently by scientists through animal cloning successes such as sheep, dogs, cats, horses, etc. (Campbell et al. 1996). Like the animal clones, it may become possible to produce human clones from a single embryo, which has not happened yet.

As soon as the technology becomes a reality, the society is bound to face great risk. Imagine the temptations that richest individuals will face upon the possibility of cloning themselves before the moment of death! Imagine the temptations that the society will face upon the possibility of replacing all the bodily organs of preeminent persons in the society before they die! For a variety of reasons which can be easily foreseen by anyone, nations will rush to utilize such technological possibilities.

Fifth, a neuroscience singularity may be difficult for casual observers to imagine at this point since it is just starting to float the idea of making consciousness out of pure matter (Tegmark 2015; Reardon 2020). A singularity event may occur through the consciousness creation experiments during which a defective consciousness or defective mental functions are given birth to (Quadrato et al. 2017; Trujillo et al. 2019; Giandomenico et al. 2019). A similar scenario can be said of the brain-reviving experiments after death (Vrselja et al. 2019).

It is possible that such beings of created minds interact with the people of natural minds through which the former starts to seriously influence the latter. The beings of created minds will likely be similar to a super-intelligent robot, if successful (NYT 2023a, 2023b; OpenAI 2023). In a more pernicious scenario, the experiments may give birth to the beings with a partially functioning brain. They would look like normal people outwardly but their mental functions would be partially damaged. From the society's perspective, many serious issues will ensue including ethics, politics, religion, and so on.

To emphasize again, each of the five singularities described above is a very low probability event. However, each of these is a truly catastrophic event. In economic or mathematical terms, each of these events has a fat-tail probability distribution or one similar to it (Schuster 1984; Weitzman 2009; Nordhaus 2011).

4 Singularities Economics

Economics is the science of the economy and markets, whose primary indicators are prices and values of the goods and services exchanged in the markets (Seo 2023, 2024a). It is very rare that economists would be concerned about the kinds of events that are described in this book, that is, the singularity events that are predicted to end the planet itself or even the universe. These singularities are not traded in any market!

Having said that, the economics of natural and man-made catastrophes is a lively field of research. The examples of such are the economic analyses of environmental disasters, of global warming, of hurricanes, and of various natural disasters (Nordhaus 1994; Hanemann 1994; Mendelsohn and Olmstead 2009; Seo and Bakkensen 2017). The primary economic instruments developed by economists to deal with these disaster events more effectively are insurances, bonds, and other financial instruments, for example, the US crop insurance against natural disasters, a flood insurance, a hurricane insurance, etc. (Seo 2018, 2021).

Another line of economic research that is pertinent to this book is the analysis of great market crashes. The great crash in 1929 of the US stock market, the Asian Financial Crisis of the 1990s, the subprime mortgage market crash of the USA in 2008 are the events that are subjects of such an analysis. The primary theory of these market crashes is the theory of bubble, which may also be called the theory of irrational exuberance. The proponents argue that the formation of a bubble and its eventual burst is propelled by personal psychology of jealousy. Everyone wants to replicate the successes of their neighbors, even if they are just rumors, by investing in an ever-higher risk asset, which propels a bubble and its burst (Shiller 2005; Seo 2022b).

A singularity economics emerged in 2009 when a Harvard economist Martin Weitzman published an article which proposed what he called a dismal theorem. To economists, it is perhaps better known as a fat-tail economics than a singularity economics (Weitzman 2009). In analyzing a climate policy, he argued that the climate change has the chance of "ending all the planetary civilizations as we know them." This phrase is exactly what the singularity refers to in mathematics and science and what the catastrophe theorists have been using for a long time (Thom 1972, 1975; Kurzweil 2005).

The economic component of his analysis was startling. The dismal theorem concludes that the human civilization should spend an infinite amount of dollars in order to prevent such a catastrophic event, even if the probability of such an event's realization is tiny. This policy proposal was called the generalized precautionary principle (Weitzman 2009). The dismal theorem is in essence a trade between the singularity and dollars proposed by Weitzman for which the humanity should place a bet.

The rationale for such a drastic policy intervention was the fat-tail distribution of the probability of climate change which he assumed. He argued that the probability distribution is not normally distributed, which is usually assumed in an economic analysis of a climate policy. As enunciated by the dismal theorem, the distribution is fat-tailed in that the probability of a planet-ending climate change cannot be reduced by any means because of deep uncertainty in climate change (Nordhaus 2011; Seo 2020).

The Weitzman theory did not succeed in convincing economists or policymakers that such an extreme climate change scenario such as a 20 °C climate warming is not unreasonable. Nor did he succeed in convincing them that the human civilization should spend unlimited resources to stop on-going climate change.

Notwithstanding, the dismal theorem has certainly opened the door to economists to the world of singularities. The singularities such as the five science-driven singularities discussed in this book. That is, if anyone has been a keen observer of this theory! To put it more modestly, the dismal theorem gives us a clue about how economists would deal with the five singularities. The economic interpretation can then be compared with the framework of Buddhist thoughts on these issues which is laid out by this book.

5 A Heartful Perspective from the Buddhist Thoughts

This book offers an analysis of the five singularity events driven by scientific pursuits and experiments from the Buddhist viewpoints. Some readers may view this book as a continuation of the present author's past works on catastrophes from the economics standpoints (Seo 2018, 2020, 2022a, 2022b). The present author relies on the vast Canons and commentaries of Buddhism since the appearance of Buddha Shakyamuni 2647 years ago in order to explicate these events of grave consequences, which are well preserved in the Pali language, the Chinese language, and the Tibetan language (Tipitaka, The Dege Edition of Tibetan Kangyur and Tengyur).[4]

Why? Some readers might wonder. The reason is simple. The present author is confident that the Buddhist thought system is especially apt and effective in elucidating these problems when properly applied, unlike any other in the human intellectual endeavors. To mention just one example of where the two intellectual endeavors intersect, neuroscientists' experiments to understand and create consciousness are not very much different from the Buddhists' 2600-year-old explorations into the minds and

[4] Refer to the Appendix for the Buddhist Sutras cited in this book from the Pali Canon and the Tibetan Kangyur and Tengyur.

consciousness of sentient beings, although the two traditions put forth starkly different views (Maha-nidana Sutta, Aryadeva's Four Hundred, Shantideva's Bodhisattva Way).

In particular, the present author relies on Lama Tsongkhapa's teachings and commentaries written over 600 years ago in Tibet, who is regarded as the Buddha in the Land of Snows (Thurman 1982; Thubten Jinpa 2019). The present author introduced him in the recent books entitled *Buddha, Wisdom and Economics* in the context of economics and *Protecting Nature with Buddha's Wisdom* in the context of nature philosophy (Seo 2024a, 2024b).

At a deeper level, my personal motivation to write this book may have arisen from one of the earliest experiences in my life. At the age of 10, I picked up a book in a children's library, which was the first ever book that I read: a children's book about a Buddhist monk with many pictures and drawings. The title of the book was *Everything is Mind-only* and the content of it was also about that doctrine (Ten Grounds Sutra, Flower Ornament, Asanga's Bodhisattva Stages, Compendium, Vasubandhu's Thirty). For over 40 years since then, the phrase has always followed me and bothered me: "What does that mean?" In my mind, I have put forth dozens of answers to that question and has heard from others dozens of explanations on that, but nothing was truly satisfying after all.

This book is a definitive answer by the present author to that enigmatic question for such a long time, which in turn is especially apposite to the scientists' pursuits in the contemporary world, as this book will demonstrate. The present author has attained a definitive answer to the question through the Lama Tsongkhapa's marvelous writings and teachings written over 600 years ago (Lama Tsongkhapa's Collected Works, Praise, Golden Rosary, Ocean of Reasoning, True Eloquence, Illuminating the Intent).

According to the grand synthesis of the Buddhist Paths referred to as the Great Stages of the Path [Lamrim in Tibetan], each of the 84,000 Dharma Teachings given by Buddha Shakyamuni is intended for a specific audience in terms of their mental capacities and propensities (Lama Tsongkhapa's Stages of the Path, Songs of Experience, Atisha's Lamp, Cutler and Newland 2000). According to this exposition, the teaching of Mind-only [*Semzam* in Tibetan, *Vijnanavada* in Sanskrit] is directed to those who have long cultivated strong attachments to the reality of things. Whatever they pursue, they cannot go without an undisputable solid reality or the truth of the things around us. To such an audience, Buddha explains that that is not the case after all. All things you see, hear, smell, taste, feel, and think are only arisen from your mind alone (Maitreya's Ornament Realization, Ornament Scripture, Lama Tsongkhapa's True Eloquence)!

The present author will provide a compendium of the Buddhist thoughts in Chap. 2, relying on the Lama Tsongkhapa's enlightened words who is reputed as Vajradhara Buddha who has elucidated the meaning of emptiness or realitylessness or truthlessness or identitylessness of all things, internal and external (Thurman 1984; Hopkins 2008; Thubten Jinpa 2021, Perfection of Wisdom Pronounced by Manjushri). This compendium will be written in the context of scientists' pursuits.

From Chaps. 3–8, after explaining the five singularities expounded by scientists, the present author will provide a brief presentation of the Buddhist perspectives in each chapter. Assembling all the pieces, the present author will then put forward a final synthesis of the Buddhist perspectives in Chap. 9, the final chapter. In that final chapter, I tell the story of the book that I picked up at the age of 10 and clarify how the teaching of "All Things are Mind-only" is a particularly apt framework for dealing with the question of science-driven singularities, both to the scientists as well as the Buddhists.

6 The Structure of the Book

This book is structured into five parts and nine chapters (Fig. 1.2). Part I is an introduction to the book.

Part II is a pithy introduction to Buddhist thoughts, which is done in Chap. 2. This chapter provides a brief and lucid exposition of the large literature of the Buddhist thoughts relying on the Lama Tsongkhapa's works. Je Lama, by which name he is known to Tibetans, is a leading philosopher in the Middle Way philosophy [Woomapa in Tibetan, Madhyamaka in Sanskrit] who established the Prasangika Middle Way School [Tel-gyu-wa in Tibetan] (Seo 2024a, 2024b, Nagarjuna's Fundamental Wisdom, Buddhapalita's Commentary, Chandrakirti's Lucid Exposition, Lama Tsongkhapa's True Eloquence). Lama Tsongkhapa is renowned for his profound synthesis of the entire range of Buddhist thoughts through his book known as *Lam-Rim-Chen-Mo* (Nagarjuna's Precious Garland, Atisha's Lamp).

Part III presents the economics literature on natural and man-made catastrophes which is germane to the analysis of the singularity events that are addressed in this book. This is done in Chap. 3. The economic analysis

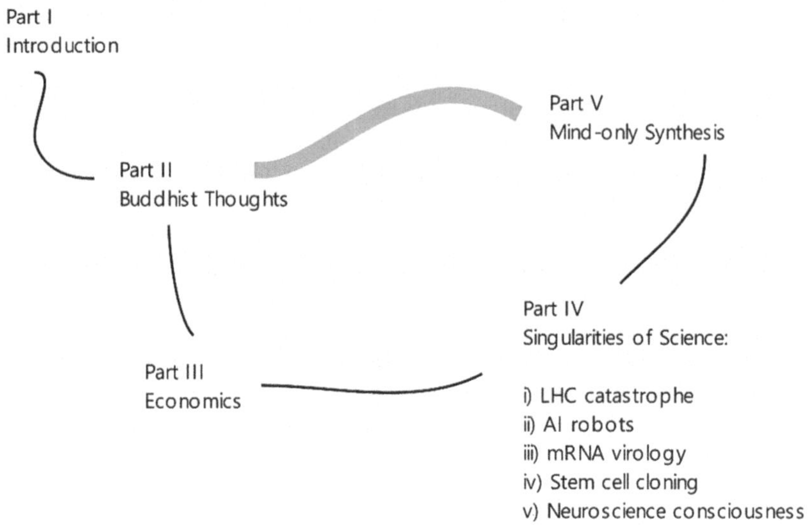

Fig. 1.2 The structure of the book

through the fat-tail events highlights the disparity as well as dissonance between the dramatic monetized consequence of a singularity event and the miniscule likelihood of such an unprecedented event.

Part IV provides a presentation of each of the five scientific singularities: the LHC strangelet singularity in Chap. 4, the AI robots singularity in Chap. 5, the mRNA virology singularity in Chap. 6, the stem cell research's cloning singularity in Chap. 7, and the neuroscience's consciousness generation singularity in Chap. 8. In each chapter, the present author also highlights the intersection between Buddhist thoughts and the respective science endeavor. For example, stem cell research as well as mRNA virology is put in contrast with the Buddhist explanations of life and death process (Khantipalo 1995, Fremantle and Trungpa 1975, Tibetan Book of the Dead, Kalacakratantra).

Part V provides a final synthesis of all the analyses offered in the book from the viewpoints of the Buddhist wisdom. The wisdom is specifically the wisdom of "all things are mind only" taught by Buddha Shakyamuni that has continued to be one of the most influential teachings of all time offered by him (Ten Grounds Sutra, Descent into Lanka Sutra, Unravelling the Intent Sutra).

7 The Road Ahead

Everything is well packed and prepared now for you to go on a journey offered in this book. In this fascinating book, you will come across a night sky, brightest stars and constellations, and endless universes. You will pass through the land of snow-covered mountains, clear water, and grasslands of wild flowers [*Gang-ri, Choo-dang-mo, Cha-tang* in Tibetan]. You will come across the tiniest of the tiny things imaginable such as an mRNA virus, a photon, and quanta. You will run into a humanoid robot, a human clone, an animal clone. You will land on glittering markets of lights, people, and money. And You will come across dead men walking or people of created consciousness. At the end of your journey, you will be greeted by a palm-sized golden Buddha sitting on a lotus smiling at you, telling "all things you have seen and ran into in your journey were just made up by your minds only" with such profundity and grandeur which will make perfect sense to you, temporarily so.

Bon Voyage!

References

Alberts B, Hopkin K, Johnson A, Morgan D, Roberts K, Walter P, and Heald R (2019) Essential Cell Biology (Sixth Edition). New York, NY: W.W. Norton & Company.

Alison MR, Poulsom R, Forbes S, and Wright NA (2002) An introduction to stem cells. The Journal of Pathology 197 (Special Issue on Stem Cells): 419–423.

Al-Khalili J (2020) The World According to Physics. Princeton, NJ: Princeton University Press.

Ananthaswamy A (2021) AI designs quantum physics experiments beyond what any human has conceived. Scientific American. Accessed from https://www.scientificamerican.com/article/ai-designs-quantum-physics-experiments-beyond-what-any-human-has-conceived/

Aryadeva (2nd century). Four Hundred Stanzas. Catuḥśatakaśāstra. Bstan bcos bzhi brgya pa. Toh 3846, dbu ma tsha.[5]

Asanga (ca. 4th century). Compendium of the Universal Vehicle. Mahāyānasaṃgraha. Theg pa chen po bsdus pa. Toh 4048, sems tsam ri.

Asanga (ca. 4th century) Stages of the Bodhisattva. Bodhisattvabhumi. Byang chub sems dpa'i sa. Toh 4037. sems tsam wi.

[5] Toh means Tohoku University Catalogue. Tohoku University (ed.) (1934). A Complete Catalogue of the Tibetan Buddhist Canons, Sde-dge Edition, Tohoku University, Japan.

Atala A, Lanza R, Mikos AG, and Nerem R (eds.) (2019) Principles of Regenerative Medicine (3rd Edition). Amsterdam, NL: Academic Press.
Atisha Dipankara Srijnana (982–1054). Bodhipathapradīpa. A Lamp for the Path to Enlightenment. Byang chub lam gyi sgron ma.
Azar II AM (2020) How Operation Warp Speed delivered a COVID vaccine in record time. Fox News. Published on 12 December 2020. Accessed from https://www.foxnews.com/opinion/hhs-azar-operation-warp-speed-covid-vaccine-record-time
Bhikkhu Khantipalo (1995) The Wheel of Birth and Death. Access to Insight. Accessed from https://www.accesstoinsight.org/lib/authors/khantipalo/wheel147.html#fn-6
Buddhapalita (ca. 5th century). Commentary. Buddhapālitamūlamadhyamakavṛtti. Dbu ma rtsa ba'i 'grel pa buddha pā li ta. Toh 3842, dbu ma tsa.
Caltech Science Exchange (2022) What is Quantum Physics. Accessed from https://scienceexchange.caltech.edu/topics/quantum-science-explained/quantum-physics
Campbell KH, McWhir J, Ritchie WA, and Wilmut I (1996) Sheep cloned by nuclear transfer from a cultured cell line. Nature 380 (6569): 64–66.
Chandrakirti (7th century) Lucid Exposition. Mulamadhyamakavrttiprasannapada. dBu ma tsal 'bai grel pa tshig gsal. Toh 3860.
Carroll S (2020) A Brief History of Quantum Mechanics. The Royal Institution, Westminster. UK.
Cutler JWC, Newland G (trans.) (2000) The Great Treatise on the Stages of the Path to Enlightenment by Tsongkhapa. Ithaca, NY: Snow Lion Publications.
Dar A, Rujula AD, and Heinz U (1999) Will relativistic heavy-ion colliders destroy our planet? Physics Letters B 470: 142–48.
Darwin C (1859) On the Origin of Species by Means of Natural Selection, or the Preservation of Favoured Races in the Struggle for Life. London, UK: John Murray.
Descartes R (1637) Discourse on the Method of Rightly Conducting One's Reason and of Seeking Truth in the Sciences. BnF, FR.
Dharmakirti (7th century) Exposition of Valid Cognition. Pramāṇavārttika. Tshad ma rnam'grel. Toh 4210, tshad ma ce.
Einstein, A (1905a) On a heuristic point of view concerning the production and transformation of light. Annalen der Physik 17: 132–148.
Einstein, A (1905b) On the movement of small particles suspended in stationary liquids required by the molecular-kinetic theory of heat. Annalen der Physik 17: 549–560.
Einstein, A (1905c) On the electrodynamics of moving bodies. Annalen der Physik 17: 891–921
Einstein A (1915a) On the General Theory of Relativity. Submitted to Prussian Academy of Science, Berlin, DE.

Einstein A (1915b) The Field Equations of Gravitation. Submitted to Prussian Academy of Science, Berlin, DE.

Einstein A, Klein MJ, and Przibram K (2015) Letters on Wave Mechanics: Correspondence with H. A. Lorentz, Max Planck, and Erwin Schrödinger. Philosophical Library/Open Road.

Ellis J, Giudice G, Mangano M, Tkachev I, and Wiedemann U (2008) Review of the Safety of LHC Collisions. Journal of Physics G: Nuclear and Particle Physics 35 (11).

European Organization for Nuclear Research (CERN) (2023) Facts and figures about the LHC. The CERN, Geneva, CH. Accessed from https://home.web.cern.ch/resources/faqs/facts-and-figures-about-lhc

Feynman R, Leighton R, and Sands M (2010) The Feynman Lectures on Physics, Volume III Quantum Mechanics. California Institute of Technology, Pasadena, CA. Accessed from https://www.feynmanlectures.caltech.edu/III_toc.html

Flower Ornament Sutra. Chapter 20. Eulogies in the Palace of the Suyama Heaven. Avatamsaka Sutra. Sans rgyas phal po che shes bya ba sintu rgyas pa chen pohi mdo. Toh 44. phal chen ka.

Forbes Magazine (2023) Top 10 Quantum Computing Companies Making Change. Published on December 11, 2023. Accessed from https://www.forbes.com/sites/technology/article/top-quantum-computing-companies/?sh=c1980463a941

Fremantle F, Trungpa C (1975) The Tibetan Book of the Dead: The Great Liberation through Hearing in the Bardo by Guru Rinpoche according to Karma Lingpa. Boulder, CO: Shambhala.

Giandomenico SL, Mierau SB, Gibbons GM, et al. (2019) Cerebral organoids at the air–liquid interface generate diverse nerve tracts with functional output. Nature Neuroscience 22: 669–679.

Gilmore R (1981) Catastrophe Theory for Scientists and Engineers. Wiley, New York, NY.

Hanemann WM (1994) Valuing the environment through contingent valuation. Journal of Economic Perspectives 8, 19–43.

Hawking S, Tegmark M, Russell S, and Wilczek F (2014) Transcending complacency on superintelligent machines. Huffington Post. Accessed from https://www.huffingtonpost.com/stephen-hawking/artificial-intelligence_b_5174265.html

Hayward J, and Varela FJ (1992) Gentle Bridges: Dialogues Between the Cognitive Sciences and the Buddhist Tradition. Boston, MA: Shambhala Press.

Heisenberg W (1930) The Physical Principles of the Quantum Theory (German: Physikalischen Prinzipien der Quantentheorie). Chicago, IL: The University of Chicago Press.

Hopkins J (2008) Tsong-Kha-Pa's Final Exposition of Wisdom. Boston, MA: Shambala.

Hubble E (1929) A relation between distance and radial velocity among extra-galactic nebulae. Proceedings of the National Academy of Sciences US.A.:15(3): 168–173.

Jaffe RL, Buszaa W, Sandweiss J, and Wilczek F (2000) Review of speculative disaster scenarios at RHIC. Review of Modern Physics 72: 1125–1140.

Kariko K, Muramatsu H, Ludwig J, and Weissman D (2011) Generating the optimal mRNA for therapy: HPLC purification eliminates immune activation and improves translation for nucleoside-modified, protein-encoding mRNA. Nucleic Acids Research 39: e142.

Kurzweil R (2005) The Singularity is Near: When Humans Transcend Biology. Penguin, New York, NY.

Lama Tsongkhapa (1357a–1419) Collected Works of the Incomparable Lord Tsongkhapa Lobsang Drakpa. Kumbum woodblock edition.

Lama Tsongkhapa (1357b–1419) Great Treatise on the Stages of the Path to Enlightenment. Byang chub lam rim chen mo. Collected Works. Vol. pa.[6]

Lama Tsongkhapa (1357c–1419) Ocean of Reasoning: An Exposition of Treatise on the Middle Way. Rtsa ba shes rab kyi rnam bshad ṭik chen rigs pa'i rgya mtsho. Collected Works. Vol. ba, 1–583.

Lama Tsongkhapa (1357d–1419) Illuminating the Intent: A Thorough Exposition of Entering the Middle Way. Dbu ma la 'jug pa'i rnam bshad dgongs pa rab gsal. Collected Works. Vol. ma, 1–605.

Lama Tsongkhapa (1357e–1419) Golden Rosary of Excellent Utterances: Extensive Exposition of "Ornament of Realization" As Well As Its Commentary (Shes rab kyi pha rol du phyin pa mngon par rtogs pa'i rgyan 'grel pa dang bcas pa rgyas par bshad pa legs bshad gser gyi phreng ba). Collected Works. Vols. tsa and tsha.

Lama Tsongkhapa (1357f–1419) In Praise of the Buddha for His Teaching of Dependent Origination. Ston pa la rten cing 'brel bar byung bar gsungs pa las brtsams te bstod pa legs bshad snying po. Portland, OR: The Foundation for the Preservation of the Mahayana Tradition (FPMT).

Lama Tsongkhapa (1357g–1419) Songs of Experience. Lam rim nyams mgur. Portland, OR: The Foundation for the Preservation of the Mahayana Tradition (FPMT).

Lama Tsongkhapa (1357h–1419) Essence of True Eloquence: Distinguishing the Provisional and the Definitive Meaning (Drang ba dang nges pa'i don rnam par 'byed pa legs bshad snying po). Collected Works. Vol. pha, 441–687.

Lemaitre G (1931) The beginning of the world from the point of view of quantum theory. Nature 127 (3210): 706.

[6] Lama Tsongkhapa (1357–1419). Collected Works of the Incomparable Lord Tsongkhapa Lobsang Drakpa. Kumbum woodblock edition.

Lenton TM, Held H, Kriegler E, Hall JW, Lucht W, Rahmstorf S, and Schellnhuber HJ (2008) Tipping elements in the earth's climate system. Proceedings of National Academy of Sciences 105: 1786–1793.

Maitreya (4th century). Ornament of Realizations. Abhisamayālaṃkāra. Mngon rtogs rgyan. Toh 3786, shes phyin ka.

Maitreya (4th century). Ornament of the Scriptures of the Great Vehicle. Mahayanasutralamkara. Mdo sde rgyan. Toh 4020.

Mendelsohn R, Olmstead S (2009) The economic valuation of environmental amenities and disamenities: methods and applications. Annual Review of Resources 34, 325–347.

Mills MJ, Toon OB, Turco RP, Kinnison DE, Garcia RR (2008) Massive global ozone loss predicted following regional nuclear conflict. Proceedings of the National Academy of Sciences of the United States of America 105: 5307–5312.

Nagarjuna (2nd century) Fundamental Wisdom on the Middle Way. Mūlamadhyamakakārikā. Dbu ma rtsa ba'i tshig le'ur byas pa (Rtsa ba'i shes rab). Toh 3824, dbu ma tsa.

Nagarjuna (2nd century) Precious Garland. Ratnāvalī. Rin chen phreng ba. Toh 4158, spriṅ yig ge.

Nagarjuna (2nd century) Sixty Stanzas of Reasoning. Yuktiṣaṣṭikākārikā. Rigs pa drug cu pa. Toh 3825, dbu ma tsa.

National Academies (2024) National Academies of Sciences, Engineering, and Medicine. NASEM, Washington, DC. Accessed from https://www.nationalacademies.org/home.

National Human Genome Research Institute (NHGRI) (2020) Cloning Fact Sheet. The NHGRI, Washington, DC. Accessed from https://www.genome.gov/about-genomics/fact-sheets/Cloning-Fact-Sheet

National Institutes of Health (NIH) (2009) NIH Guidelines for Human Stem Cell Research. Bethesda, MD: The NIH.

New York Times (2023a) Microsoft says new A.I. shows signs of human reasoning. Published on May 16, 2023.

New York Times (2023b). A.I. poses 'risk of extinction,' Industry leaders warn. Published on May 30, 2023.

Newton, I (1687) Philosophiæ Naturalis Principia Mathematica. London.

Nobel Prize (2012). The Nobel Prize in Physiology or Medicine 2012: Sir John B. Gurdon and Shinya Yamanaka "for the discovery that mature cells can be reprogrammed to become pluripotent." Accessed from https://www.nobelprize.org/prizes/medicine/2012/summary/

Nobel Prize (2013) The Nobel Prize in Physics 2013: "for the theoretical discovery of a mechanism that contributes to our understanding of the origin of mass of subatomic particles, and which recently was confirmed through the discovery of the predicted fundamental particle, by the ATLAS and CMS experiments at CERN's Large Hadron Collider." Accessed from https://www.nobelprize.org/nobel_prizes/physics/laureates/2013/

Nobel Prize (2023). The Nobel Prize in Physiology or Medicine 2023: Katalin Karikó and Drew Weissman "for their discoveries concerning nucleoside base modifications that enabled the development of effective mRNA vaccines against COVID-19." Accessed from https://www.nobelprize.org/prizes/medicine/2023/summary/

Nordhaus W (1994) Managing the Global Commons. Cambridge, MA: MIT Press.

Nordhaus W (2011) The economics of tail events with an application to climate change. Review of Environmental Economics and Policy 5: 240–257.

OpenAI (2023) Introducing ChatGPT. Accessed from https://openai.com/blog/chatgpt

Pakkenberg B, Gundersen HJG (1997) Neocortical neuron number in humans: Effect of sex and age. Journal of Comparative Neurology 384: 312–320.

Panchen Lama (4th) Guru Puja Ritual. Berzin Archives. Accessed from https://studybuddhism.com/bo/tshad-mtho-i-slob-sbyong/zhal-don-dang-cho-g-i-rigs/sngags-kyi-nymas-len/bla-ma-mchod-p-i-cho-ga

Pardi N, Hogan MJ, Porter W, and Weissman D (2018) mRNA vaccines – A New Era in Vaccinology. Nature Reviews Drug Discovery 17: 261–279.

Peskin ME (2008) The end of the world at the Large Hadron Collider? Physics 1 (14).

Pierce BA (2019) Genetics: A Conceptual Approach (7th Edition). New York, NY: W.H. Freeman.

Plaga R (2009) On the potential catastrophic risk from metastable quantum-black holes produced at particle colliders. arXiv:0808.1415 [hep-ph].

Poincaré H (1880–1890) Mémoire sur les Courbes Définies par les Équations Différentielles I-VI, Oeuvre I. Gauthier-Villars, Paris.

Posner RA (2004) Catastrophe: Risk and Response. Oxford, UK: Oxford University Press.

Potter CW (2001) A history of influenza. Journal of Applied Microbiology 91(4):572–579.

Purves D, Augustine GJ, Fitzpatrick D, Hall WC, LaMantia A-S, White LE (Editors) (2011) Neuroscience (5th edition). Sunderland, MA: Sinauer Associates.

Quadrato G, Nguyen T, Macosko EZ, Sherwood JL, Yang SM, Berger DR, Maria N, Scholvin J, Goldman M, Kinney JP, Boyden ES, Lichtman JW, Williams ZM, McCarroll SA, and Arlotta P (2017) Cell diversity and network dynamics in photosensitive human brain organoids. Nature 545: 48–53.

Reardon S (2020) Can lab-grown brains become conscious? Nature. Published on October 27, 2020.

Reuters (2021) Former CDC chief Redfield says he thinks COVID-19 originated in a Chinese lab. Published on March 27, 2021. Accessed from https://www.reuters.com/article/us-health-coronavirus-origin-redfield-idUSKBN2BI2R6.

Schopenhauer A (1818) Die Welt als Wille und Vorstellung [The World as Will and Representation]. Translated into English by Haldane RB, Kemp J (London UK: Routledge & Kegan Paul, 1883–1886).

Schrodinger E (1935) Die gegenwärtige Situation in der Quantenmechanik (The present situation in quantum mechanics). Naturwissenschaften. 23 (48): 807–812

Schuster EF (1984) Classification of probability laws by tail behavior. Journal of the American Statistical Association 79 (388): 936–39.

Seo SN (2018) Mathematical Foundations of Catastrophe and Chaos Theories and Their Applications. In: Seo SN (2018) Natural and Man-made Catastrophes: Theories, Economics, and Policy Designs. Wiley-Blackwell, John Wiley & Sons.

Seo SN (2020) The Economics of Globally Shared and Public Goods. Amsterdam, NL: Academic Press.

Seo SN (2021) Climate Change and Economics: Engaging with Future Generations with Action Plans. Palgrave Macmillan, London, UK

Seo SN (2022a) The Economics of Pandemics: Exploring Globally Shared Experiences. Palgrave Macmillan, London, UK.

Seo SN (ed.) (2022b) Handbook of Behavioral Economics and Climate Change. Edward Elgar, Cheltenham, UK.

Seo SN (2023) The Economics of Optimal Growth Pathways: Evaluating the Health of the Planet's Natural and Ecological Resources. Palgrave Macmillan, London, UK.

Seo SN (2024a) Buddha, Wisdom and Economics: A Contribution to the Art of Happiness. Edward Elgar, Cheltenham, UK.

Seo SN (2024b) Protecting Nature with Buddha's Wisdom: A Contribution to Environmental and Nature Studies. Edward Elgar, Cheltenham, UK.

Seo SN, Bakkensen LA (2017) Is tropical cyclone surge, not intensity, what kills so many people in South Asia? Weather, Climate, and Society 9 (2): 171–181.

Shantideva (8th century) Guide to the Bodhisattva Way. Bodhicaryāvatāra. Byang chub sems dpa'i spyod pa la'jug pa. Toh 3871, dbu ma la.

Shiller RJ (2005) Irrational Exuberance (2nd edition). Princeton, NJ: Princeton University Press.

Singer W (1999) Neuronal Synchrony: A Versatile Code for the Definition of Relations? Neuron 24: 49–65.

Spinoza B (1677) Ethics. In: The Chief Works of Benedict de Spinoza: Volumes 1 and 2 (Kb Classics). Translated from Latin by RHM Elwis in 1883. London, UK: George Bell and Sons.

Soft Bank Robotics (2019) Pepper. Soft Bank, Tokyo, Accessed from https://www.softbankrobotics.

Tegmark M (2015) Consciousness as a state of matter. Chaos, Solitons & Fractals 76: 238–270. arxiv.org/abs/1401.1219

Takahashi K, Yamanaka S (2006) Induction of pluripotent stem cells from mouse embryonic and adult fibroblast cultures by defined factors. Cell 126(4): 663–676

Tesla (2023) AI & Robotics. Tesla, Austin, TX. Accessed from https://www.tesla.com/AI

Thom R (1972) Stabilité Structurelle et Morphogenèse: Essai d'une Théorie Générale des Modèles. Benjamin, New York.

Thom R (1975) Structural stability and morphogenesis. Benjamin-Addison-Wesley, New York, NY.

Thomson JA, Itskovitz-Eldor J, Shapiro SS, Waknitz MA, Swiergiel JJ, Marshall VS, Jones JM (1998) Embryonic stem cell lines derived from human blastocysts. Science 282 (5391): 1145–1147.

Thubten Jinpa (2019) Tsongkhapa: A Buddha in the Land of Snows. Boston, MA: Shambala.

Thubten Jinpa (2021) Illuminating the Intent: An Exposition of Candrakirti's Entering the Middle Way. Wisdom Boston, MA: Wisdom Publications.

Thurman RAF (1982) Life and Teachings of Tsongkhapa. Dharamsala, India: Library of Tibetan Works & Archives.

Thurman RAF (1984) Tsong Khapa's Speech of Gold in the Essence of True Eloquence: Reason and Enlightenment in the Central Philosophy of Tibet. Princeton, NJ: Princeton University Press.

Tohoku University (ed.) (1934). A Complete Catalogue of the Tibetan Buddhist Canons, Sde-dge Edition, Tohoku University, Japan.

Trujillo CA, Gao R, Negraes PD, Gu J, Buchanan J, Preissl S, Wang A,Wu W, Haddad GG, Chaim IA, Domissy A, Vandenberghe M, Devor A, Yeo GW, Voytek B, and Muotri AR (2019) Complex oscillatory waves emerging from cortical organoids model early human brain network development. Cell Stem Cell 25, 558–569.

Turco RP, Toon OB, Ackerman TP, Pollack JB, and Sagan S (1983) Nuclear winter: global consequences of multiple nuclear explosions. Science 222: 1283–1292.

United States Department of Interior (USDOI) (2024) Re: U.S. Geological Survey (USGS) Freedom of Information Act (FOIA) Tracking # DOI-USGS-2023-000257 – Response. Washington, DC: US DOI.

United States Energy Information Administration (USEIA) (2024) Energy Explained. US EIA, Department of Energy, Washington, DC.

United Nations Population Division (2022) World Population Prospects 2022. Department of Economics and Social Affairs, United Nations, New York, NY.

Varela FJ, Rosch E, and Thomson E (1992) The Embodied Mind: Cognitive Science and Human Experience. Cambridge, MA: The MIT Press.

Vasubandhu (4th century) Thirty Verses on Consciousness Only. Triṃśikā Vijñaptimātratā. Taishō Tripiṭaka Volume 31, Number 1586.[7]
Vrselja Z, Daniele SG, Silbereis J, et. al. (2019) Restoration of brain circulation and cellular functions hours post-mortem. Nature 568: 336–343.
Wade N (2024) Where Did Covid Come From? Wall Street Journal. Published on February 28, 2024. Accessed from https://www.wsj.com/articles/where-did-covid-come-from-new-evidence-lab-leak-hypothesis-78be1c39
Wadhwa V (2022) Why Quantum Computing Is Even More Dangerous Than Artificial Intelligence. Foreign Policy. Accessed from https://foreignpolicy.com/2022/08/21/quantum-computing-artificial-intelligence-ai-technology-regulation/
Weiss SR (2020) Forty years with coronaviruses. Journal of Experimental Medicine 217 (5): e20200537. https://doi.org/10.1084/jem.20200537
Weitzman ML (2009) On modeling and interpreting the economics of catastrophic climate change. The Review of Economics and Statistics 91 (1): 1–19.
World Health Organization (WHO) (2021) Press Conference on February 12th, 2021. The joint World Health Organization-China Mission to Investigate the Origins of COVID-19. Geneva, CH: WHO. Accessed from https://www.who.int/emergencies/diseases/novel-coronavirus-2019
Zeeman EC (1977) Catastrophe theory-selected papers 1972–1977. Addison-Wesley, Reading, MA.

[7] Taishō Shinshū Daizōkyō, Tokyo, Japan.

CHAPTER 2

A Compendium of Buddhist Thoughts for Scientists as Elucidated by Lama Tsongkhapa

1 Introduction

This chapter introduces a basket of Buddhist thoughts to scientists and economic scientists that are apposite to the analyses of science and science singularities to be conducted throughout this book. The goal of the book is to lead readers to an opportunity to view the singularity events of science, each of which is predicted to be utterly catastrophic and even planetary civilizations-ending, from the fresh perspective grounded on this basket of Buddhist ideas (Tipitka, Kangyur and Tengyur, Lama Tsongkhapa's Collected Works).[1] The exposition in this chapter relies on the marvelous writings of Lama Tsongkhapa during the fifteenth century, also known to Tibetans as Je Rinpoche or Manjushri the Buddha of Wisdom (Thubten Jinpa 2019).

Therefore, the importance of the task that this book takes on can be measured only by the graveness and inextricability of the singularity events of science to be clarified in the book as well as the intractability of them through the existing science knowledge and technologies including the relevant economic analyses.

[1] Throughout the book, the Buddhist scriptures from the Pali Tipitaka, the Tibetan Kangyur and Tengyur, and the Chinese Dazangjing are referenced in the Book bibliography at the end of the book (THL 2009, Tohoku 1934).

S. N. Seo, *The Economics of Singularities of Science Elucidated with Buddhist Thoughts*,
https://doi.org/10.1007/978-3-031-69118-8_2

This book puts forth the five singularity events of science selected relying on the present author's research experiences of the past two decades. The present author has delved into the questions of global climate change and other global public good challenges during this period (Seo 2020, 2021, 2022a, 2022b, 2023). This in turn has created an atmosphere in which the present author can appreciate the crossroads of science and economics, especially when they are concerned with truly big events, say, planetary-scale events or universal events (Seo 2018).

The five singularity events are intimately associated with the five major fields of science, as such, comprehensive of scientific endeavors in the contemporary world: relativity physics, quantum mechanics, genetics/virology, medicine/biology, neuroscience. Without doubt, this comprehensive coverage is also by intention of the present author.

The five singularity events are a physics singularity caused by the Large Hadron Collider (LHC) experiment or alternatively the God Particle experiment by the European Organization for Nuclear Research (CERN) (Chap. 4), a quantum mechanics singularity through artificial intelligence (AI) robot supremacy (Chap. 5), a genetics/virology singularity through a super virus such as one caused by an mRNA virus and vaccines (Chap. 6), a medicine/biology singularity through stem cell research such as human organ regenerations and cloning (Chap. 7), a neuroscience singularity such as one caused by consciousness manufacturing in a laboratory (Chap. 8).

The risk that any of the five scientific endeavors poses is unmistakable. To quote a preeminent physicist, Stephen Hawking, right before his passing away, called the above AI singularity as "the greatest achievement by the humanity but the last achievement" written with prominent experts on AI (Hawking et al. 2014). Here the AI singularity in the quote refers to the point in time when the robot's intelligence equals human intelligence (Kurzweil 2005).

For another illuminating remark, Martin Weitzman, a late Harvard economist, called the global warming risk as "the end of all civilizations on the planet as we know them." This phrase succinctly captures the salient characteristic of the singularity risk introduced in this book, although I need to clarify that global warming is not one of the five singularity events explained in the book (Weitzman 2009). The risk that some of the five singularity events poses is even bigger, as is described by concerned scientists. The God particle experiment through the CERN reactors can even destroy the current universe itself, far beyond this planet Earth, according to concerned scientists (Dar et al. 1999; Jaffe et al. 2000).

Given this magnitude of risk posed on humanity and other sentient beings through the frontier scientific experiments, it would be natural for Buddhists, adherents of a rational religion, to be curious about what these singularity events are and how humankind may deal with these challenges (Dignaga's & Dharmakirti's Valid Cognition, Bhaviveka's Wisdom Lamap, Lama Tsongkhapa's Ocean of Reasoning). Up until now, however, there has been no attempt by Buddhists to explain the science-caused challenges in a systematic and comprehensive manner. This is not that they are ignorant of these issues or intentionally ignoring these issues. It is that these humanity-wide concerns remain at the level of a chatter among them.

From another viewpoint, this book takes a form of an introduction of Buddhist thoughts to scientists as well as economists to some degree in the context of these challenges. What would be the rationale for this approach? First and foremost, the singularities examined in this book all have arisen from the scientific and technological progresses at which people have also marveled. Many Nobel prizes have been awarded to the five scientific experiments dealt with in this book, which will be clarified shortly.

The teachings and commentaries of Buddhism, being a system of rational minds often called the path of reasoning (Lama Tsongkhapa's Ocean of Reasoning, Realization Narrative, Ngawang Samten and Garfield 2006), deal with the issues to some degrees that the scientists are attempting to address through the five experiments/researches, even if not directly. For example, the question of how the universe began or the life on Earth began is not strange to the Buddhist philosophers. About the question of how to create consciousness out of pure matter attempted by neuroscientists today is something that the Buddhist thinkers can easily take a position about. In fact, the present author would argue that the corpus of Buddha's teachings and commentaries is a rich treasure trove of ideas pertinent to these scientific questions.

The Buddhist exposition will be split into two chapters. In this chapter, the present author offers an introduction to Buddhist thoughts intended for scientist readers, which is composed of four sections: Buddhism in a nutshell, the question of "I," the question of life, and the question of the universes. This will be followed by six chapters on science: Chap. 3 on singularities economics, Chap. 4 on physics, Chap. 5 on quantum mechanics, Chap. 6 on mRNA virology, Chap. 7 on stem cell, and Chap. 8 on neuroscience. The final chapter of the book, Chap. 9, offers a grand synthesis of all these scientific endeavors from the Buddhist platform of ideas.

2 Buddhism in a Nutshell According to Je Rinpoche

Science is the investigation of the reality of the world. So is Buddhism. The two endeavors are the same in that sense. But the two endeavors put forth a starkly different answer on reality. In that sense, they are different. As a sixteen-year-old youthful Manjushri says "jokingly," all the things are unreal, false, and deceptive (Lama Tsongkhapa's Stages, Nagarjuna's Fundamental Wisdom, Aryadeva's Four Hundred, King of Meditations, Entering Truths Sutra).[2]

Let me begin this exposition from where it began, the Buddha There is much suffering in the world, including in yourself. Would you agree on this? I think many of you would agree, if not most of you. Then, let me ask you this. Why is there so much suffering? You will be hesitant even if you have an answer to put forth. Let me further ask: Is there an end to all of these sufferings at all, thoroughly and completely? You will be utterly bewildered.

Buddhism was founded upon the unexcelled enlightenment of Shakyamuni under the Bodhi Tree at Bodhgaya, whose first teaching was the Four Noble Truths given at the Deer Park at Sarnath (Wheel of Dharma Sutra, Naga King Sagara, Walpola Rahula 1974). This happened a long time ago, around 2612 years ago according to Tibetans. Notwithstanding, this first teaching thoroughly addresses the above questions that I put forth after so many years since his Pari Nirvana and further completely elucidates the end of suffering and the path toward it (Maha Vibhanga Sutta, Maha Nidana Sutta, Watanabe 2005).

As Lama Tsongkhapa succinctly summarizes Shakyamuni's teachings and praises him in the opening verse of his famous Praise of Buddha Shakyamuni, Buddha realized the ignorance and taught as he saw it the removal of it as the path to the end of suffering (Lama Tsongkhapa's Praise):

[2] The historical Buddhist commentaries are cited by the author's name and the two-letter short title of the corresponding work.

> He who speaks on the basis of seeing,
> This makes him a knower and teacher unexcelled,
> ......
> You saw and taught
> whatever degenerations there are in the world,
> The root of all these is ignorance.

What is ignorance [Ma-rik-pa in Tibetan]? According to Lama Tsongkhapa, it is not simple unknowing. For example, you may not know the name of the galaxy next to the Milky Way or you may believe white lilies blossom in the autumn. It is neither an objective obscuration, that is, a distorted mental tendency. To give the simplest example pertinent to scientists: you may believe that scientists are superior to common people.

The ignorance that Lama Tsongkhapa refers to is afflictive ignorance [*nyon mongs can gyi ma rik pa* in Tibetan; *klistavidaya* in Sanskrit].[3] The afflictive ignorance is the ignorance that afflicts [*nyon mongs* in Tibetan; *klesa* in Sanskrit] the mind of the ignorant, which propels the ignorant into the cycle of suffering of existence (Lama Tsongkhapa's True Eloquence, Thurman 1984; Hopkins 2008). These are the unconscious and intellectual views that are held by sentient beings from the moment of one's birth, more precisely, from beginningless time.

What is the afflictive ignorance? What is that unconsciously held futile view? To put it more directly, what is the afflictive ignorance that brings such pain and suffering to sentient beings and the worlds without ends? I am hesitant to give you an answer directly here. Because I know it will be thoroughly perplexing to most readers of this book including scientists and economists. I know this because I have witnessed for thousands of years that even brightest of the brightest students of Shakyamuni did not understand it (Perfection of Wisdom in 700 Lines & 8000 Lines, Nagarjuna's Sixty Reasoning, Chandrakirti's Clear Words).

From the bottom of my heart, there is no intention at all to belittle you here, scientists, economists, and philosophers. Rather, this is to clarify that the Buddha's perfect wisdom sees things upside down, which may feel to you a mass of contradictions or even non-senses. This is also one of the reasons that the present author offered an exposition in the context of

[3] The Tibetan letters of the Tibetan words used in the book are collected in the Appendix at the end of the book. In converting the Tibetan letters to English, the present author relied on the actual pronunciation method and avoided the transliteration method.

economics in "Buddha, Wisdom and Economics," an exposition in the context of environmental and nature philosophy in "Protecting Nature with Buddha's Wisdom," and now an exposition in the context of science in this book (Seo 2024a, 2024b).

Having clarified that, let me take you this way. Ordinary people have an innate belief that there is I. "I am here right now. I am looking at you, talking to you, and can even touch you. How can I not exist?" they would argue with total confidence. Some might even say that Buddhism is just nonsense. To ordinary people, this belief is innate in that it is habitual, unconsciously held, and not questioned.

This is a belief in intrinsic self in which the "I" that ordinary people assume to exist as the true identity of themselves is an intrinsic self. Under the belief, they assume this self to be substantial, self-sufficient, and distinct in nature from the five aggregates. To them, this self is the master and the five aggregates are servants (Maha-satipatthana Sutta, Maha-Nidana Sutta, Nidana Sutta, Dhammpada, Sutta Nipata). This view is held intellectually by philosophers and scientists after a rational examination, that is, other than common people who hold in an unreflective manner.

It is not the self that people are experiencing day to day, but the self that people hold on to habitually as their true identity. More generally, it is not the self that sentient beings are experiencing day to day, but the self that sentient beings hold on to as their true identity habitually. From this divide between reality and perception arise afflictions which propel people through the ocean of cyclic existence in pain and suffering (Aryadeva's Four Hundred, Lama Tsongkhapa's Intent). The Buddha declared that there is no such self (Sutta-Nipata, Naga King Sagara).

This process of cycle of existence in the ocean of suffering was expounded in the following way by the Buddha as the rule of dependent origination [Dren-drel-jung-wa in Tibetan] (Bodhi Sutta, Paticasamupada Sutta);

> From ignorance arises volition,
> From volition arises consciousness,
> From consciousness arises name and form,
> ....
> From birth arises aging and death, sorrow, lamentation, pain, distress, and despair. Such is the origination of this entire mass of suffering.

The teachings of no-self and dependent origination thus expounded by the Buddha were well received especially by his top students who would become the Theras of Buddhism after Shakyamuni's Parinirvana. Having said that, as it has turned out through history, his followers would struggle mightily to clarify what the true intention of Shakyamuni's vast teachings is (Lama Tsongkhapa's Stages of the Path, True Eloquence, Thurman 1984, Rizong Rinpoche's Teaching).

On the other hand, the Buddha's teachings thoroughly baffled his contemporaneous rivals who were of 62 kinds including realists, materialists, and nihilists. If there is no I, where is your morality? Who am I then? How can one go from one life to another life? They were baffled thus (Nagarjuna's Fundamental Wisdom, Reasoning Sixty, Emptiness Seventy).

The teaching of dependent origination was given in order to destroy the extreme views: the view of existence as well as the view of non-existence (Kacayana Sutta, Mother Scripture). Hence, the middle way devoid of the extremes. The extreme views are expressed as the view of annihilation and the view of permanence (Nagarjuna's Fundamental Wisdom). They are also expressed as the view of reification and the view of repudiation (Asanga's Bodhisattva Stages, Compendium). As Lama Tsongkhapa quotes from the scripture (Naga King Anavatapta, Lama Tsongkhapa's Ocean of Reasoning):

> The wise, having understood dependently originated phenomena,
> Do not rely on extreme views.
> They understand that phenomena have causes and conditions,
> And that no phenomena exist without causes and conditions.

Having said that, even the sharpest disciples of the Buddha during his time as well as afterward may not have understood what the Buddha realized and taught, whose points became clear through Lama Tsongkhapa's elucidations, to which the present author referred as falsity of the world (Buddhapalita's Commentary, Chandrakirti's Middle Way, Lama Tsongkhapa's Illuminating the Intent, Thubten Jinpa 2021; Seo 2024a):

> Even though things have no existence,
> they appear as if they do,
> hence, they are all false.

In the falsity [juen-pa in Tibetan] of all things internal as well as external, the reality [de-nyi in Tibetan] is realityless, the truth is truthless, the form is formless, the world is worldless, the nature is natureless, the Buddha is Buddhaless (Perfection of Wisdom in 700 Lines, King of Meditations Sutra, Ajatasatru Sutra). In the falsity of all things, there is not a single thing that exists ultimately [don-dam-den-pa in Tibetan]; there is not a single thing you can pinpoint to. Neither any mental phenomenon nor any external phenomenon. Neither the God nor the truth. Neither the eternality nor the nothingness itself (Chandrakirti's Clear Words, Lama Tsongkhapa's True Eloquence). Ultimately, all phenomena are unborn, unarisen, and unreal. All phenomena and all terms are false and deceptive (Entering Truths Sutra).

As the Great Charioteer Noble Nagarjuna puts it (Nagarjuna's Fundamental Wisdom, Lama Tsongkhapa's Ocean of Reasoning, Ngawang Samten and Garfield 2006):

> Everything is such; and is not such;
> Both such and not such;
> Neither such nor not such.
> This is the Lord Buddha's teaching.

Shakyamuni, Nagarjuna, Je Rinpoche all repeatedly warn their students that the incurable disease of all is the clinging to emptiness (Seo 2024a, 2024b). In the empty world, what remains are the cause and effects, karma and consequences, and the conventions of the world [kun-job in Tibetan] (Mother Scripture, Engaging the World Sutra, Entering Truths Sutra). As is elucidated by Lama Tsongkhapa, to complete the quotation in the beginning of this section (Lama Tsongkhapa's Praise, Stages of the Path):

> Whatever degenerations there are in the world,
> The root of all these is ignorance;
> You taught that it is dependent origination,
> The seeing of which will undo this ignorance.

The undoing of the afflictive ignorance [Ma-rik-pa in Tibetan] is dependent origination devoid of the extremes, also known as the Middle Way, which is the end of all suffering in the world that the Buddha and Je Rinpoche assured us to deliver for the endless time of this limitlessly limited universes (Lama Tsongkhapa's Beginning-Middle-End Prayer, Cutler and Newland 2000, Shantideva's Bodhisattva Way).

3 The Question of "I": Where It All Begins in Time and Space

Like all ordinary people, scientists are also grappling with the fundamental questions of life as a human being. The range of scientific inquiries to be elaborated in this book is an honest attempt to address these fundamental questions, not satisfied with "religious" expositions or a life of acceptance without questioning. Unlike ordinary people, scientists including economists rely on concepts, theories, rational analyses, empirical data, social experiments, and scientific experiments to address them (Galilei 1632; Newton 1687). Henceforth, the present author will clarify the Buddhist expositions of the most fundamental questions of life pursued by both ordinary people and scientists. These expositions can serve as a platform for the family of analyses of the five major science experiments and associated singularities to be explained in the succeeding chapters.

What are the fundamental questions of life? There is a large basket of frequently recurring questions that people struggle to answer in their life, but only unsuccessfully. The present author will categorize them into the following three baskets. The first category is the question of self, which can be posed more directly but silently with "Who am I?" in one's mind. The second category is the question of the other. The other includes fellow human beings including family members, friends, and foes. The other also includes non-human beings like animal beings, gods, hell beings, ghosts, etc. The Buddhist terminology for them is sentient beings and their abodes are referred to as six realms of existence. So, the second category is also the question of life. The third category is the question of the world or the universe. The inquiries belonging to this category includes such questions as "How was this world born?," "Will the universe end at some point?," "Is the universe finite?," and "Are there other beings in the universe?" The third category is concerned with the external world that ordinary people consider to be purely matter alone and beyond us.

The most persistent question to any human being that follows in one's life is that of "Who am I?" (Anatta Sutta, Sagara Sutta). It is the most fundamental in that the "I" question will follow one all the time as soon as one is born, that is, even if one is not sane or not a human being. Even though it is always true that one does not have a clear answer to this question, one will always say without being bothered the least bit "I am X, or Y, or Z"; "I did this, or that, or something else"; "I own A, or B, or C"; "I am going to here, or there, or somewhere else"; "I believe in α, or β, or γ"; "I have the right to Δ, or Φ, or Ω". The marvelous teachings by Buddha Shakyamuni, especially those recorded in the Pali tradition, are indeed his kind instructions on how to avoid such a mistaken belief about self which leads inescapably to immense suffering of individuals (Maha-sattipathana Sutta, Lama Tsongkhapa's Stages).

To common people who do not analyze the true meaning of the word, there is I or the self that exists intrinsically in them from beginningless time. One accepts without doubt that there is the self that is the master of their five aggregates and six sense faculties, that is, one's mind and body (Milarepa's Songs). Without the slightest doubt, people grasp onto it, namely, the notion of intrinsic I thus held (Lama Tsongkhapa's Stages, Nagarjuna's Precious Garland, Atisha's Lamp). As declared in the United States Declaration of Independence, an individual is entitled to the pursuit of their happiness and when one does pursue that goal, they are rooted on such mistaken grasping on the self, that is, the innate self (US National Archives 2024). Similarly, when a Buddhist begins its path to end their suffering, they do so beginning with the concept of inherent I, even if they are reciting the truth of no-self outwardly (Lama Tsongkhapa's Songs, Seo 2024a, 2024b).

The myriad scientific endeavors which have yielded many remarkable achievements thus far in human history, which are the primary subjects of this book, are largely founded on the individuals' unrestrained pursuits of happiness in their lives. To give salient examples, recent advances in stem cell research, regenerative medicine, mRNA virology, and neuroscience are primarily driven by the common people's desire for enjoying a healthier, prettier, and longer life (Alison et al. 2002; Tegmark 2015; Pardi et al. 2018). The same can be said of the economic achievements of the past two centuries (Seo 2022a, 2023).

Having introduced the concept of intrinsic self in the previous section and having explained that the myriad of common people's behaviors and scientific progresses are made rooted on the inherent self thus held, the present author is curious how you would feel that Buddha the Omniscient One declares that there is no I, or there is no such self as people hold on to. Neither in a casual manner nor in a light manner, but in all seriousness and rigor, known to be the perfection of wisdom [*she-rab-gyi-pa-rol-tu-chin-pa* in Tibetan], with millions of his top students, noble bodhisattvas, and Buddhas present as his audience! In fact, you can still easily come across in India and elsewhere people who are shocked at what the Buddha said.

How would you feel that the Buddha goes further to say that there is in fact no no-self either. In fact, he declares that there is neither self nor no-self. Here is how it is stated in the Fundamental Wisdom of Middle Way by Nagarjuna (Nagarjuna's Fundamental Wisdom, Kacayana Sutta):

> The Buddhas have explained what a self is;
> And have taught that there is no self;
> And he also has taught that
> There is neither self nor selflessness.

Scientists are not common people who do not question what the truth or true nature of things is, but reflective individuals (Lama Tsongkhapa's True Eloquence). They may be unsettled but still would counter as follows: Isn't it evident that there is a self? We all experience it and everybody knows it, perhaps even if one cannot explain what it exactly is. They may even put forth a road map and set up concrete experiments to create the self (Thomson et al. 1998; Quadrato et al. 2017).

To this, the Omniscient Ones [Kun-kyen in Tibetan] of Buddhism will say to scientists that "Bring me the self if you have found one or if you have succeeded in creating one." They will then clarify. To the Buddhas, the self exists like a horn of a rabbit. Everybody talks about it, imagines about it, writes a book about it, but it does not exist. Have you seen a horn of a rabbit? For another simile, it is like the son of a barren woman. People can talk about it, think about it, and act based on this idea, but in fact the son of a barren woman does not exist from beginningless time (Lama Tsongkhapa's Illuminating the Intent).

The self is the same concept as the intrinsic nature [Rang-shin-gyi-drup-pa in Tibetan], as Lama Tsongkhapa brilliantly elucidated. Emptiness [Tong-pa-nyi in Tibetan] is the lack of the self, which is the same with the absence of intrinsic existence [rang-shin-gyi-drup-pa in Tibetan]. The proof of emptiness, which is the heart of the Buddha's perfection of wisdom, is done through the proof of absence of four extreme productions relying on the royal principle of dependently arisen phenomena (Lama Tsongkhapa's True Eloquence).

In short, Je Rinpoche asks "what is a chariot?" to those who are so confident (Buddhapalita's Commentary, Aryadeva's Four Hundred). In Fig. 2.1, the present author provides an illustration of a chariot which is composed of individual parts: two wheels, an axle, hubs, spokes, a carriage, a shaft, and a yoke. The present author also inserts the seven

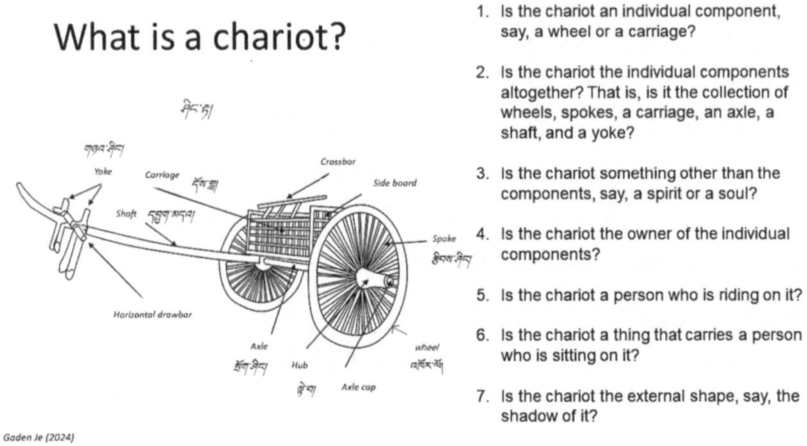

Fig. 2.1 An analysis of what is a chariot
Note: The chariot illustration on the low left side is from Philg88 (2017)

analyses of a chariot. What is called a chariot? Is it the parts of it, for example, a wheel? Is it other than the parts of it, say, a spirit or a soul? Is it the parts of it put together in one place? Is it the owner of individual parts or the collection of them? Does it refer to the external shape, like a shadow of it? Is it the person who is riding on it? Or is it the thing that carries a person who is riding on it? None of these answers is a chariot (Lama Tsongkhapa's Illuminating the Intent)!

This inherent notion of the self or intrinsic nature or true identity, which is held by all sentient beings, is the very beginning from which all the things you know, touch, experience, and imagine have arisen as they are. Including the universes themselves. That is to say, that is the Buddha's omniscient point of view!

4 The Question of Life: Sentient Beings in the Cycle of Existence

The question of life is perhaps the biggest question for scientists (Darwin 1859). There are numerous fields of science that directly address the question of life including life sciences, biological sciences, microbiology, cell biology, physiology, medical sciences, genetics, virology, animal sciences, plant sciences, and so on. There are also many other fields that deal with the question in a more indirect way such as exoplanets, aliens, habitable planets, the origin of the universe, etc.

Who are the sentient beings who turn in the cycle of existence endlessly and how? This is how Buddhists posit the question of life (Tibetan Book of the Dead, Fremantle and Trungpa 1975, The Wheel of Birth and Death Sutta). Since scientists and common people do not believe in the truthfulness of the cycle of existence, they do not ask this question exactly as Buddhists put it. Notwithstanding, they all carry this question whether they realize it or not. They are putting the same question in slightly different ways.

To mention some of these scientific inquiries, scientists are intrigued by what animals are out there; how many of them there are; how they were originated initially; how they survive, function, and live under external conditions; how some of them go extinct and some of them newly emerge; how they migrate from one place to another; and how they are related to each other (Linnaeus 1758; Mora et al. 2011; Seo 2021). They are also super sensitive on human bodies and internal organs. There is none that they are not interested in: brain sizes, eye colors, skin colors; how to make one taller, slimmer, faster, and stronger; what causes heart failures, lung diseases, cancers, diabetes; how failed organs such as a liver can be regrown and replaced; how air pollutants enter the bodies and harm a human body; how mRNA (Messenger Ribonucleic Acid) viruses are transmitted among people and kill some of them; in what processes babies are conceived and given birth; what genes in the body cause what personal characteristics; how humans learn language; in what ways humans became conscious (NIH 2009; Purves et al. 2011; Pardi et al. 2018; Alberts et al. 2019; NHGRI 2021; Mayo Clinic 2023; Seo 2022a). These are only a small fraction of what scientists are putting their minds on regarding the question of life.

The term "a sentient being" is not a modern science concept. It is a Buddhist concept of a being, more generally an Indian concept. The sentience in Buddhism is defined as having consciousness, based on which a sentient being can experience happiness and suffering (Vasubandhu's Abhidharmakosa, Shantaraksita's Ornament, Kamalasila's Stages). Humans and animals are sentient beings. But, where the boundary between sentience and non-sentience lies in a totality of a pool of species on Earth is difficult to perceive (Linnaeus 1758). For example, is a snail a sentient being? Or, is a mosquito or an earthworm a sentient being?

Even in modern science, this boundary is difficult to pinpoint. The question of where sentience begins is the question of where and how consciousness begins. This is one of the hottest pursuits by contemporary scientists (Singer 1999; Tegmark 2015; Quadrato et al. 2017). To understand this frontier endeavor, we can ask a far more difficult question. Is an amoeba, that is, a single-celled organism, a sentient being, that is, a consciousness possessor? Further, is an mRNA virus like the novel Coronavirus a sentient being, that is, a consciousness possessor? These beings are as tiny as no one can see or "experience," that is, it is small at an atomic level or at a nanometer scale. To uncover the mystery of consciousness, scientists explore even tinier things such as a quantum.

Still, the Buddhist concept of a sentient being stands. What is critical in this concept is that these beings can experience feelings such as happiness, sadness, suffering, etc. because they are mind possessors [sem-chen in Tibetan]. As such, they are the objects of compassion of Buddhas and bodhisattvas (Nagarjuna's Bodhicitta Commentary, Shantideva's Bodhisattva Deeds). They are the ones who can, relying on the teachings of the Buddhas and lamas, achieve the liberation and perfect wisdom of the Buddha even if it would take a multitude of eons.

Sentient beings are born again and again by their fundamental ignorance of the reality of existence. This again is due to the very fact that they are mind possessors. They accumulate karma [Le or Tin-le in Tibetan], according to which they are born in one of the six realms of existence [Do-wa-rik-druk in Tibetan] (Lama Tsongkhapa's Stages of the Path, Khantipalo 1995; HAR 2023). This is the cycle of existence through which one is born and relocated. When the fundamental ignorance is removed, one is liberated from the cycle of existence, called *samsara* in Sanskrit and *korwa* in Tibetan. The liberation is *nirvana*, which is utter peace. In Tibetan, it is *nyang-en-de* or *namtar*. The fundamental ignorance here is the afflictive ignorance, explained in the preceding section, about the self-nature of things.

As per this cycle of existence, all sentient beings can be classified to be primary residents in one of the six realms of existence [*do-wa-rik-druk* in Tibetan]. The six realms are the realm of Gods, the realm of humans, the realm of asura, the realm of animals, the realm of hungry ghosts, and the realm of hell beings (HAR 2023).

The beings in the Gods' realm have supernatural power but do not have a "physical" form. They too, however, turn in the *samsaric* cycle because of their karma accumulated on from fundamental ignorance, for which reason they always request and listen to the teachings of the Buddha.

That means they can fall to a lower realm. The beings in asura are demigods or the lower gods who are always engaged in conflicts and wars.

The beings in the animal realm are animals. They are four-legged creatures who do not have a language system and are with a much inferior mental capacity than humans. They are taken advantage of by humans for manual works, for meat consumption, and for various products like milk and wool. The life of an animal is a miserable life, as such, and is regarded as one of the lower realms of existence. But they can be reborn as a human through meritorious acts such as helping other fellow animals or even humans. The Jataka stories of the Buddha describe the Buddha Shakyamuni's former births as animal beings such as a monkey, a lion, a deer, an elephant, a bird, a fish, etc. (Jataka, Aryasura's Jatakamala, Chalmers 1895).

The beings in the realm of hungry ghosts are always starved to death but they have a throat which is too narrow to swallow anything. People can be born in the hungry ghost realm [*pretas* in Sanskrit, *yi-dak* in Tibetan] from a human realm because of extreme miserliness to others. This realm is another lower realm of existence. In this realm, it is also extremely difficult to find an opportunity to be reborn as a human being, that is, by performing virtuous acts.

The beings in the hell realm [Sem-chen-nyel-wa in Tibetan] are in the lowest realm of existence. The pain and suffering are so overwhelming that hell beings cannot do anything but cry, regret, and despair. There are many different hells described in the Buddhist canons, one of which is the cauldron hell and another of which is the no-gap hell. In the no-gap hell, there is practically no space among the barriers where the beings in hell should remain trapped. One falls into the hell realm by committing a root infraction, for example, harming a Buddha physically, or killing another human being. However, even in such an ocean of unbearable suffering, there is a bodhisattva who is working to save sentient beings, who is renowned as Ksitigarbha [Sai-ning-bo in Tibetan], without whom it is impossible to escape hell (Ksitigarbha's Fundamental Vows, Medicine Buddha Sutra, Akasagarbha Sutra, Samantabhadra Vows).

Of the six realms, the human realm is praised as the best place for the pursuit and attainment of Buddhahood. This is because there are happiness and suffering abundant in this realm while beings thereof can learn and practice through languages and scriptures. Lama Tsongkhapa calls it the realm of leisure and opportunities, that is, del-jor in Tibetan (Lama Tsongkhapa's Principal Aspects, Stages). Literally, del means free time and jor means wealth. Shakyamuni was born into this realm as a prince in the Shakya country in the Himalayas. In this realm, however, it is also easy for one to fall into one of the lower realms such as asura, animals, hungry ghosts, and hells owing to abuses and misuses of the mental capacity.

For this reason, Lams Tsongkhapa calls the human rebirth more precious than the wish-fulfilling jewels [*yi-shin-norbu* in Tibetan] (Lama Tsongkhapa's Stages, Three Principal Aspects, Foundation of All). According to him, the human life is endowed with leisure and opportunity which enables one to pursue and ultimately achieve the perfection of wisdom, that is the Buddhahood. In Tibetan, the leisure (or free time) and opportunity (or wealth) is called *del-jor* while the human life is described as the life of leisure and opportunity which is *del-jor-tob-pa* (Lama Tsongkhapa's Songs);

> This life of leisure is even more precious than a wish-granting jewel;
> That I have found such an existence is only this once;
> So hard to find yet like a flash of lightning it is easy to vanish;
> Contemplating this situation it's vital to realize that all mundane pursuits
> Are like the empty grain husks floating in the winds.

Scientists do not subscribe to the idea of the six realms of cyclic existence, whose view is similar to Lokayata nihilists who considered that all the things in the world are naturally existent. As such, they reject the rule of karma and its effects (Chandrakirti's Clear Words). Lama Tsongkhapa describes their viewpoints thus: The living beings who are now here were not seen arriving in this life from a former life. Neither are they seen leaving it for a future life. Therefore, they are naturally existent (Lama Tsongkhapa's Stages of the Path).

This cycle of existence through the six realms is depicted as the wheel of life in the Buddhist literature [bhavacakra in Sanskrit, kor-wai-kor-lo in Tibetan]. A schematic bhavacakra diagram is drawn by the present author in Fig. 2.2. The innermost circle shows the three poisonous minds [duk-sum in Tibetan] as the three causes of the cyclic existence: desire, hatred, and ignorance [doichak, shedang, timuk in Tibetan]. The innermost circle and the six realms circle are intervened by the depiction of the Bardo [which is a Tibetan word], the intermediate state from one life to another according to the karma accumulated, either black or white. The outermost circle depicts the twelve factors of dependent origination which is the mechanism through which one is born in one realm and then reborn in

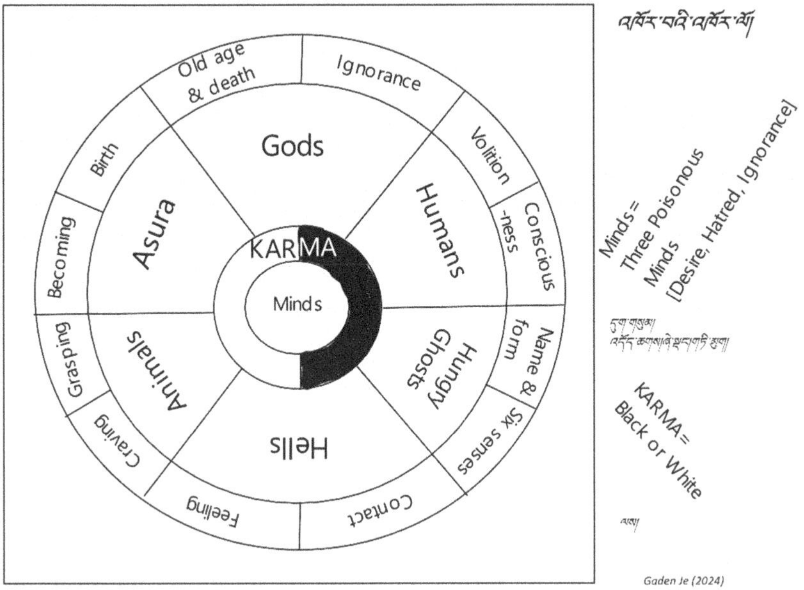

Fig. 2.2 The wheel of life schematic

another realm. This is the cycle of samsara [korwa in Tibetan], which is the cycle of existence.

Outside the wheel stands the Buddha who points to Nirvana, the end of suffering [Nyang-en-de in Tibetan]. This is not depicted in the figure. As Lama Tsongkhapa puts it (Lama Tsongkhapa's Songs):

I have made meaningful human existence that I have obtained.

དལ་འབྱོར་ཐོབ་པ་དོན་དང་ལྡན་པར་བྱས།།

5 The Question of the Worlds: Things "Beyond Us"

Everyone is curious about the worlds around us but perhaps even more so about the worlds "beyond us." What is really out there in the universe? How did it begin at all in the first place? Is there a limit, a boundary in the outer space unthinkably far away by human perception? Are there alien worlds out there somewhere humans cannot fathom to get to? Will the universe of ours end at some point in time? These are some of the questions ordinary people struggle to face with. Sometimes, not always!

Scientists are not an exception in this. Astronomers strive to see through the space as far as they can reach with the help of a telescope as far-reaching as the Hubble or the James Webb telescope (NASA 2024). They produce the photos of stars millions or even billions of years away from us or the photos of a spiraling black hole. Physicists endeavor to prove the very first state of the universe through a large-scale high-risk experiment such as the CERN (European Organization of Nuclear Research) experiment calling it a God particle experiment (Jaffe et al. 2000; CERN 2023). Engineers build and send the rovers to Mars to explore a human settlement there. They send space shuttles and rockets with an aim of carrying ordinary people for a travel through the unknown space in the universe (SpaceX 2024). However, the most powerful of them all is the unseen world of the smallest which is too fine to be perceived by human perception, for example, mRNA virus or quantum bits or photons (Einstein 1905; Kariko et al. 2011; Carroll 2019; Weiss 2020).

Looking deep into the Buddhist literature, you will find that some traditions have long wondered about the stars, planets, their cyclical patterns, and seasons. There are also some traditions which attempt to explain the earthly phenomena, including sentient beings' and nations' fortunes, through these heavenly phenomena. We may call it a Buddhist astrology (Kalachakratantra, Aryamanjushrimulakalpasutra). However, this approach is far more developed in non-Buddhist thought systems, for example, China's *I Ching* (Chinese Text Project 2024).

In Buddhism, the "universe" is not a single entity. Neither is it an entity that has a definite beginning. It begins without beginning. In fact, there is no "universe" in the Buddhist cosmology as scientists or ordinary people are understanding it. What? You may be puzzled. Let me begin by saying that there are not a few ways that express this Buddhist cosmology among which the principle of dependent origination is supreme (Lama Tsongkhapa's Praise, Buddhapalita's Commentary).

The external world or the material world in Buddhism is explained as dependently originated and designated phenomena (Paticca-samuppada Sutta, Bodhi Sutta). In this cosmology, if you will, the things around us as well as beyond us exist in dependence on other things. They are interdependent. In the interdependent cosmology, how can there be a universe or the universe that stands alone? In the interdependent cosmology, how can there be the end of a universe or the universe? In the interdependent cosmology, how can there be a beginning of the universe? These commonly held conclusions both by common people and scientists are impossible and irrational. As the Flower Ornament Sutra succinctly puts it (Ten Abodes Chapter):

> One is many, many are one.

Neither is the universe an entity that has a definite beginning. It begins without beginning. It ends without ending. What? Readers may be puzzled. To give you a clear example, reconsider the wheel of life in Fig. 2.2. Where is the beginning in the cycle of existence depicted in Fig. 2.2?

Let me give a more familiar example to scientists. Imagine a waterwheel with eight spokes, at each of which is a water bucket. It rotates on its own. It is well-known to scientists as an energy generator and especially to mathematicians. To understand the concept of the universe in Buddhism, imagine this waterwheel turns endlessly from the beginningless time!

The concept of time is analyzed in Buddhism also according to the rule of dependent origination and emptiness of intrinsic nature of anything. According to this, time does not exist on its own. You might ask: "But, doesn't the present exist at the very moment we are discussing this topic?" In response, I can direct you to think a little bit deeper about the dependently designated nature of time. To put it in simpler terms: the past is gone, the future is not here. With neither the past nor the future, where can the present be?

The reasonings that the present author just displayed are the rational analysis best elucidated by the acclaimed treatise of Nagarjuna entitled the Fundamental Verses of the Middle Way (Nagarjuna's Fundamental Wisdom; Lama Tsongkhapa's Ocean of Reasoning). In turn, the Nagarjuna's Fundamental Wisdom treatise is rooted on the teachings by Buddha Shakyamuni in numerous teachings such as the King of Meditations Sutra and the Mother Scripture, whose core message is the emptiness of all things internal as well as external without exception (Conze 1973, 1975). Nagarjuna [Lu-drup in Tibetan] is regarded as the founder of the Middle Way School of Buddhism [Woo-ma-pa in Tibetan], attributable to the title of his treatise (Aryadeva's Four Hundred, Buddhapalita's Commentary).

The reasoning of dependent origination as demonstrated by Nagarjuna has since then known to be the king of reasonings or the king of analyses, which had since then been upheld by such moon-like teachers as Buddhapalita [Sang-gye-kyang in Tibetan] and Chandrakirti [Da-wa-drak-pa in Tibetan] (Buddhapalita's Commentary, Chandrakirti's Clear Words, Entering Middle Way). Since then, the Buddhist scholarship would evolve over time for a period of about 800 years to reach a grand synthesis by Lama Tsongkhapa as the Prasangika Middle Way School [Woo-ma-tel-gyu-wa] where Prasanga means the absurd consequences, which has flourished up to this moment for over 600 years (Lama Tsongkhapa's True Eloquence). To quote directly from Lama Tsongkhapa (Ocean of Reasoning),

> If the past and the future
> Depended on the present,
> Therefore, neither the past nor
> The future could exist.

Perhaps, what is more tasteful to scientists is the Buddhist description of the cosmos which is far more colorful. In the interdependent world system, the Buddhist literature describes a billionfold universes. Start with a single world like the universe scientists know it. There are a thousand such worlds, which constitutes the first order world system. In turn, there are a thousand first-order world systems, which constitute the second-order world system. Again, there are a thousand second-order world systems, which constitute the third-order world system. In the third-order world system, therefore, there a billion worlds or universes, each of which is like the universe as scientists know it. The billionfold world system is referred to as a *trichiliocosm* in Sanskrit (Vasubandhu's Abhidharmakosa, Srikalacakra, Aryamanjusrimulakalpa). Again, do not be fooled by the large number here. The billionfold worlds are just one world system and there are again a billionfold such world systems. Remember one is many and many are one in Buddhism (Flower Ornament Sutra)!

This description of the Buddhist world system can be best visualized by the concept of Indra's Net [Indrajala in Sanskrit] (The Incalculable in Avatamsaka). Indra is the king of gods and devas in heaven who, in this metaphor, is depicted to hold a giant net all over the billionfold universes. At each knot of Indra's Net is attached a spherical crystal jewel. A single jewel is a single world. In the scripture, it is depicted as a particle or an atom (Cleary 1993):

> If untold buddha-lands are reduced to atoms,
> In one atom are untold lands,
> And as in one, so in each.
> The atoms to which these buddha-lands are reduced in an instant are unspeakable,
> And so are the atoms of continuous reduction moment to moment going on for untold eons;
> These atoms contain lands unspeakably many,
> And the atoms in these lands are even harder to tell of.

Let me help you visualize this metaphor. Refer to Fig. 2.3, which is the present author's rendition of Indra's Net. There are incalculable crystal jewels in Indra's Net. Since each jewel is crystal clear, it reflects the other

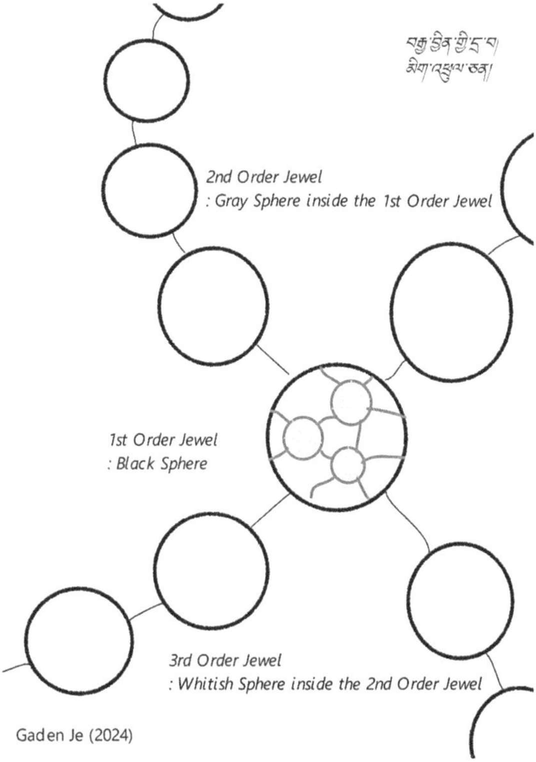

Fig. 2.3 An illustration of Indra's Net

jewels like a mirror. All the jewels in Indra's Net are reflected in that jewel like a good mirror of all directions does.

To understand the Buddhist meaning of this metaphor, pick one crystal jewel of all the incalculable jewels in Indra's Net. Let us call it the 1st order jewel. The 1st order jewels are incalculable. A single 1st order jewel reflects all the jewels in Indra's Net. In Fig. 2.3, it is the black spherical jewel in the middle. Of the reflected jewels inside the 1st order jewel, let us pick one jewel and call it the 2nd order jewel. It is the gray spherical jewel inside the black jewel in the figure. Since the 2nd order jewel, which is the reflected image in the 1st order jewel, is also crystal clear, it also reflects on its surface all the 2nd order jewels which are all reflected images, not the real jewels, but also all the 1st order jewels. Once again, let us pick one of the jewels reflected in the 2nd order jewel which is reflected on the surface of the 1st order jewel. Let us call it the 3rd order jewel which is the whitish spherical jewel in the figure. This process goes on without an end. It is an endless process, that is, we can keep finding 2nd order, 3rd order, 4th order jewels, and so on without end.

So, what scientists are seeing, when they are experimenting on something, is a reflection of a reflection of a reflection of a reflection of … of a crystal jewel. As Lama Tsongkhapa so eloquently elucidates it, the world exists like an illusion, or if you will, the reality is as such (Lama Tsongkhapa's True Eloquence, Illuminating the Intent, Nagarjuna's Sixty Reasoning Stanzas, Seventy Emptiness Stanzas).

What is fascinating in the Indra's Net metaphor is that any single crystal ball in Indra's Net reflects all the crystal balls in the billionfold universes. A single spherical jewel is equivalent to the billionfold universes. The present author can venture to say that that single crystal is known to many Buddhists as your mind [sem in Tibetan], that is, your consciousness [nam-she in Tibetan] (Ten Grounds Sutra, Descent int Lanka Sutra, Unravelling the Intent Sutra, Uttaratantra, Asanga's Compendium, Bodhisattva Stages). The mind is the creator of all the worlds and the beings therein (Flower Ornament Sutra's 20th Chapter):

> Mind is like an artist,
> Able to paint the worlds:
> The five clusters all are born thence;
> There's nothing it doesn't make.
> …
> If people know the actions of mind

Create all the worlds,
They will see the Buddha
And understand Buddha's true nature.

This is the central message that the present author hopes to deliver regarding all scientific inquiries and pursuits: all things are mind only. The present author will come back to this mind-only [*cittamatra* in Sanskrit, *semzam* in Tibetan] philosophy again at the final synthesis chapter of this book (Asanga's Compendium, Bodhisattva Stages, Maitreya's Ornament Realizations, Scripture Ornament). All the analyses on relativity physics, quantum mechanics, genetics and virology, stem cell research, and neuroscience, which are done from Chaps. 3–8, will be synthesized through the theory of mind-only, that is, the mind creator. That this theory of Buddhism is a proper rational framework for analyzing science endeavors is made clear to the present author while reading Je Rinpoche's analyses on this doctrine (Lama Tsongkhapa's True Eloquence, Golden Rosary, Sparham 2016).

6 Buddha the Teacher of Gods and Humans

This chapter explained Buddhism or the Perfect Wisdom expounded by the Buddha for the sake of scientists and engineers. As such, the exposition was organized appropriately into the question of the self, the question of life, and the question of the world. This chapter will serve as the anchor of this book's analysis of the five major science experiments and singularities that are currently under way with fervor.

Buddha Shakyamuni and Je Rinpoche taught the teaching of perfect wisdom not for the sake of the pleasure of intelligence but for the sake of liberating living beings from the unbearable ocean of suffering (Lama Tsongkhapa's Prayers of Goodness, Lotus Sutra, Diamond Sutra, Vimalakirti Sutta). The only door to such liberation is the perfection of wisdom [she-rab-gyi-pa-rol-tu-chin-pa in Tibetan] on reality [de-nyi in Tibetan], for the reason of teaching which the Buddha is called the Teacher of Gods and humans (Maha Parinibbana Sutta, Buddha Carita, Abhiniṣkramaṇa, Lalitavistara).

The truths, doctrines, concepts, and ideas of Buddhism explained in this chapter should not be interpreted with an absolutist attitude. Nothing mentioned in this chapter is presumed by the present author to exist ultimately (Perfection of Wisdom Sutra Condensed & 18000 Lines, King of

Meditations Sutra, Aksayamati Sutra). What that means is that nothing explained in this chapter exists in the way it appears, including the Buddha himself (Lama Tsongkhapa's True Eloquence). In the words of Lama Tsongkhapa, the world of the seen only exists in dependence of the seer. The seer in turn exists only in dependence on seeing. Seeing in turn depends on the seen. How can there be a seer without seeing (Lama Tsongkhapa's Ocean of Reasoning)?

7 Manjushri the Buddha of Wisdom

Manjushri is renowned as the Buddha of wisdom, but he is still called as the youthful Manjushri. His statues and tangkas depict him as a young boy like a sixteen-year-old youth. Je Rinpoche is renowned as Manjushri to Tibetans as his life-long experiences of meeting with and receiving teachings from Manjushri (Panchen Lama's Ritual, Thubten Jinpa 2019). Manjushri is also a teacher of Buddha Shakyamuni in previous lives, as such, regarded in the Buddhist Canons as the only one who can exchange jokes with Buddha Shakyamuni or give teachings to him (Adornment of Trees Sutra, Ajatasatru Sutra). Let me conclude this chapter with some of Manjushri's profound teachings because this chapter is written from the Lama Tsongkhapa's truly eloquent writings.

When a prostitute's daughter or a prostitute herself asks Manjushri how to attain enlightenment, he answers that "you yourself are enlightenment." He explains to her that the real nature of the delusional minds is enlightenment (Manjushri's Miraculous Play).

On another occasion, Buddha Shakyamuni said to Manjushri, "If there are no sentient beings, why do you speak of sentient beings, and even of a realm of sentient beings?" Manjushri the youth responded to the Buddha, "The realm of sentient beings is the same as the realm of Buddhas" in his youthful voice (Perfection of Wisdom Pronounced by Manjushri).

Shariputra, the foremost disciple of the Buddha, was among the audience of tens of thousands of bodhisattvas and Buddhas, was startled, and inquired of Manjushri, "Hasn't the Buddha realized unexcelled complete and perfect enlightenment?" Manjushri replied, "Neither is the case, Shariputra" in his youthful gentle voice (Perfection of Wisdom in 700 Lines).

Completed by Gaden Je at Lamajel Ling
June 30, 2024

References

Alberts B, Hopkin K, Johnson A, Morgan D, Roberts K, Walter P, and Heald R (2019) Essential Cell Biology (Sixth Edition). New York, NY: W.W. Norton & Company.

Alison MR, Poulsom R, Forbes S, and Wright NA (2002) An introduction to stem cells. The Journal of Pathology 197 (Special Issue on Stem Cells): 419–423.

Aryadeva (2nd century). Four Hundred Stanzas. Catuḥśatakaśāstra. Bstan bcos bzhi brgya pa. Toh 3846, dbu ma tsha.[4]

Aryashura (ca. 4th century). Jatakamala. Garland of the Buddha's Past Lives. Toh 4150.

Asanga (ca. fourth century). Compendium of the Universal Vehicle. Mahāyānasaṃgraha. Theg pa chen po bsdus pa. Toh 4048, sems tsam ri.

Asanga (ca. 4th century) Stages of the Bodhisattva. Bodhisattvabhumi. Byang chub sems dpa'i sa. Toh 4037. sems tsam wi.

Atisha Dipankara Srijnana (982–1054). Bodhipathapradīpa. A Lamp for the Path to Enlightenment. Byang chub lam gyi sgron ma.

Bhaviveka (sixth century). Lamp of Wisdom. Prajnapradipa. Shes rab sgron ma. Toh 3853, dbu ma tsha.

Bhikkhu Khantipalo (1995) The Wheel of Birth and Death. Access to Insight. Accessed from https://www.accesstoinsight.org/lib/authors/khantipalo/wheel147.html#fn-6

Buddhapalita (ca. fifth century). Commentary. Buddhapālitamūlamadhyamakavṛtti. Dbu ma rtsa ba'i 'grel pa buddha pā li ta. Toh 3842, dbu ma tsa.

Carroll S (2019) Something Deeply Hidden: Quantum Worlds and the Emergence of Spacetime. Boston, MA: E.P. Dutton.

CERN (European Organization for Nuclear Research) (2023) The Large Hadron Collider. CERN, Geneva, Switzerland. Accessed from https://www.home.cern/science/accelerators/large-hadron-collider

Chalmers R (1895) The Jataka or Stories of the Buddha's Former Births (Volume 1–6). Accessed from https://www.wisdomlib.org/buddhism/book/jataka-tales-english

Chandrakirti (seventh century). Clear Words. Prasannapada. Tshig gsal. Tengyur. Beijing: Comparative edition. Vol. 60, 3–483.

Chandrakirti (seventh century). Entering the Middle Way. Madhyamakāvatāra. Dbu ma la 'jug pa. Toh 3861, dbu ma'a.

Chinese Text Project (2024) Book of Changes: Yi Jing. Available at https://ctext.org/book-of-changes/yi-jing.

[4] Tohoku University (ed.) (1934). A Complete Catalogue of the Tibetan Buddhist Canons, Sde-dge Edition, Tohoku University, Japan.

Cleary T (1993) The Flower Ornament Scripture: A Translation of the Avatamsaka Sutra. Boston, MA: Shambala.
Conze E (1973) Perfect Wisdom: The Short Prajnaparamita Texts. London, UK: The Buddhist Publishing Society.
Conze E (1975) The Large Sutra on Perfect Wisdom with the divisions of the abhisamayālaṃkāra. Berkeley, CA: The University of California Press.
Cutler JWC, Newland G (trans.) (2000) The Great Treatise on the Stages of the Path to Enlightenment by Tsongkhapa. Ithaca, NY: Snow Lion Publications.
Dar A, Rujula AD, and Heinz U (1999) Will relativistic heavy-ion colliders destroy our planet? Physics Letters B 470: 142–48.
Darwin C (1859) On the Origin of Species by Means of Natural Selection, or the Preservation of Favoured Races in the Struggle for Life. London, UK: John Murray.
Dharmakirti (seventh century) Exposition of Valid Cognition. Pramāṇavārttika. Tshad ma rnam'grel. Toh 4210, tshad ma ce.
Dignaga (c. 480–540 CE) Synthesis of Valid Cognition. Paramanasamuccaya. Tshad ma kun las btus pa. Toh 4203.
Einstein, A (1905) On a Heuristic Point of View Concerning the Production and Transformation of Light. Annalen der Physik 17: 132–148.
Flower Ornament Sutra. Chapter 15. Ten Abodes. Avatamsaka Sutra. Sans rgyas phal po che shes bya ba sintu rgyas pa chen pohi mdo. Toh 44. Phal chen ka.
Flower Ornament Sutra. Chapter 20. Eulogies in the Palace of the Suyama Heaven. Avatamsaka Sutra. Sans rgyas phal po che shes bya ba sintu rgyas pa chen pohi mdo. Toh 44. Phal chen ka.
Flower Ornament Sutra. Chapter 30. The Incalculable. Avatamsaka Sutra. Sans rgyas phal po che shes bya ba sintu rgyas pa chen pohi mdo. Toh 44. Phal chen ka.
Fremantle F, Trungpa C (1975) The Tibetan Book of the Dead: The Great Liberation through Hearing in the Bardo by Guru Rinpoche according to Karma Lingpa. Boulder, CO: Shambhala.
Galilei G (1632) Concerning the Two Chief World Systems (Dialogo sopra i due massimi sistemi del mondo). Fiorenza, Per Gio: Batista Landini.
Hawking S, Tegmark M, Russell S, Wilczek F (2014) Transcending Complacency on Superintelligent Machines. Huffington Post. Accessed from https://www.huffingtonpost.com/stephen-hawking/artificial-intelligence_b_5174265.html
Himalayan Art Resources (HAR) (2023) Wheel of Life Schematic. Accessed from https://www.himalayanart.org/pages/wheeloflife2/index.html
Hopkins J (2008) Tsong-Kha-Pa's Final Exposition of Wisdom. Boston, MA: Shambala.
Jaffe RL, Buszaa W, Sandweiss J, Wilczek F (2000) Review of speculative disaster scenarios at RHIC. Review of Modern Physics 72: 1125–1140.
Kamalasila (ninth century). Stages of Meditation. Bhāvanākrama. Sgom pa'I rim pa. Toh 3915, dbu ma ki.

Kariko, K., H. Muramatsu, J. Ludwig, and D. Weissman. 2011. Generating the Optimal mRNA for Therapy: HPLC Purification Eliminates Immune Activation and Improves Translation for Nucleoside-modified. Protein-encoding mRNA. Nucleic Acids Research 39: e142.

Kurzweil R (2005) The Singularity is Near. New York, NY: Penguin.

Lama Tsongkhapa (1357a–1419). Collected Works of the Incomparable Lord Tsongkhapa Lobsang Drakpa. Kumbum woodblock edition.

Lama Tsongkhapa (1357b–1419) In Praise of the Buddha for His Teaching of Dependent Origination. Ston pa la rten cing 'brel bar byung bar gsungs pa las brtsams te bstod pa legs bshad snying po. Miscellaneous Writings of the Incomparable Lord Tsongkhapa, 30–36.

Lama Tsongkhapa (1357c–1419) Great Treatise on the Stages of the Path to Enlightenment. Byang chub lam rim chen mo. Collected Works. Vol. pa.[5]

Lama Tsongkhapa (1357d–1419) Ocean of Reasoning: An Exposition of Treatise on the Middle Way. Rtsa ba shes rab kyi rnam bshad ṭik chen rigs pa'i rgya mtsho. Collected Works. Vol. ba, 1–583.

Lama Tsongkhapa (1357e–1419) Illuminating the Intent: A Thorough Exposition of Entering the Middle Way. Dbu ma la 'jug pa'i rnam bshad dgongs pa rab gsal. Collected Works. Vol. ma, 1–605.

Lama Tsongkhapa (1357f–1419) Golden Rosary of Excellent Utterances: Extensive Exposition of "Ornament of Realization" As Well As Its Commentary (Shes rab kyi pha rol du phyin pa mngon par rtogs pa'i rgyan 'grel pa dang bcas pa rgyas par bshad pa legs bshad gser gyi phreng ba). Collected Works. Vols. tsa and tsha.

Lama Tsongkhapa (1357g–1419) Essence of True Eloquence: Distinguishing the Provisional and the Definitive Meaning (Drang ba dang nges pa'i don rnam par 'byed pa legs bshad snying po). Collected Works. Vol. pha, 441–687.

Lama Tsongkhapa (1357h–1419). Three Principal Aspects of the Path. Lam gyi gtso bo rnam pa gsum. Miscellaneous Writings, 463–65.

Lama Tsongkhapa (1357i–1419) Realization Narrative. Rtogs brjod 'dun legs ma. Portland, OR: The Foundation for the Preservation of the Mahayana Tradition (FPMT).

Lama Tsongkhapa (1357j–1419). Songs of Experience on the Stages of the Path. *Lam rim nyams mgur*). *Miscellaneous Writings*, 127–33.

Lama Tsongkhapa (1357k–1419). Prayers for Goodness in the Beginning, the Middle, and the End. Thog mtha' bar gsum du dge ba'i smon lam. Portland, OR: The Foundation for the Preservation of the Mahayana Tradition (FPMT).

[5] Lama Tsongkhapa (1357–1419). Collected Works of the Incomparable Lord Tsongkhapa Lobsang Drakpa. Kumbum woodblock edition.

Lama Tsongkhapa (1357l–1419). Foundation of All Good Qualities. Yon ten kun gyi gsir gyur. Portland, OR: The Foundation for the Preservation of the Mahayana Tradition (FPMT).
Linnaeus, Carolus. 1758. Systema naturæ per regna tria naturæ, secundum classes, ordines, genera, species, cum characteribus, differentiis, synonymis, locis. Stockholm, SE: Laurentius Salvius.
Mayo Clinic (2023) Stem cells: What they are and what they do. Rochester, MN: Mayo Clinic. Accessed from https://www.mayoclinic.org/tests-procedures/bone-marrow-transplant/in-depth/stem-cells/art-20048117
Maitreya (4th century). Ornament of Realizations. Abhisamayālaṃkāra. Mngon rtogs rgyan. Toh 3786, shes phyin ka.
Maitreya (4th century). Ornament of the Scriptures of the Great Vehicle. Mahayanasutralamkara. Mdo sde rgyan. Toh 4020.
Milarepa (1052–1135) The Hundred Thousand Songs of Milarepa: A New Translation (translated by Stagg C, 2017. Boulder, CO: Shambhala).
Mora, Camilo, Derek P. Tittensor, Sina Adl, Alastair G.B. Simpson, and Boris Worm. 2011. How Many Species Are There on Earth and in the Ocean? PLoS Biology 9 (8): e1001127. https://doi.org/10.1371/journal.pbio.1001127.
Nagarjuna (second century). Commentary on the Awakening Mind. Bodhicittavivaraṇa. Byang chub sems kyi 'grel pa. Toh 1801, rgyud 'grel ngi.
Nagarjuna (second century). Fundamental Wisdom on the Middle Way. Mūlamadhyamakakārikā. Dbu ma rtsa ba'i tshig le'ur byas pa (Rtsa ba'i shes rab). Toh 3824, dbu ma tsa.
Nagarjuna (second century). Precious Garland. Ratnāvalī. Rin chen phreng ba. Toh 4158, spriṅ yig ge.
Nagarjuna (second century). Sixty Stanzas of Reasoning. Yuktiṣaṣṭikākārikā. Rigs pa drug cu pa. Toh 3825, dbu ma tsa.
Nagarjuna (2nd century). Seventy Stanzas on Emptiness. Śūnyatāsaptatikārikā. Stong nyid bdun cu pa. Toh 3827, dbu ma tsa.
National Aeronautics and Space Administration (NASA) (2024) Webb Space Telescope. NASA, Washington, DC. Accessed from https://webb.nasa.gov/
National Human Genome Research Institute (NHGRI). 2021. The Human Genome Project. The NHGRI, National Institutes of Health, Bethesda, MD. https://www.genome.gov/human-genome-project.
National Institutes of Health (2009) NIH Guidelines for Human Stem Cell Research. Bethesda, MD: National Institutes of Health.
Newton, I (1687) Philosophiæ Naturalis Principia Mathematica. London, UK: The Royal Society.
Ngawang Samten, and Garfield JL (tras.) (2006) Ocean of Reasoning: A Great Commentary on Nagarjuna's Mulamadhyamakakarika. Oxford, UK: Oxford University Press.

Panchen Lama (4th) (17th century). Guru Puja Ritual. Berzin Archives. Accessed from https://studybuddhism.com/bo/tshad-mtho-i-slob-sbyong/zhal-don-dang-cho-g-i-rigs/sngags-kyi-nymas-len/bla-ma-mchod-p-i-cho-ga

Pardi, N., M.J. Hogan, F.W. Porter, and D. Weissman. 2018. mRNA vaccines—A New Era in Vaccinology. Nature Reviews Drug Discovery 17: 261–279.

Philg88 (2017) Chinese Chariot Design. World History Encyclopedia. Retrieved from https://www.worldhistory.org/image/6849/chinese-chariot-design/

Purves D, Augustine GJ, Fitzpatrick D, Hall WC, LaMantia A-S, White LE (Editors) (2011) Neuroscience (5th edition). Sunderland, MA: Sinauer Associates.

Quadrato G, Nguyen T, Macosko EZ, et al. (2017) Cell diversity and network dynamics in photosensitive human brain organoids. Nature 545: 48–53.

Rizong Sras Rinpoche (2013) The Ganden Tripa Teaching on "In Praise of Dependent Arising." A teaching give at Kurukulla Center, Medford MA.

Seo SN (2018) Natural and Man-made Catastrophes: Theories, Economics, and Policy Designs. Wiley-Blackwell, John Wiley & Sons.

Seo SN (2020) The Economics of Globally Shared and Public Goods. Amsterdam, NL: Academic Press.

Seo SN (2021) Climate Change and Economics: Engaging with Future Generations with Action Plans. London UK: Palgrave Macmillan.

Seo SN (2022a) The Economics of Pandemics: Exploring Globally Shared Experiences. Palgrave Macmillan, London, UK

Seo SN (2022b) Handbook of Behavioral Economics and Climate Change. London, UK: Palgrave Macmillan.

Seo SN (2023) The Economics of Optimal Growth Pathways: Evaluating the Health of the Planet's Natural and Ecological Resources. London, UK: Palgrave Macmillan

Seo SN (2024a) Buddha, Wisdom, and Economics: A Contribution to the Art of Happiness. Edward Elgar, Cheltenham, UK.

Seo SN (2024b) Protecting Nature with Buddha's Wisdom: A Contribution to Environmental and Nature Studies. Edward Elgar, Cheltenham, UK.

Shantarakṣita (9th century). Ornament of the Middle Way. Madhyamakālaṃkāra. Dbu ma rgyan. Toh 3884, dbu ma sa.

Shantideva (eighth century). Guide to the Bodhisattva Way. Bodhicaryāvatāra. Byang chub sems dpa'i spyod pa la'jug pa. Toh 3871, dbu ma la.

Singer W (1999) Neuronal Synchrony: A Versatile Code for the Definition of Relations? Neuron24: 49–65.

SpaceX (2024) Mission. Space Exploration Technologies Corp., Hawthorne, CA. Accessed from https://www.spacex.com/mission/

Sparham G (2016) Golden Garland of Eloquence: Legs Bshad Gser Phreng by Tsong Kha Pa. New Delhi, IN: Jain Pub.

Tegmark M (2015) Consciousness as a State of Matter. Chaos, Solitons & Fractals 76: 238–270. arxiv.org/abs/1401.1219

The Tibetan and Himalayan Library (THL) (2009) The Tibetan Buddhist Canon. Accessed from https://www.thlib.org/encyclopedias/literary/canons/index.php

Thomson JA, Itskovitz-Eldor J, Shapiro SS, Waknitz MA, Swiergiel JJ, Marshall VS, Jones JM (1998) Embryonic stem cell lines derived from human blastocysts. Science 282 (5391): 1145–1147.

Tohoku University (ed.) (1934). A Complete Catalogue of the Tibetan Buddhist Canons, Sde-dge Edition, Tohoku University, Japan.

Thubten Jinpa (2019) Tsongkhapa: A Buddha in the Land of Snows. Boston, MA: Shambala.

Thubten Jinpa (2021) Illuminating the Intent: An Exposition of Candrakirti's Entering the Middle Way. Wisdom Boston, MA: Wisdom Publications.

Thurman RAF (1984) Tsong Khapa's Speech of Gold in the Essence of True Eloquence: Reason and Enlightenment in the Central Philosophy of Tibet. Princeton, NJ: Princeton University Press.

United States (US) National Archives (2024) Declaration of Independence: A Transcription. Accessed from https://www.archives.gov/founding-docs/declaration-transcript

Vasubandhu (ca. 4th century). Treasury of Abhidharma. Abhidharmakośa. Chos mngon pa mdzod. Toh 4089, mngon pa ku.

Walpola Rahula (1974) What the Buddha Taught: Revised and Expanded Edition with Texts from Suttas and Dhammapada. New York, NY: Grove Press.

Watanabe S (2005) Buddha Shakyamuni. Tokyo, JP: Chikumashobo.

Weis SR (2020) Forty Years with Coronaviruses. Journal of Experimental Medicine 217 (5): e20200537. https://doi.org/10.1084/jem.20200537.

Weitzman ML (2009) On modeling and interpreting the economics of catastrophic climate change. Review of Economics and Statistics 91: 1–19.

CHAPTER 3

The Economics of Singularities and Civilizations-Ending Catastrophes

1 Introduction

Having introduced the basket of Buddhist thoughts that are broadly pertinent for the reviews and assessments of the five singularities that are originating from the major science experiments today, the present author will in this chapter offer a brief review of the economic models and theories that are concerned with planet-ending catastrophes. As this chapter will show, the economic models will highlight the intersection between science and Buddhist thoughts on this topic.

The economics on such singularity events as analyzed in this book is very sparse, if not nonexistent, as of yet. The reason for that is not hard to imagine. Economists are by far more accustomed to analyzing daily transactions of goods and services as well as economy-wide events at the national level. The latter encompasses economic growth, inflation, an interest rate, an unemployment rate, housing markets, governmental policies, etc. (Mas-Colell et al. 1995; Mankiw 2014). Economists very rarely ask a question about a planet-ending catastrophe, even if they are concerned with a global market crash (Galbraith 1954; Shiller 2005).

The pioneering effort of William Nordhaus for developing the economic model of a global climate change policy can be credited, which is known as the DICE model (Nordhaus 1994). However, it was not a catastrophe model or analysis (Nordhaus 2008). A planet-ending catastrophe

S. N. Seo, *The Economics of Singularities of Science Elucidated with Buddhist Thoughts*,
https://doi.org/10.1007/978-3-031-69118-8_3

economic model can be credited to Martin Weitzman for his fat-tail economic model known as the dismal theorem, the term he coined (Weitzman 2009). However, the economic models do not as of yet have the sophistication for accounting for the adaptive capabilities and capacities of people and anthropogenic systems in responding to any catastrophic possibilities, which may lie at the heart of economics (Seo 2016, 2020a, 2020b, 2023).

This chapter will review the latter literature, that is, the fat-tail economics of planet-ending catastrophes. As will be made clearer, it is meaningful to begin with the scientific theories of a catastrophe, that is, the definitions of a catastrophe by scientists, before jumping into an economic analysis (Seo 2018a, 2018b). The two theories are particularly apposite. One is the catastrophe theory advanced through the concept of a tipping point put forth from a biological/ecological model (Thom 1975). The tipping point is also referred to as a bifurcation point or a singularity point in mathematics. The other is the chaos theory put forth by a meteorologist through such concepts as initial conditions and butterfly effects (Lorenz 1963).

The two scientific theories are in fact applied at one level or another across all the chapters of this book and as such are essential components of this book. The term "singularities" in the book title refers to such concepts as a bifurcation point, singularity, a tipping point, a catastrophe, a critical point, which are advanced in mathematics, biology, and ecology and recently applied to other areas of science (Thom 1972, 1975; Kurzweil 2005; Hawking et al. 2014).

The economic models such as the dismal theorem and the scientific models such as the catastrophe theory and the chaos theory share in common that they are a model or another that explains how a "truly" catastrophic event can befall. The former, however, is driven by the role of uncertainty. In addition, they also share in common that they do not take into account, or put differently, do not have the sophistication of accounting for the adaptive behaviors of the people and anthropogenic systems faced with an existential threat (Seo 2018a, 2018b).

Interestingly, should the full adaptive capacity be introduced into a catastrophe model or another, the expected or assumed catastrophe disappears from the model in most cases, which means that the model itself is no longer appropriate for explaining the core mechanism that it tried to explain in the first place. This is the quandary of the catastrophe modelers: how much the adaptative system should be assumed, that is, included in the model to keep the catastrophe or chaos outcome alive?

This chapter proceeds with the following five topics in sequence: an introduction to the mathematical bifurcation theory and singularity, an introduction to the catastrophe theory, an introduction to the chaos theory, an introduction to the economics of fat-tails, and a critique against the fat-tail economics of catastrophes from behavioral standpoints.

2 The Bifurcation Theory and Singularity in Mathematics

For the description of the major scientific theories applicable to the economic models of catastrophes, we can start with their origin in mathematics. The catastrophe theory, as was introduced to the public during the 1970s, was originated from and is recognized as a part of the bifurcation theory in mathematics. The term "bifurcation" does not connote any implication of a catastrophe.

The bifurcation theory in mathematics is a study of changes in a family of curves in terms of its qualitative or topological nature. The family of curves represents a dynamical system, which can be a biological system or an economic system or something else. The family of curves is described by a set of differential equations (Teschl 2012). A bifurcation occurs when a small change in the value of a parameter in the system causes a sudden qualitative change in the system (Gilmore 1981; Rosser 2007).

The term "bifurcation" originated from Henri Poincare (1854–1912), a French mathematician, who is credited to have invented the bifurcation theory of mathematics while he was researching the celestial mechanics. He asked whether the orbits of the planets in the solar system would escape without bounds, or be kept within certain bounds, or whether the planets in the solar system would crash into each other or the Sun. It was many decades before Einstein's publications on general relativity, but centuries after Newton's publication of the "Principia" in the seventeenth century (Newton 1687; Einstein 1915). This investigation by Poincare regarding the stability of the solar system in the event of a small perturbation in the system had led to the discovery of the bifurcation theory of mathematics (Poincare 1880–1890).

Poincare's orbit problem provides an apt visual example for the defining feature of the various singularities of science that are dealt with in this book. A singularity or a bifurcation is at the point where the orbit of a planet starts to diverge from the "normal" orbit, after which point a return to the "normal" orbit is no longer possible. The singularity is irreversible by definition. It is a degenerate critical point in mathematical terms (Zeeman 1977; Gilmore 1981).

The singularity point is not strange to economists, either, although it is not mentioned in the economic literature as such. The opposite of it is the most familiar concept to economists, that is, an equilibrium. To elaborate it, when there is a perturbation in an equilibrium, the process that takes place after the perturbation leads the system back to the equilibrium point. That is why it is called an equilibrium. It is a stable point, like a ping pong ball placed inside a round mixing bowl (Dixit 1990; Mas-Colell et al. 1995).

The bifurcation point, which will be graphically explained shortly relying on mathematical equations, is a point at which a sudden qualitative change occurs in the system. Once a tiny perturbation is stirred at the singularity point, the system is forever deviating from the normal state. It is therefore irreversible. The bifurcation point is therefore a type of a disequilibrium, like a golf ball placed on top of a dome (Arrow and Intriligator 1981).

3 A Singularity in the Catastrophe Theory

The catastrophe theory was developed during the 1970s by French mathematician Rene Thom and others (Thom 1972, 1975, 1977). It is a special case of the bifurcation theory of mathematics, which is asserted by mathematicians. Thom, on the other hand, defined the catastrophe as a biological or ecological event. At the bifurcation point in his model, the stability of a biological system is gone forever. The bifurcation point in his model is a singularity point, which is again a tipping point which is a more popular term in applied sciences such as climate change.

Thom's catastrophe model is a functional representation of a dynamic system whose dynamic changes depend on state variables and parameters, in which a catastrophe is inherent (Thom 1975; Zeeman 1977). He defined multiple such systems of equations, each of which is referred to as an elementary catastrophe. Limiting the number of state variables to two and the number of parameters to four, there are seven elementary catastrophes Thom offered.

In Thom's catastrophe model, the solutions of the system under investigation depend on the parameters in the system. A stable equilibrium is where a potential function is at the minimum. A catastrophe is identified where a small change in a certain parameter causes the equilibrium in the system to disappear.

To explain what that means, let us consider a fold catastrophe, the simplest of the elementary catastrophe models. The fold catastrophe has one control parameter (φ) and one state variable (x), whose potential function is defined as follows (Zeeman 1977):

$$G(x;\varphi) = x^3 + \varphi x. \tag{3.1}$$

It is difficult for most people to understand why Eq. (3.1) is a catastrophe model, at least at first sight. Figure 3.1 explains why, as suggested by Thom. The two-dimensional figure is the plot of the potential function G given the state variable x, depending on the value of the control parameter, φ. The four relationships are drawn for the four values of the control parameter. Notice that at the negative values of the control parameter ($\varphi < 0$), the potential function has two equilibria. The first is a stable equilibrium which exists at the local minimum of $G(x)$. The other is an unstable equilibrium which exists at the local maximum of $G(x)$. As φ gradually increases ever closer to zero, the system behaves as it was before, with the stable equilibrium moving ever closer to the left.

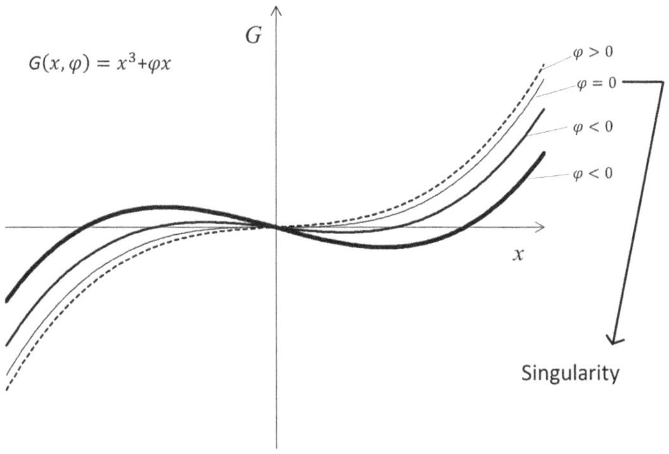

Fig. 3.1 Illustrating a fold catastrophe

Notice that when $\varphi = 0$, the system is fundamentally changed: There is no equilibrium in the system. A strange phenomenon suddenly appears at that value of the control parameter. That is, the equilibrium suddenly disappears. That value of the control parameter on which the system abruptly loses equilibria is called a bifurcation point. The bifurcation point is also referred to as a singularity (Zeeman 1977).

The other elementary catastrophe models put forth by Rene Thom, seven in total, can be explained the same way. There are only seven generic structures of an elementary catastrophe, that is, when the number of x is no larger than two and the number of φ is no larger than four. Thom gave the following colorful names to them: fold catastrophe, cusp catastrophe, swallowtail catastrophe, butterfly catastrophe, hyperbolic umbilic catastrophe, elliptic umbilic catastrophe, and parabolic umbilic catastrophe.

They all have the same characteristic as just explained through Fig. 3.1. So, the catastrophe theory is an exposition of what a catastrophe looks like. It does not explain why such a catastrophe occurs. Neither does it explain how such a catastrophe can be prevented by regulating mechanisms, for example, an anthropogenic intervention in the biological/ecological system (Seo 2018a, 2018b).

4 A Chaos Theory

In the fold catastrophe above (Fig. 3.1), the system has no equilibrium when the value of the control parameter is zero or positive. The system without an equilibrium is also referred to as a chaos or a chaotic system. The chaos theory was developed from a different line of inquiry, specifically, the study of weather. The chaos theory is the field of research on the systems that are in chaos (Gleick 1987; Strogatz 1994). The chaos is defined as absence of order in the system.

The first experimenter of the chaos theory was Edward Lorenz, a meteorologist at the Massachusetts Institute of Technology (Gleick 1987; Emanuel 2011). How he found the chaos theory is a tale of serendipity, which is how it has been described. In the 1960s, he was constructing a computer model to predict the weather in Boston. His model had the set of 12 equations (Lorenz 1963). He failed, but was able to produce a set of solutions relying on the 1960s' computing capabilities, that is, a long sequence of a set of numbers produced by the equations, which is then printed on a paper. It was a ticker tape era of computing. One year later, he wanted to reproduce the sequence. In order to save time, he started from the set of numbers at the middle of the sequence. He expected to produce the same sequence again as last year's but the program produced a wildly different set of numbers. Against his expectation, a minute difference in the starting point was resulting in a starkly different sequence of numbers as well as a strange destination.

This phenomenon was termed the butterfly effect in such presentations by Lorenz as "Does the Flap of a Butterfly's Wings in Brazil Set Off a Tornado in Texas?" at a meeting in Washington D.C. (Lorenz 1969a, 1969b, 1993). When the present author began studying at a college in Seoul during the 1990s, it was a fancy term among the students there. In the chaos theory literature, the butterfly effect is more formally referred to as sensitive dependence on the initial conditions (Strogatz 1994).

If you are wondering why this phenomenon matters, imagine that the world system we are in now is not controllable at all because it depends so sensitively to a minor disturbance or another, as is depicted in the chaos theory. The minor disturbance can occur through many routes, for example, experimental noises that are not noticeable, background noises that cannot be controlled, tiny discrepancies that occur in the equipment or laboratories, or researchers' habits and preferences (Seo 2022a).

Let me give readers a brief taste of his model. Continuing with the set of differential equations developed for his weather prediction model, Lorenz came to formally present a mathematical representation of a chaotic system. The three-dimensional system is referred to as the Lorenz system which is a set of three ordinary differential equations as follows: (Lorenz 1963; Strogatz 1994):

$$\begin{aligned} \dot{x} &= \sigma(y - x); \\ \dot{y} &= \gamma x - y - xz; \\ \dot{z} &= xy - \rho z. \end{aligned} \tag{3.2}$$

In the Lorenz system in Eq. (3.2), there are three state variables—x, y, z—and three system parameters—σ, γ, ρ. Setting the parameters to specific values, namely, setting initial conditions, he drew the sequence of the solution set on a three-dimensional plane, which is depicted in Fig. 3.2 (Hirsch et al. 2003). Notably, the solution sets always stayed on a double spiral as in Fig. 3.2. The double spiral was called the Lorenz attractor (Lorenz 1963, 1993).

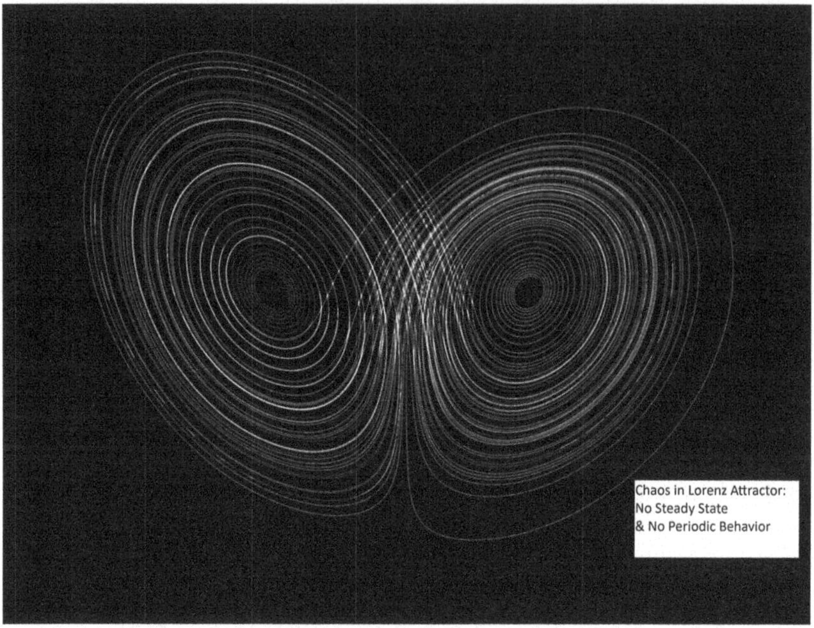

Fig. 3.2 The Lorenz attractor: a system of chaos
Note: The Lorenz attractor was simulated by the present author using the Interactive Lorenz Attractor provided online by Cristersson (2017)

The Lorenz attractor represents a chaos, more formally, a chaotic system. You might wonder why. As graphically presented in Fig. 3.2, the Lorenz system goes into a loop in the double spiral and does not rest on any steady or equilibrium state at all. It randomly takes on a different loop each time, which also depends on the initial values of the parameters, and repeats its spiral action. It is a nonlinear, non-periodic, and deterministic system.

The Lorenz attractor is a system of chaos in that there is no order in it. There is no order in the sense that the Lorenz system fails to exhibit either of the two features of an orderly system. First, it does not contain a steady state solution. Second, it does not contain a periodic behavior (Gleick 1987; Tziperman 2017). The note box at the bottom-right corner of Fig. 3.2 states these two features of the Lorenz attractor.

The development of the field of the chaos theory over time since its first emergence through Lorenz, however, took a somewhat unexpected turn, which is notable considering the nature of a chaos that its founders strove to explicate. Contrary to the seminal work of presenting a chaos, its followers delved in an effort to discover an order in a chaotic system thus put forth. What they found is also notable. Although a system may look like a chaos at one scale of time or space, it may reveal an orderly structure in another scale of time or space (Feigenbaum 1978; Alligood et al. 1996; Tziperman 2017).

5 The Economics of Fractals and Fat-Tails

An economic analysis of catastrophes was presented by Martin Weitzman through his analysis of on-going climate change policy negotiations. He asked, to paraphrase it slightly: Faced with the truly catastrophic possibilities (of climate change) through such processes as explained in the catastrophe theory or the chaos theory, what should be the best policy approach for the human society to adopt (to deal with climate change)?

Although neither the catastrophe theory nor the chaos theory may appear at first to be a meaningful idea for an economic analysis, a wide range of economic matters is indeed dependent, in a major or minor way, on such processes as elucidated by scientists. As for the Weitzman's analysis, he relied on the process that has been known variously to economists as a fractal or a power function or a fat-tail distribution (Schuster 1984; Mandelbrot 1997; Seo 2018a, 2018b). These probability distributions were adopted by economists in the expositions of a once-in-a-century great market crash (Mandelbrot 1997; Taleb 2007; Shiller 2005; Gabaix 2009). They may be derived from Thom's catastrophe or Lorenz's chaos.

The dismal theorem (DT) of climate change economics, as Weitzman referred to it as such, is succinctly expressed as:

$$\lim_{\lambda \to \infty} E\left[M|\lambda\right] = +\infty. \tag{3.3}$$

The E[M] is the stochastic discounting factor, which expresses the dollar amount that the present time period is willing to sacrifice in order to secure one dollar in the future period. It is a simplistic two-period model: now and the future. The dismal theorem in Eq. (3.3) says that it is infinite in the case of global warming policy.

Another critical parameter in Eq. (3.3) is λ. This is roughly the value of all the civilizations on the planet (VACP). It is interpreted as an extension of the economic concept of value of statistical life (VSL) in the environmental literature (Viscusi and Aldy 2003). It is assumed to be infinite in the dismal theorem.

The DT expressed in Eq. (3.3) can be succinctly explained with several equations (Seo 2020b). The primary variable of interest is the degree of climate change. Let X be a random variable of that variable of interest. For all practical purposes, it corresponds to the global temperature anomaly which is reported every month and projected into the future for the next 100-year period and more (Le Treut et al. 2007; IPCC 2021).

The critical assumption of the DT is that this random variable has a fat-tail probability distribution, the distribution of which can be written with a power law function as follows in the probability density form:

$$\Pr\left[X = x\right] = cx^{-(1+\alpha)}. \tag{3.4}$$

This distribution has been known as the Pareto distribution to most economists named after Italian economist Vilfred Pareto in the nineteenth century who applied it for an analysis of income distribution, or the Pareto-Levy-Mandelbrot distribution, or the Zipf distribution to some (Pareto 1896; Zipf 1949; Mandelbrot 1963; Gabaix 2009). The c is a constant. The α (>0) is the shape parameter. Importantly, when $\alpha \to 0$, the distribution becomes fat-tailed. When $\alpha \to \infty$, the distribution approximates a Gaussian (Normal) distribution (Schuster 1984).

Another key assumption that the value of all civilizations on the planet (VACP) is unbounded was already mentioned:

$$\lambda \to +\infty. \tag{3.5}$$

Given the assumption of the VACP, the damage from an exceptionally high degree of global warming would be exponentially harmful. Weitzman cites a 10 °C increase as well as a 20 °C increase in global average temperature. An exponential damage function such as Eq. (3.6) is what is needed to represent the assumed damage from climate change (in the dismal theorem). In other words, it is a function of λ. With two parameters k and β of the exponential function:

$$D(x|\lambda) = ke^{\beta x}. \tag{3.6}$$

The fat-tail distribution or the power law distribution function in Eq. (3.4) is interpreted as a posterior-predictive distribution function in that the climate change uncertainty is so large that, however much time and resources were to be committed by the global community to resolve this uncertainty, it cannot be reduced (Bayes 1763). In other words, the fatness of the tail distribution cannot be made thinner.

These assumptions were radically different from William Nordhaus's climate change economic model which was awarded the Nobel Prize in 2018. Specifically, the latter relies on the Gaussian probability for Eq. (3.4) and the power function with specific parameters for Eq. (3.6) (Nordhaus 2008; Nobel Prize 2018).

With the assumptions of Eqs. (3.4–3.6) combined, the dismal theorem in Eq. (3.3) can be written slightly differently. Let x_0 be the degree of climate change that is irreversible, then the DT at that point is:

$$E\left[D(x_0)|\lambda\right] = \Pr(x_0) * D\left[x_0|\lambda\right] = +\infty. \tag{3.7}$$

If you are an economist, you might ask why the middle part of the equation in Eq. (3.7) diverges to infinity. Under the customary assumption of economics, the probability distribution in the middle of Eq. (3.7) would be a Normal distribution or another medium-tailed distribution under any of which Eq. (3.7) would converge to zero. So, the Eq. (3.7) hinges on the assumption of a fat-tail distribution critically.

To show why graphically or intuitively, the present author draws two probability distribution functions in Fig. 3.3. The top figure is a Normal distribution and the bottom figure is a fat-tail distribution. There is a tipping point mark in each figure. To give readers a motivation, the tipping point mark is set at 10 °C temperature increase in the Z axis which can be interpreted as the range of global temperature rise.

As you can see, if the distribution is a Normal distribution, the probability approximates to zero at the tipping point, which would make Eq. (3.7) to converge to zero. On the other hand, when the distribution is a fat-tailed one, the probability does not converge to zero at the tipping point. In such a case, Eq. (3.7) would diverge to infinity because of the damage function which explodes to infinity under the Weitzman assumption of λ.

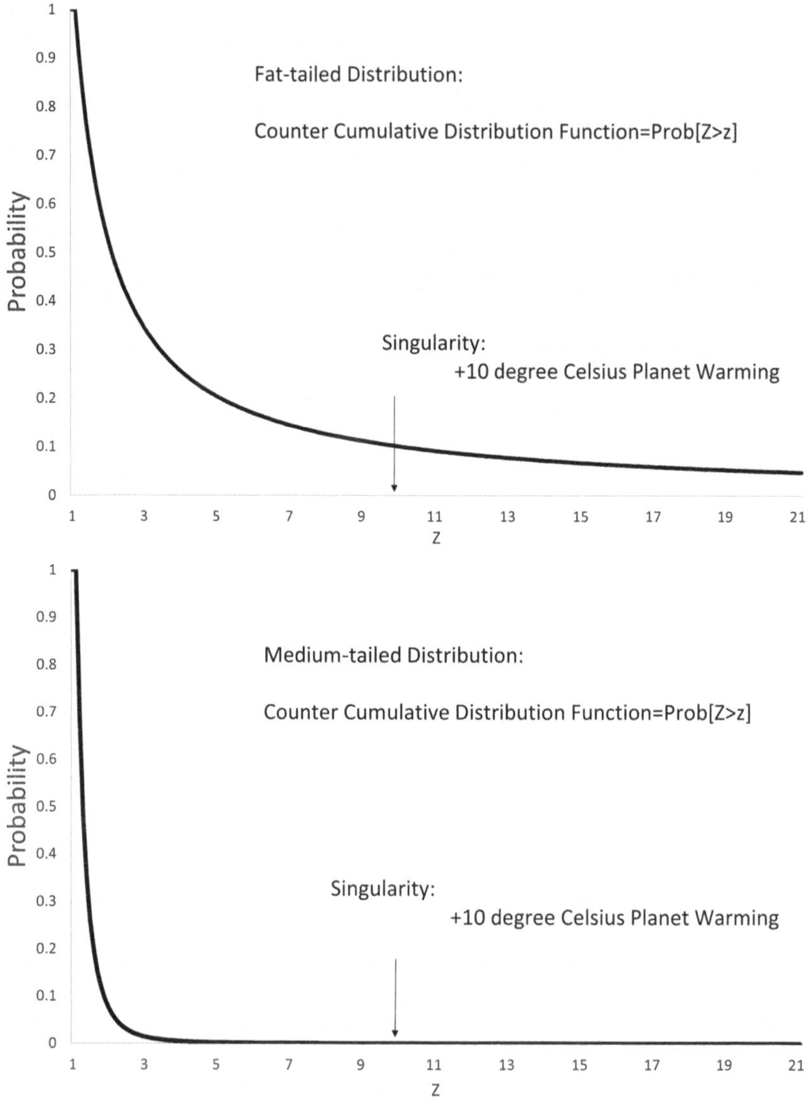

Fig. 3.3 Fat-tail (bottom) versus normal (top) distribution

6 A Behavioral Economics Critique

Thus far, the present author gave an exposition of the three theories that are pertinent to the discussion of singularities of science: a catastrophe theory, a chaos theory, and the dismal theorem. These theories were either developed in the economics literature or applied to the economics analyses in meaningful ways (Seo 2018a, 2018b).

They, however, have been met, especially their applications to an economic analysis, for example, the dismal theorem, with various criticisms from the economic points of view. The present author called these critiques on various occasions a behavioral economics critique (Nordhaus 2011; Seo 2020a, 2020b). The essence of this line of critique is that the catastrophe models of economics are not adequate for accounting for behaviors of individuals or social regulation mechanisms in the system (Seo 2022b).

To give a taste of the behavioral economics critique, let's assume that the human and non-human biological communities on the planet are well-versed on the changes in the climate system since they have survived there for millions of years, so will adapt efficiently to the changes, that is, in the best ways possible (Seo 2006, 2016). Efficient adaptations will take place across the full range of economic sectors, biomes, and technologies, including agriculture, natural resource uses, energy generations, building constructions, natural disaster management, information technologies, ecologies, and climate engineering at the local level (IPCC 2014; Seo 2017, 2018a, 2018b, 2019).

The full range of adaptation behaviors can be parameterized to enter the dismal theorem. First, we can enter it as the adaptation delta into the fat-tail distribution, which would make the tail thinner. Let δ_1 be a positive parameter:

$$\Pr[X = x] = cx^{-(1+\alpha+\delta_1)}. \quad (3.8)$$

Second, the range of adaptation behaviors will also enter the damage function. With δ_2 being a positive parameter:

$$D(x|\lambda) = ke^{(\beta-\delta_2)x}. \quad (3.9)$$

The δ_1 includes planetary climate engineering such as solar radiation reflector or carbon dioxide capture and storage (NRC 2015a, 2015b); regional climate engineering such as rainmaker or space road technologies; transitions to novel energy technologies such as solar energy or batteries (Seo 2021a, 2021b). The δ_2 includes a vast array of adaptation behaviors or adaptive systems such as agricultural adaptations, coastal adaptations, hurricane adaptations, housing and infrastructure adaptations, etc. (Bakkensen and Blair 2022; Lanfranco et al. 2022; Mendelsohn 2022; Seo 2021a, 2022b).

What it takes to a disproof of the dismal theorem is to show the following, with a constant m and any x_0 (Seo 2020b):

$$E\left[D\left(x_0\right)|\lambda\right] = m < +\infty, \forall x_0. \tag{3.10}$$

This equation can be proven after writing out the expected damage, the left-hand side of the equation, at any x_0:

$$\frac{e^{\beta x_0}}{\left(x_0^{\alpha+\delta_1}\right)\left(e^{\delta_2 x_0}\right)} = m < +\infty, \forall x_0. \tag{3.11}$$

To give readers a taste of the proof, imagine that β and δ_2 get ever closer as x_0, that is, the degree of climate change ever gets larger. Or, for even a simpler case, imagine that β and δ_2 always remain closer. In another scenario, you can imagine that δ_1 is very large to make the power-law distribution to approximate an exponential distribution in an appropriate range of x. In economic terms, these conditions mean that adaptations by human, biological, and physical communities on the planet will be substantial and effective.

This behavioral critique does not mean that climate adaptations will overwhelm all planet-wide climate change occurrences. Neither does it mean that climate change will bring no damage at all to the planet communities (Mendelshon 2000; Hanemann 2000; Schlenker and Roberts 2009).

7 Moving Forward from Economics to Science Singularities

The economics of singularities does not exist yet in the economic literature. This book may become the first one to explore this idea and define the field. For that, this book will proceed to introducing the five science singularities to be explained in the succeeding five chapters from the next chapter onward. The five singularities to be introduced are encompassing: from a high-risk physics experiment, artificial intelligence and quantum mechanics, mRNA virology and vaccinology, stem cell research, and neuroscience of consciousness.

This chapter provided the definitions of the central concept of this book: a singularity. It showed that it is referred to by economists as different terms such as a tipping point, a critical point, a catastrophe. The applications of these terms to the economic policy decision-making settings are found in such theories as the dismal theorem and the precautionary principle. The behavioral critique emphasizes the possibilities of human, biological, and physical adaptations to a foreseen catastrophe risk. All these aspects of the economics of catastrophes will play out in the next five chapters.

References

Alligood KT, Sauer TD, Yorke JA (1996) Chaos: An introduction to dynamical systems. Springer, New York.

Arrow KJ, and Intriligator MD (1981) Handbook of Mathematical Economics: Volume 1. Amsterdam, NL: North-Holland.

Bakkensen LA and Blair L (2022) The economics of tropical cyclone adaptation. In: Seo SN (ed.), Handbook of Behavioral Economics and Climate Change. Cheltenham, UK and Northampton, MA, USA: Edward Elgar Publishing.

Bayes T (1763) An essay towards solving a problem in the doctrine of chance. Philosophical Transactions of the Royal Society of London 53: 370–418.

Cristersson M (2017) Interactive Lorenz Attractor. Available online at http://malinc.se/m/lorenz.php.

Dixit AK (1990) Optimization in Economic Theory, 2nd edition Oxford University Press, Oxford.

Einstein A (1915) On the General Theory of Relativity. Submitted to Prussian Academy of Science.

Emanuel K (2011) Edward Norton Lorenz (1917–2008): A biographical memoir by Kerry Emanuel. National Academy of Sciences. Washington DC.

Feigenbaum MJ (1978) Quantitative universality for a class of non-linear transformations. Journal of Statistical Physics 19: 25–52.
Gabaix X (2009) Power laws in economics and finance. Annual Review of Economics 1: 255–293.
Galbraith JK (1954) The Great Crash 1929. Boston, MA: Houghton Mifflin.
Gilmore R (1981) Catastrophe Theory for Scientists and Engineers. Wiley, New York, NY.
Gleick J (1987) Chaos: Making a New Science. Penguin Books, London.
Hanemann WM (2000) Adaptation and its management. Climatic Change 45: 571–581.
Hawking S, Tegmark M, Russell S, Wilczek F (2014) Transcending complacency on superintelligent machines. Huffington Post. Accessed from https://www.huffingtonpost.com/stephen-hawking/artificial-intelligence_b_5174265.html
Hirsch MW, Smale S, and Devaney RL (2003) Differential Equations, Dynamical Systems, and an Introduction to Chaos (2nd edition). Boston, MA: Academic Press.
Intergovernmental Panel on Climate Change (IPCC) (2014) Climate Change 2014: Impacts, adaptation, and vulnerability. The Fifth Assessment Report of the IPCC. Cambridge, UK: Cambridge University Press.
Intergovernmental Panel on Climate Change (IPCC) (2021) AR6 Climate Change 2021: The Physical Science Basis. Cambridge, UK: Cambridge University Press.
Kurzweil R (2005) The Singularity is Near: When Humans Transcend Biology. New York, NY: Penguin.
Lanfranco B, Fernández E, Ferraro B, and de Lima JMS (2022) Historical changes in the Pampas biome, land use, and climate change. In: SN Seo (ed.), Handbook of Behavioral Economics and Climate Change. Cheltenham, UK and Northampton, MA, USA: Edward Elgar.
Le Treut H, Somerville R, Cubasch U, Ding Y, Mauritzen C, Mokssit A, Peterson T, Prather M (2007) Historical overview of climate change. In Solomon S et al. (eds.) Climate Change 2007: The Physical Science Basis. The Fourth Assessment Report of the Intergovernmental Panel on Climate Change. Cambridge, UK: Cambridge University Press.
Lorenz EN (1963) Deterministic nonperiodic flow. Journal of the Atmospheric Sciences 20: 130–141.
Lorenz EN (1969a) Atmospheric predictability as revealed by naturally occurring analogues. Journal of the Atmospheric Sciences 26: 636–646.
Lorenz EN (1969b) Three approaches to atmospheric predictability. Bulletin of the American Meteorological Society 50: 345–349.
Lorenz EN (1993) The Essence of Chaos. University of Washington Press, Seattle.
Mandelbrot B (1963) The variation of certain speculative prices. The Journal of Business 36 (4): 394–419.

Mandelbrot B (1997) Fractals and Scaling in Finance. New York, NY: Springer.
Mankiw NG (2014) Principles of Economics, (7th edition). Stamford, CT: Cengage Learning.
Mas-Colell A, Whinston MD, Green JR (1995) Microeconomic Theory. Oxford, UK: Oxford University Press.
Mendelshon R (2000) Efficient adaptation to climate change. Climatic Change 45: 583–600.
Mendelsohn R (2022) The economics of efficient adaptation to sea level rise. In SN Seo (ed.), Handbook of Behavioral Economics and Climate Change. Cheltenham, UK and Northampton, MA, USA: Edward Elgar.
National Research Council (NRC) (2015a) Climate Intervention: Reflecting Sunlight to Cool Earth. Committee on Geoengineering Climate: Technical Evaluation and Discussion of Impacts. Washington, DC: National Academies Press.
National Research Council (NRC) (2015b) Climate Intervention: Carbon Dioxide Removal and Reliable Sequestration. Washington, DC: National Academies Press.
Newton I (1687) Philosophiæ Naturalis Principia Mathematica. London, UK.
Nobel Prize (2018) The Sveriges Riksbank Prize in Economic Sciences in Memory of Alfred Nobel 2018 was divided equally between William D. Nordhaus "for integrating climate change into long-run macroeconomic analysis" and Paul M. Romer "for integrating technological innovations into long-run macroeconomic analysis." Stockholm, SE: Nobel Foundation.
Nordhaus W (1994) Managing the Global Commons. Cambridge, MA: MIT Press.
Nordhaus WD (2008) A Question of Balance: Weighing the Options on Global Warming Policies. New Haven, CT: Yale University Press.
Nordhaus W (2011) The economics of tail events with an application to climate change. Review of Environmental Economics and Policy 5: 240–257.
Pareto V (1896) Cours d'Economie Politique. Droz, Geneva.
Poincaré H (1880–1890) Mémoire sur les Courbes Définies par les Équations Différentielles I-VI, Oeuvre I. Gauthier-Villars, Paris.
Rosser, JB Jr. (2007) The rise and fall of catastrophe theory applications in economics: Was the baby thrown out with bathwater? Journal of Economic Dynamics and Control 31: 3255–3280.
Schlenker W, Roberts M (2009) Nonlinear temperature effects indicate severe damages to crop yields under climate change. Proceedings of the National Academy of Sciences 106, 15594–15598.
Schuster EF (1984) Classification of probability laws by tail behavior. Journal of the American Statistical Association 79 (388): 936–39.
Seo SN (2006) Modeling Farmer Responses to Climate Change: Climate Change Impacts and Adaptations in Livestock Management in Africa. PhD Dissertation, Yale University, New Haven.

Seo SN (2016) Microbehavioral Econometric Methods: Theories, Models, and Applications for the Study of Environmental and Natural Resources. Amsterdam, NL: Academic Press.
Seo, SN (2017) Measuring policy benefits of the cyclone shelter program in North Indian Ocean: Protection from high winds or high storm surges? Climate Change Economics 8(4): 1–18.
Seo SN (2018a) Natural and Man-made Catastrophes: Theories, Economics, and Policy Designs. Hoboken, NJ: Wiley-Blackwell.
Seo SN (2018b) Two tales of super-typhoons and super-wealth in Northwest Pacific: Will global-warming-fueled cyclones ravage East and Southeast Asia? Journal of Extreme Events. https://doi.org/10.1142/S2345737618500124.
Seo SN (2019) The Economics of Global Allocations of the Green Climate Fund: An Assessment from Four Scientific Traditions of Modeling Adaptation Strategies. Cham: Springer Nature.
Seo SN (2020a) The Economics of Globally Shared and Public Goods. Amsterdam, NL: Academic Press.
Seo SN (2020b) Appendix A: A succinct mathematical disproof of the dismal theorem of economics. In Seo SN, The Economics of Globally Shared and Public Goods. Amsterdam, NL: Academic Press.
Seo SN (2021a) Climate Change and Economics: Engaging with Future Generations with Action Plans. Cham, CH: Palgrave Macmillan.
Seo SN (2021b) Energy revolutions: A story of the Three Gorges dam in China. In Seo SN, Climate Change and Economics: Engaging with Future Generations with Action Plans. Cham, CH: Palgrave Macmillan.
Seo SN (2022a) The Economics of Pandemics: Exploring Globally Shared Experiences. Cham: Palgrave Macmillan.
Seo SN (ed.) (2022b) Handbook of Behavioral Economics and Climate Change. Cheltenham, UK: Edward Elgar.
Seo SN (2023) The Economics of Optimal Growth Pathways: Evaluating the Health of the Planet's Natural and Ecological Resources. Palgrave MacMillan, London, UK.
Shiller RJ (2005) Irrational Exuberance (2nd ed.) Princeton, NJ: Princeton University Press.
Strogatz SH (1994) Nonlinear Dynamics and Chaos: With Applications to Physics, Biology, Chemistry, and Engineering. Addison-Wesley, MA.
Taleb NN (2007) The Black Swan: The Impact of the Highly Improbable (1st ed.). London, UK: Penguin.
Teschl G (2012) Ordinary Differential Equations and Dynamical Systems. Graduate Studies in Mathematics, Vol. 140. Providence, RI: American Mathematical Society.
Thom R (1972) Stabilité Structurelle et Morphogenèse: Essai d'une Théorie Générale des Modèles. New York, NY: Benjamin.

Thom R (1975) Structural stability and morphogenesis. New York, NY: Benjamin-Addison-Wesley.
Thom R (1977) What is catastrophe theory about? In Haken H (ed.) Synergetics. Springer Series in Synergetics, vol 2. Heidelberg, DL: Springer.
Tziperman E (2017) Chaos Theory: A Brief Introduction. Boston, MA: Harvard University.
Viscusi WK, Aldy JE (2003) The value of a statistical life: a critical review of market estimates throughout the world. Journal of Risk and Uncertainty 5, 5–76.
Weitzman ML (2009) On modeling and interpreting the economics of catastrophic climate change. Review of Economics and Statistics 91: 1–19.
Zeeman EC (1977) Catastrophe theory-selected papers 1972–1977. Reading, MA: Addison-Wesley.
Zipf GK (1949) Human Behavior and the Principle of Least Effort. Cambridge, MA: Addison-Wesley.

CHAPTER 4

The Physics of Relativity and the Strangelet Singularity

1 Introduction

From this point on, the present author will lead the readers through the world of science in the next five chapters with a series of analyses on five singularity events that could be realized from major scientific experiments that are vigorously as well as competitively pursued today. The five singularities are as wide-ranging as the entire range of science, covering the physics of relativity, quantum mechanics, mRNA virology, stem cell research, and neuroscience of consciousness.

To begin with, let me tell you first how the present author has come in to contact with science. Growing up, my favorite subjects were language, mathematics, English, philosophy, and perhaps Buddhism. Ever since enrolling in a college, my primary field of study has been economics. My first encounter with science probably occurred through Buddhism in which some of the theories of science are also discussed albeit marginally, for example, the theory of relativity and the theory of evolution (Darwin 1859; Einstein 1915a, 1915b). It was a vague encounter. The real encounter with science began when I started to pursue a doctoral degree at Yale University with climate economists. At first, the economic aspects of it were of concern to me. But gradually and expectedly, I began to meet with climate scientists in conferences and lectures. At the same time, I started

S. N. Seo, *The Economics of Singularities of Science Elucidated with Buddhist Thoughts*,
https://doi.org/10.1007/978-3-031-69118-8_4

to read climate scientists' works far beyond the IPCC (Intergovernmental Panel on Climate Change) scientific reports.

For clarifications, climate science is wide-ranging: it is not limited to the science of climate and weather. It did not even begin by climate scientists (Arrhenius 1889; Revelle and Suess 1957). It involves atmospheric science, physics of energy and radiation, biology, chemistry, geology, biogeochemistry, engineering, plant science, animal science, nuclear science, ocean science, marine biology, virology, epidemiology, psychology, etc. (IPCC 2021). From reading the wide range of climate science articles, I have gradually become very confident about the science and scientific theories. This was especially because I have written more than ten books on the topics of climate change and other globally shared goods such as worldwide pandemics, which positioned me to read closely and think about the scientific debates keenly (Seo 2020, 2021, 2022).

From then on, my scientific understanding has become very sharp through my continued study in Buddhist scriptures and commentaries. Although they do not specifically mention the scientific principles and theories as we know them today, they are very perceptive of the problems that the scientists in the contemporary world are striving to solve. From the extensive reading of the Buddhist commentaries and my own analysis of them, I have come to obtain a unique interpretation of the science and scientific theories (Refer to Seo 2024a, 2024b).

With this introduction, I can begin the discussion of the first singularity of science, namely, the strangelet singularity. This singularity was first proposed in the background of the Large Hadron Collider (LHC) experiment conducted by the European Organization for Nuclear Research (CERN) (CERN 2023a, 2023b). This research is sometimes called the God Particle experiment since it tries to create the first atmospheric condition after the Big Bang. The Big Bang theory is in turn a theory of an expanding universe with a tiny particle origin (Lemaître 1931; Hubble 1929).

The nature of singularity from the LHC experiment has been the subject of scientific debates for some time among the scientists (Dar et al. 1999; Jaffe et al. 2000). The singularity is such that once the strangelet, which is a dark matter, is created accidently from the LHC experiment, it will suck up in an instance the entire universe created by the Big Bang. The dark matter would create a giant black hole which would draw in everything in the universe.

In the following sections, the present author will review the physics and the theory of relativity, introduce the LHC experiment, and explain the strangelet hypothesis. As these sections will show, the big concern on the strangelet preceding its experiment has ebbed for now (Nobel Prize 2013; CERN 2023b). It is hard to say, however, that the risk is completely gone. For an analogy, it is like the scientists' attitude about a worldwide spread of a coronavirus before the actual outbreak of the COVID-19 pandemic or their concern about the risk of experimenting on an mRNA virus in a laboratory (Coleman and Frieman 2014).

At the end of this chapter, the present author will share some insights from the economics and especially the Buddhist literature on how this singularity event should be interpreted. These insights will be the basis of the comprehensive presentation of the Buddhist insights to be offered in the final chapter of this book.

2 Physics in a Nutshell

Physics is a branch of science whose inquiry is the nature and properties of matter or, more simply put, the science of matter. In a more elaborate definition, it is the science of matter, motion, space, and energy. In the acclaimed Feynman lectures on physics, it has headings of mechanics, radiation, heat, electromagnetism, and matter (Feynman et al. 2010a, 2010b). Alternatively, physics is defined to be the science of how the universe works.

What does it mean to be the science of matter, motion, space, and energy? Consider the famed Einstein's energy-mass equation (Einstein 1905c, 1905d):

$$E = m * c^2, \tag{4.1}$$

where E is the amount of energy generated by a moving object; m is the mass of the moving object; c is the speed of light. In this equation, physics is expressed as the relationship between energy and mass moderated by the speed of light.

For another example, if you were wondering how much energy the planet receives from the Sun, which is the basis of global warming and climate change, you can go out to a flat plain on a high mountain where the solar radiation directly falls in order to measure the magnitude of the solar energy received there. This measurement is the basis of the idea of

Radiative Forcing (RF) in climate change literature which is the magnitude of energy added to Earth because of an increase in carbon dioxide concentration in the atmosphere. Specifically, it is +3.8 Watts per square meter (W/sq) under carbon dioxide doubling (Le Treut et al. 2007; Ciais et al. 2013).

To grasp what physics is and does, it is far easier for readers to go back to the physics before Albert Einstein's theory came along in the early 1900s (Beck and Havas 1990). The three laws of motion put forth in Isaac Newton's masterpiece entitled *Philosophiæ Naturalis Principia Mathematica* and referred to as in a short form *Principia* defined the physics of the era (Newton 1687; Cohen et al. 1999):

(a) Inertia: Objects in motion stay in motion, unless an external force is applied.
(b) Force: The force acting on an object is equal to the mass of the object multiplied by its acceleration.
(c) Reaction: For every action, there is an equal and opposite reaction.

The most important contribution of the *Principia* was the explanation of gravity for which he invented the calculus as we know it today in order to explain the motion of a falling moon (Strang 1991). In this, he sets forth the physics of the universe as the calculus of his equations (Kaku 2021). His calculation has proven to be right.

Does Newton's physics explained in the *Principia* explain without flaws, perhaps almost without flaws, the natural phenomena around us? Scientists during the latter half of the nineteenth century started to see that Newton's laws of motion and gravity only work in some situations but not in other situations. That other situation was light and the speed of light, the contemplations on which led to the emergence of Albert Einstein's theory of relativity (Al-Khalili 2020).

What about light? Scientists came to the problem of light on several fronts of physics. The present author may explain the problem thus. According to Newton, gravity exists, which pulls the moon toward Earth. In the same way, all heavenly objects hanging up in the sky could be understood. They all would behave according to the Newton's calculus of gravity. Someone might have asked at the end of the nineteenth century: what about light? Light is another thing high up in the sky. Light is the only source of energy, which sustains all life on Earth. Can Newton's physics explain its locations, movements, and energy of light?

3 The Theory of Relativity in a Nutshell

In 1905, young Einstein published four scientific papers in the *Annals of Physics* (Annalen der Physik in German), then a leading scientific journal published in German (Einstein 1905a, 1905b, 1905c, 1905d, 2001). These papers proposed new theories on light, energy, matter, space, which included a special theory of relativity. A decade later, he presented his general theory of relativity to the Prussian Academy of Science, which dealt with the all-important physical inquiry of gravity (Einstein 1915a, 1915b; Beck and Havas 1990).

The special theory of relativity is an exposition of how speed of light affects mass, time, and space. It includes an exposition of how the speed of light defines the relationship between energy and matter, that is, the aforementioned $E = m * c^2$. The theory is called the special theory because it deals with special cases of physical phenomena involving huge energies, extreme speeds, astronomical distances (Feynman et al. 2010a, 2010b, 2010c; Stein 2022). In these special cases which are all so important in the explanations of universe, space, and light, the rules of Newton's physics outlined in the previous section cannot be a useful guide any longer.

What the theory of relativity says can be understood from the basic knowledge that all things are already in motion at some speed. Therefore, the rule of physics based on the assumption that things are stationary when in rest cannot explain the reality of Einstein, that is, all in-rest things are in movement according to his view. Einstein put forth his imagination as a 16-year-old kid. He imagined himself chasing light to catch up with it. The light moves, say, at the speed of light. So, it moves really fast. When he finally caught up with light, that is, at the same speed as light, he imagined that he is seeing the frozen electromagnetic field. Since he is flying at the speed of light, it is as if he cannot feel the light any more (Stein 2022).

Another thought experiment he put forth was the lightning strike on a train track. A train is moving. There are two trees: one in front of the train and the other behind the train. When the lightning strikes, it would hit both trees at the same time. So, an observer beside the train track would see that the lightning strikes both trees at the same time. However, a man on a train would see that the lightning strikes the tree in the front first and the tree behind later, which is because the train is moving toward the tree in the front.

These thought experiments tell the theory of relativity's core argument put forth by Albert Einstein. Physical phenomena cannot be understood properly without correctly accounting for their differential speeds of movement. Applied to the heavenly phenomena, the so-called special cases of physics—universe, space, solar radiation, and stars—cannot be explained without correctly considering the speed of an observer.

In the relativity theory, the speed of an observer can be measured with reference to the speed of light. Einstein argued that the light is a photon, that is, a particle not a wave that people before him assumed it to be (Einstein 1905a). The light is not transmitted through a certain physical basis like a luminiferous ether that some people before him assumed it to be. He said that the light moves in vacuum. Therefore, no matter moves faster than the speed of light which is the cosmic speed limit. How fast is that? It is 299,792,458 meters per second, which is approximately 1.08 billion kilometers per hour. For your reference, a commercial airplane moves at about 1000 kilometers per hour at 10 km above the ground where there is "little" interference. So, human aircrafts are nowhere near to having the ability to move at the speed of light.

Within the context of the special theory of relativity, there is a phenomenon of time dilation put forth by Einstein and others (Botermann et al. 2014). It is an interesting hypothesis about time and has also fascinated common people. According to this hypothesis, time goes slower in a fast-moving vehicle than time in a slow-moving vehicle. Put differently, a fast-moving clock ticks slower than a stationary non-moving clock.

With regard to this time dilation, the following thought exercise has become very popular even among the public, adding to the legend of Einstein. Let's imagine that one of the identical twins who is 15 years old chooses to live in New York for the rest of her life while the other of the identical twins who is also of the same age embarks on a travel through space aboard an aircraft which moves near to the speed of light. Let's say that the latter—the lucky one—travels for five years "in her time" and returns to New York. In the latter's time, the latter will have aged five years exactly, but the other twin on Earth would have aged, say, 50 years to be 65 years old.

From the present author's points of view, this time dilation hypothesis may give a false idea to physics students that there is an absolute time with reference to which the lucky one's travel is measured to be 5 years and the unlucky one's residence on Earth is measured to be 50 years. "For some reason, the former time is dilated": They may falsely conclude like this. But the fact is that, according to science, time is measured only through relations among Sun, Moon, and Earth. As shown in Fig. 4.1, imagine the

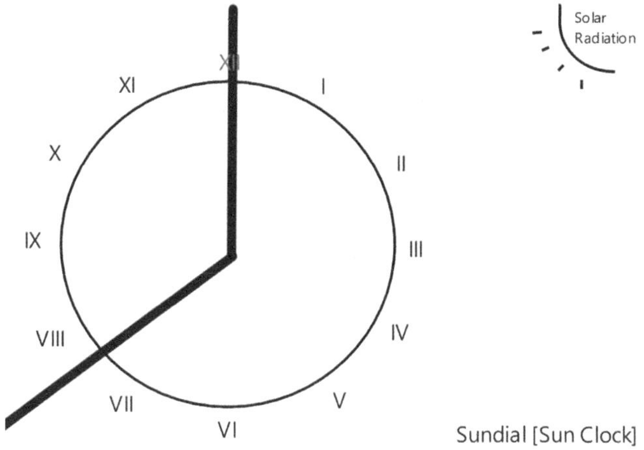

Fig. 4.1 Sundial: the concept of time

sun clock or sundial which tells the exact time of the moment by the solar radiation's footprint on the table, namely, the sundial, on Earth. This is the time people know and scientists rely upon. From this basic mechanics, people know an hour, a day, a half-month season, a month, a year, and a 60-year cycle. This time would certainly not exist outside the solar system. There is no time other than the relationships between Sun, Moon, and Earth (Nagarjuna's Fundamental Wisdom, Precious Garland).

In Buddhist wisdom, time does not exist (Aryadeva's Four Hundred, Buddhapalita's Commentary, Chandrakirti's Clear Words). As physics theories would agree, time cannot be separately defined without movement—the distance moved. However, the movement does not exist, nor does the mover (Nagarjuna's Sixty Reasoning Stanzas, Seventy Emptiness Stanzas, Lama Tsongkhapa's Ocean of Reasoning). What does that mean? You might ask. It means that there is no single time in the above time dilation hypothesis. I will add a clarification on this later in this chapter.

The special theory of relativity was built without consideration of gravity which was at the heart of the Newtonian physics regarding heavenly objects, that is, the falling apple exposition. Without gravity, how can you possibly explain stars, planets, radiation, and universe? For it to have a shot at offering a new paradigm of physics, it had to explain gravity. Preeminent scientists at that time such as Max Planck urged Einstein to pursue the general theory of relativity which includes an explanation of gravity, which resulted in his presentations at the Prussian Academy of Science a decade later (Einstein 1915a, 1915b).

In the general theory, whose term in fact Einstein used in his presentations entitled "On the General Theory of Relativity," Einstein argued that there is no gravity. Instead, he explained the movement of heavenly objects like the moon, solar system, stars, and others from a time-space curvature. The universe is curved in that way in the time-space dimension, which forces the moon to rotate the Earth in the way it does, and the planets in the solar system rotate the Sun in their ways as they do (Engel 1997). For example, the Sun's extremely high energy would curve the space around it in a certain way. Similarly, a black hole would be formed in the universe, which is a curvature in the universe, whose energy is so intense that it sucks everything in (Feynman et al. 2010a, 2010b, 2010c; Carroll 2020).

The curved universe? The warped heaven? The convoluted outer space? People were puzzled and continue to be by Einstein's suggestion about the universe while physicists once in a very long while would argue that they proved one tiny aspect of the theory or another (NYT 2013; Witze 2014; Kaku 2021). How can it, that is, the time-space curvature, be so strong as well as stable to hold everything together? Is there someone who is pulling all the strings? Or more properly, is there some underlying force that makes the universe curved in the way Einstein saw it? People have wondered.

A common response scientists give is that the theory of relativity is described as a smooth model of the universe because it deals with the extremely large distances, objects, and speeds in a "smooth" way. The events in the smooth universe are continuous and deterministic. This means that there are things that cannot be explained or are poorly explained by the general theory of relativity, especially the things that are miniscule, say, microscopic, things that are disruptive, things that are complex like New York city, things that are always unstable and chaotic.

A notable scientific field that points out the problems of the general theory of relativity and offers an alternative is, for example, quantum physics (Heisenberg 1930). It deals with really tiny things, that is, quantum. Quantum events occur in leaps or jumps with probabilistic outcomes, not definite outcomes (Feynman et al. 2010a, 2010b, 2010c; Stein 2022). The quantum world is saliently different from what the general theory describes about the heavenly objects and the universe, which is the subject of next chapter of this book.

4 The God Particle Experiment

Over time, the theories of relativity would gain wider acceptance across the scientific community owing in part to the testability of many of what Einstein posited (Beck and Havas 1990). Physicists found ways to test some aspects of his theories empirically including the time-space curvature that explains the planets' rotations around the Sun, the existence of a black hole, the time dilation, etc.

One of such tests is the test of the beginning of the universe (NYT 2013). The Big Bang theory of the universe says that the universe began from a big loud explosion of an extremely high-density energy matter, from which it expanded ever since. The universe is still expanding. This means that the solar system and Earth that we live in are at some point in that expansion of the universe. This also means that if scientists can send an object at near the speed of light into the universe, it will go back through the universe's historical time and near the time of Big Bang. The Big Bang theory was first suggested by Lemaître and the evidence of an expanding universe was first presented by Hubble (Lemaître 1931; Hubble 1929). Einstein also accepted it to be agreeable with the general theory.

The Large Hadron Collider (LHC) experiment by the European Organization of Nuclear Research (CERN) is an experiment designed to test the theory of the universe's beginning. The LHC is the world's largest particle accelerator built at the France-Switzerland border during the 10-year period from 1998 to 2008. It is argued to be the largest single machine in the world with 27 km long in circle and 175 meters deep underground. It consists of a 27-km long ring of superconducting magnets to which a number of accelerating structures are attached to boost the energy of the particles inside the tube (CERN 2023a).

The LHC is a particle accelerator and collider through which scientists aim to observe the state of the universe at the time of its origin, including the existence of a God particle more formally referred to as the Higgs boson (NYT 2013). The basic function of the LHC, as described in the following by the CERN, is simple: to make two light beams travel through the "ultrahigh" vacuum at "near" the speed of light and collide (CERN 2023a):

> Inside the accelerator, two high-energy particle beams travel at close to the speed of light before they are made to collide. The beams travel in opposite directions in separate beam pipes—two tubes kept at ultrahigh vacuum.

They are guided around the accelerator ring by a strong magnetic field maintained by superconducting electromagnets.

The collisions of light beams are observed at four locations situated around the LHC ring by four particle detectors: ATLAS, CMS, ALICE, and LHCb. The ATLAS (A Toroidal LHC Apparatus) detector, for example, is a cylinder whose height is 46 meters and diameter is 25 meters built at 100 meters below the ground. The other detectors are CMS (Compact Muon Solenoid), ALICE (A Large Ion Collider Experiment), LHCb (Large Hadron Collider beauty).

The LHC completed two runs successfully: the first run from 2009 to 2013, the second run from 2015 to 2018. It began its third operational run from 2022. The first run was reported to have found the Higgs boson, with the Nobel Prize awarded for the discovery in the following year (Nobel Prize 2013).

5 A Strangelet Singularity

A singularity can be defined for the LHC experiment, based on what concerned scientists have posited (Dar et al. 1999; Plaga 2009; Peskin 2008). The mechanism through which a truly catastrophic event is realized is as follows. The acceleration and collisions of the particle beams which travel at the speed of light in the utter vacuum may produce a strangelet, which is considered to be a dark matter that then creates a black hole in the universe. A black hole is a region in the spacetime where gravity is so strong that nothing escapes from it, whose existence can be derived from the general theory of relativity. The black hole would suck the entire universe in, demolishing the current universe with all beings on it. This process would unfold in the blink of an eye, taking less than a split second. The scale of such a catastrophe is that it would not only end Planet Earth and sentient beings, but the universe itself (Posner 2004; Weitzman 2009).

There are fascinating debates in the scientific community of particle physics on how likely it is for the LHC experiments to create a strangelet and then a destruction of the universe ensued. It seems, however, that no scientist denies a "possibility" of such an occurrence according to particle physics (Ellis et al. 2008; CERN 2023b).

What is a strangelet? It is a hypothetical particle or a small fragment of a strange matter. What does that mean? In Fig. 4.2, the basic concepts of particle physics are illustrated. Particle physicists define an ordinary

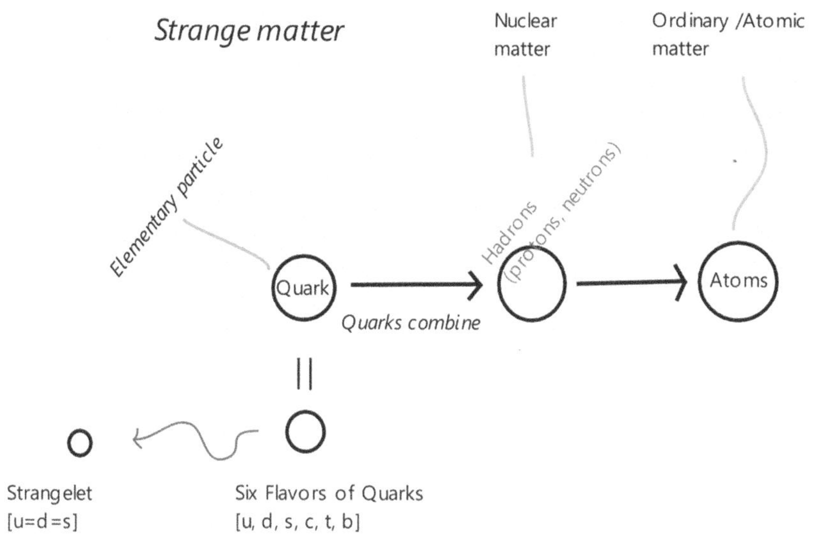

Fig. 4.2 Strangelet: basic concepts of particle physics

matter, a nuclear matter, and a strange matter. An ordinary matter is also called an atomic matter. Hadrons such as protons and neutrons are the basis for a nuclear matter (Larkoski 2019). A strange matter is also called a quark matter or just a quark. A quark is an elementary particle which combines to form hadrons, the most stable of which are protons and neutrons. According to the Standard Model, there are six flavors of quarks: up (u), down (d), strange (s), charm (c), top (t), bottom (b) (Gell-Mann 1964). A strangelet is a quark matter composed of equal numbers of up, down, strange quarks.

There is the LHC Safety Assessment Group as part of the CERN. This group's report concludes that the LHC experiments present "no" danger (Jaffe et al. 2000; Ellis et al. 2008). There are two reasons for this conclusion presented by the group. The first is that such collisions occur naturally:

> We recall the rates for the collisions of cosmic rays with the Earth, Sun, neutron stars, white dwarfs and other astronomical bodies at energies higher than the LHC. The stability of astronomical bodies indicates that such collisions cannot be dangerous.

The second is that, based on the laboratory-controlled experiments conducted by the group in which the generation of a strangelet is tested, they conclude that there are a number of physical mechanisms in the physical world that prevent a universal catastrophe by a black hole even if it were to be generated from the LCH experiments (Ellis et al. 2008):

> Specifically, we study the possible production at the LHC of hypothetical objects such as vacuum bubbles, magnetic monopoles, microscopic black holes and strangelets, and find no associated risks. Any microscopic black holes produced at the LHC are expected to decay by Hawking radiation before they reach the detector walls. If some microscopic black holes were stable, those produced by cosmic rays would be stopped inside the Earth or other astronomical bodies. The stability of astronomical bodies constrains strongly the possible rate of accretion by any such microscopic black holes, so that they present no conceivable danger. In the case of strangelets, the good agreement of measurements of particle production at RHIC with simple thermodynamic models constrains severely the production of strangelets in heavy-ion collisions at the LHC, which also present no danger.

This conclusion is shared widely among the scientists, including the American Physical Society (APS), according to whom the possibility of a strangelet-caused universal catastrophe is absurdly small (Dar et al. 1999; Jaffe et al. 2000; Peskin 2008).

The CERN reported in 2013 that the first LHC run successfully detected the Higgs boson, the so-called God particle, that was long sought-after by physicists. The LHC experiments are on-going with its third operational run since 2022. These experiments have not resulted in any major disaster event.

6 The Buddhist Wisdom of Light, Time, and Space

There are different levels or kinds of relativity (Lama Tsongkhapa's Stages of the Path). The first and elementary is the relativity against the reference point. Like in the Einstein theory, everything can be explained in relation to the reference point, for example, the speed of light. This is a rudimentary relativity, but still a vision superior than the Newton physics. The relativity physics is a theory of the physical world viewed from the perspective of two moving objects, but ultimately the reference point.

The reference point is conspicuous in the theory of relativity. One is the speed of light already mentioned. Another is a particle, a photon, which is the basis of the light and other physical phenomena of Einstein. The other is the time measured against the reference point of space or distance, or alternatively, the space measured against the time.

The consequences of the Einstein physics or the modern pursuits of physicists, which rely on the concept of relativity as prescribed by its pioneers, can be described as the pursuits of the following two referents or reference points. One is the pursuit of the speed of light against which everything else is measured. The other is the high-density matter from which everything else began.

Viewed from the palace of Einstein's absolutistic physical world, it is not difficult for us to understand why Einstein objected so vehemently to the superposition theory put forth by quantum physicists or other quantum principles (Schrodinger 1935). He even put forth an experiment that disproves the superposition theory, that is, the white gloves-black gloves experiment (Einstein et al. 1935). According to Einstein, all the things in the universe are already there without human intervention. That is, the white gloves are always there regardless of any observer (Al-Khalili 2020). This is despite the fact that what is in the box cannot be determined without the observer, according to the relative world where Einstein lives, opening the box. When the observer opens the box, he will see either a dead cat or a live cat. Before he opens the box, the cat is in an "entangled" state in which the cat is both dead and alive according to probability (Heisenberg 1930). This will be further elaborated in the next chapter when we deal with quantum physics. From Einstein physics, he cannot take anything so "magic-like." To him, it just meant superstition, perhaps.

From this interpretation of relativity physics, we can offer a fresh insight on the strangelet singularity as well as the Large Hadron Collider experiments. From the Buddha's perfect wisdom, it is not wise to pursue to discover the absolute beginning of the universe (Lama Tsongkhapa's True Eloquence, Illuminating the Intent, Chandrakirti's Entering the Middle Way). Further, there is just not a single universe: there are billions of universes (Vasubandhu's Treasury, Flower Ornament Sutra, Aryamanjusrimulakalpa). As such, what scientists are attempting at the CERN is not actually a pursuit for a discovery of the very beginning state of the universe. What they are doing can be more properly understood to be an effort to understand the states of matter, especially those subatomic matters including the strange matter, quarks, and photons.

The world according to the perfect wisdom of the Buddha is the dependently originated and designated convention. The meaning of that wisdom is emptiness of any existence on its own right, that is, emptiness of intrinsic existence (Lama Tsongkhapa's Praise, True Eloquence, Seo 2024a, 2024b). It is a starkly different world from what physicists describe in the theory of relativity. As clarified in this chapter, there is little reason for Buddhists to indulge in this theory of relativity as some do (Thurman 1984; Dalai Lama 2005).

Does this new insight have any bearing on the analysis of singularity potentially caused by a strangelet or the LHC experiment? At first glance, it may not be obvious to non-Buddhist thinkers including scientists. A more careful examination will reveal over time that the Buddhist insight plays a big role in bounding the possibility of the strangelet singularity. The reason is that if it were not "the very first particle" of the universe that is recreated by scientists through such experiments, we would be able to view them as "regular particles with some strange characteristics." This strikes at the heart of the singularity argument. I hope readers can see through it.

References

Al-Khalili J (2020). The World According to Physics. Princeton, NJ: Princeton University Press.

Arrhenius SA (1889) U¨ ber die Dissociationsw¨arme und den Einfluß der Temperatur auf den Dissociationsgrad der Elektrolyte. Z. Phys. Chem. 4, 96–116.

Aryadeva (2nd century). Four Hundred Stanzas. Catuḥśatakaśāstra. Bstan bcos bzhi brgya pa. Toh 3846, dbu ma tsha.

Beck A, Havas P (trans.) (1990) The Collected Papers of Albert Einstein: Volume 2: The Swiss Years: Writings, 1900–1909. Princeton, NJ: Princeton University Press.

Botermann B, Bing D, Geppert C, Gwinner G, Hänsch TW, Huber G, Karpuk S, Krieger A, Kühl T, Nörtershäuser W, Novotny C, Reinhardt S, Sánchez R, Schwalm D, Stöhlker T, Wolf A, and Saathoff G (2014) Test of time dilation using stored Li+ ions as clocks at relativistic speed. Physics Review Letters 113, 120405.

Buddhapalita (ca. 5th century). Commentary. Buddhapālitamūlamadhyamakavṛtti. Dbu ma rtsa ba'i 'grel pa buddha pā li ta. Toh 3842, dbu ma tsa.

Carroll S (2020) A Brief History of Quantum Mechanics. The Royal Institution, Westminster. UK.

CERN (European Organization for Nuclear Research) (2023a) The Large Hadron Collider. CERN, Geneva, Switzerland. Accessed from https://www.home.cern/science/accelerators/large-hadron-collider

CERN (European Organization for Nuclear Research) (2023b) The safety of the LHC. CERN, Geneva. Accessed from https://press.cern/backgrounders/safety-lhc

Chandrakirti (7th century). Clear Words. Prasannapada. Tshig gsal. Tengyur. Beijing: Comparative edition. Vol. 60, 3–483.

Chandrakirti (7th century). Entering the Middle Way. Madhyamakāvatāra. Dbu ma la 'jug pa. Toh 3861, dbu ma'a.

Ciais P, Sabine C, Bala G, et al. (2013) Carbon and other biogeochemical cycles. In T.F. Stocker et al. (eds.), Climate Change 2013: The Physical Science Basis. Cambridge, UK: Cambridge University Press.

Cohen IB, Whitman A, Budenz J (trans.) (1999) The Principia: Mathematical Principles of Natural Philosophy. Berkeley CA: University of California Press.

Coleman CM, and Frieman MB (2014) Coronaviruses: Important Emerging Human Pathogens. Journal of Virology 8: 5209–5212.

Dalai Lama (2005) The Universe in a Single Atom: The Convergence of Science and Spirituality. New York, NY: Harmony Books.

Dar A, Rujula AD, Heinz U (1999) Will relativistic heavy-ion colliders destroy our planet? Physics Letters B 470: 142–48.

Darwin C (1859) On the Origin of Species by Means of Natural Selection, or the Preservation of Favoured Races in the Struggle for Life. London, UK: John Murray.

Einstein, A (1905a) On a heuristic point of view concerning the production and transformation of light. Annalen der Physik 17: 132–148.

Einstein, A (1905b) On the movement of small particles suspended in stationary liquids required by the molecular-kinetic theory of heat. Annalen der Physik 17: 549–560.

Einstein, A (1905c) On the electrodynamics of moving bodies. Annalen der Physik 17: 891–921.

Einstein, A (1905d) Does the inertia of a body depend upon its energy content?. Annalen der Physik 18: 639–641.

Einstein A (1915a) On the general theory of relativity. Submitted to Prussian Academy of Science.

Einstein A (1915b) The field equations of gravitation. Submitted to Prussian Academy of Science.

Einstein A (2001) Relativity: The Special and General Theory. Mineola, NY: Dover Publications.

Einstein A, Podolsky B, and Rosen N (1935) Can quantum-mechanical description of physical reality be considered complete? Physical Review 47: 777–780.

Ellis J, Giudice G, Mangano M, Tkachev I, Wiedemann U (2008) Review of the safety of LHC collisions. Journal of Physics G: Nuclear and Particle Physics 35 (11).

Engel A (trans.) (1997) The Collected Papers of Albert Einstein: Volume 6: The Berlin Years: Writings, 1914–1917. Princeton, NJ: Princeton University Press.

Feynman R, Leighton R, Sands M (2010a) The Feynman Lectures on Physics, Volume I: Mainly Mechanics, Radiation, and Heat. California Institute of Technology, Pasadena, CA. Accessed from https://www.feynmanlectures.caltech.edu/III_toc.html

Feynman R, Leighton R, Sands M (2010b) The Feynman Lectures on Physics, Volume II: Mainly Electromagnetism and Matter. California Institute of Technology, Pasadena, CA. Accessed from https://www.feynmanlectures.caltech.edu/III_toc.html

Feynman R, Leighton R, Sands M (2010c) The Feynman Lectures on Physics, Volume III quantum mechanics. California Institute of Technology, Pasadena, CA. Accessed from https://www.feynmanlectures.caltech.edu/III_toc.html

Gell-Mann M (1964) A schematic model of baryons and mesons. Physics Letters. 8 (3): 214–215.

Heisenberg W (1930). The Physical Principles of the Quantum Theory (German: Physikalischen Prinzipien der Quantentheorie). Chicago, IL: The University of Chicago Press.

Hubble E (1929) A relation between distance and radial velocity among extra-galactic nebulae. Proceedings of the National Academy of Sciences US.A.:15(3): 168–173.

Intergovernmental Panel on Climate Change (IPCC) (2021) AR6 Climate Change 2021: The Physical Science Basis. Cambridge, UK: Cambridge University Press.

Jaffe RL, Buszaa W, Sandweiss J, Wilczek F (2000) Review of speculative disaster scenarios at RHIC. Review of Modern Physics 72: 1125–1140.

Kaku M (2021) The God Equation: The Quest for a Theory of Everything. New York, NY: Doubleday.

Lama Tsongkhapa (1357a–1419) In Praise of the Buddha for His Teaching of Dependent Origination. Ston pa la rten cing 'brel bar byung bar gsungs pa las brtsams te bstod pa legs bshad snying po. Miscellaneous Writings of the Incomparable Lord Tsongkhapa, 30–36.

Lama Tsongkhapa (1357b–1419) Great Treatise on the Stages of the Path of Tantra. Sngags rim chen mo. Collected Works, Vol. ga.

Lama Tsongkhapa (1357c–1419) Essence of True Eloquence: Distinguishing the Provisional and the Definitive Meaning (Drang ba dang nges pa'i don rnam par 'byed pa legs bshad snying po). Collected Works. Vol. pha, 441–687.

Lama Tsongkhapa (1357d–1419) Ocean of Reasoning: An Exposition of Treatise on the Middle Way. Rtsa ba shes rab kyi rnam bshad ṭik chen rigs pa'i rgya mtsho. Collected Works. Vol. ba, 1–583.

Lama Tsongkhapa (1357e–1419) Elucidation of the Intent: A Thorough Exposition of Entering the Middle Way. Dbu ma la 'jug pa'i rnam bshad dgongs pa rab gsal. Collected Works. Vol. ma, 1–605.

Larkoski AJ (2019) Elementary Particle Physics: An Intuitive Introduction. Cambridge, UK: Cambridge University Press.

Lemaitre G (1931) The beginning of the world from the point of view of quantum theory. Nature 127 (3210): 706.

Le Treut H, Somerville R, Cubasch U, Ding Y, Mauritzen C, Mokssit A, Peterson T, Prather M (2007) Historical overview of climate change. In Solomon S et al. (eds.) Climate Change 2007: The Physical Science Basis. The Fourth Assessment Report of the Intergovernmental Panel on Climate Change. Cambridge, UK: Cambridge University Press.

Nagarjuna (second century). Fundamental Wisdom on the Middle Way. Mūlamadhyamakakārikā. Dbu ma rtsa ba'i tshig le'ur byas pa (Rtsa ba'i shes rab). Toh 3824, dbu ma tsa.

Nagarjuna (2nd century). Precious Garland. Ratnāvalī. Rin chen phreng ba. Toh 4158, spriṅ yig ge.

Nagarjuna (2nd century). Sixty Stanzas of Reasoning. Yuktiṣaṣṭikākārikā. Rigs pa drug cu pa. Toh 3825, dbu ma tsa.

Nagarjuna (2nd century). Seventy Stanzas on Emptiness. Śūnyatāsaptatikārikā. Stong nyid bdun cu pa. Toh 3827, dbu ma tsa.

Newton, I (1687) Philosophiæ Naturalis Principia Mathematica. London.

New York Times (NYT) (2013) Chasing the Higgs Boson. NYT, New York. Accessed from http://www.nytimes.com/2013/03/05/science/chasing-the-higgs-boson-how-2-teams-of-rivals-at-CERN-searched-for-physics-most-elusive-particle.html?pagewanted=all

Nobel Prize (2013) The Nobel Prize in Physics 2013: François Englert, Peter W. Higgs. Accessed from https://www.nobelprize.org/nobel_prizes/physics/laureates/2013/

Peskin ME (2008) The end of the world at the Large Hadron Collider? Physics 1 (14).

Plaga R (2009) On the potential catastrophic risk from metastable quantum-black holes produced at particle colliders. arXiv:0808.1415 [hep-ph].

Posner RA (2004) Catastrophe: Risk and Response. New York, NY: Oxford University Press.

Revelle, R., Suess, H.E., 1957. Carbon dioxide exchange between atmosphere and ocean and the question of an increase of atmospheric CO2 during the past decades. Tellus 9, 18–27.

Schrödinger E (1935). Die gegenwärtige Situation in der Quantenmechanik (The present situation in quantum mechanics). Naturwissenschaften. 23 (48): 807–812

Seo SN (2020) The Economics of Globally Shared and Public Goods. Amsterdam, NL: Academic Press.

Seo SN (2021) Climate Change and Economics: Engaging with Future Generations with Action Plans. London, UK: Palgrave Macmillan.

Seo SN (2022) The Economics of Pandemics: Exploring Globally Shared Experiences. London, UK: Palgrave Macmillan.

Seo SN (2024a) Buddha, Wisdom and Economics: A Contribution to the Art of Happiness. Cheltenham, UK: Edward Elgar.

Seo SN (2024b) Protecting Nature with Buddha's Wisdom: A Contribution to Environmental and Nature Studies. Cheltenham, UK: Edward Elgar.

Stein V (2022) Einstein's Theory of Special Relativity. Space.com.

Strang G (1991) Calculus (2nd edition). Wellesley, MA: Wellesley-Cambridge Press.

Thurman RAF (1984) Tsong Khapa's Speech of Gold in the Essence of True Eloquence: Reason and Enlightenment in the Central Philosophy of Tibet. Princeton, NJ: Princeton University Press.

Weitzman, M.L. (2009). On modeling and interpreting the economics of catastrophic climate change. Review of Economics and Statistics 91: 1–19.

Witze A (2014) Special relativity aces time trial. Nature News. Published on 19 September 2014. https://doi.org/10.1038/nature.2014.15970

CHAPTER 5

The Quantum Physics and an Artificial Intelligence Singularity

1 Introduction

This chapter deals with a singularity of artificial intelligence (AI) or, more plainly, super-intelligent robots (Kurzweil 2005). The present author will explain it in terms of the relationship between the development of artificial intelligence and quantum mechanics. The two forces tend to reinforce each other, making a foreseen AI singularity far more likely and far sooner to arrive, as will be clarified in this chapter.

The AI-driven singularity was foreseen by many notable scientists who predicted that it will arrive very soon, say, within a decade as of their writing. To be specific, when Stephen Hawking and coauthors wrote the article in 2014, they predicted it will happen within a decade. For your reference, today is March 23, 2024. To my sadness, Hawking passed away in around 2018, not witnessing "the last great achievement" of humanity he predicted (Hawking et al. 2014).

The artificial intelligence is simply put a robot. An intelligent robot can perform many functions that a human being performs as of today. According to physicists, the AI singularity occurs when the robots are as intelligent as human beings. At that point, humans will no longer be in control of the robots who will then control the planet as well as the universe. Robots will become the most powerful beings on Earth.

S. N. Seo, *The Economics of Singularities of Science Elucidated with Buddhist Thoughts*,
https://doi.org/10.1007/978-3-031-69118-8_5

The present author explained the concept of a singularity developed in mathematics in Chap. 3 (Poincare 1880–1890, Thom 1975). The AI singularity offers the readers of this book the clearest example of the definition of a singularity offered by physicists. Simply and without any ambiguity, it is the point in time in which robot intelligence equals human intelligence (Hawking et al. 2014).

This doomsday prediction, as will be clarified shortly, is quite appealing to as well as felt and shared by many observers. This is because ordinary people are by now rather used to numerous machines doing the human jobs. For example, Pepper was first unveiled in 2014 as the first humanoid robot because it can read human emotions and talk to them in 15 languages (SoftBank Robotics 2019). After about a decade since then, humanoids are commonly seen in the society: in restaurants, airports, universities, offices, hospitals, etc. Pepper is even friendly and with many gestures.

A more cryptic AI robot which is by far more influential as well as pernicious is an information super robot, sometimes called a ChatBot. The examples include ChatGPT (Chat Generative Pre-trained Transformer), Google search engine, etc. (OpenAI 2023). The ChatBot does not have a friendly face, hands, and legs like Pepper. But it has, generates, spreads the information about all the people and things on and off the Internet. It will give you an answer of its own to any problem or question you might have.

Quantum mechanics is on the other hand the science of matter at the most fundamental level, that is, the tiniest form of matter. Through examinations of such tiny particles as quantum and their behaviors, physicists strive to find the fundamental aspects of nature (Caltech Science Exchange 2022). It is often described by scientists that the theory of relativity and quantum mechanics are the two most promising theories of modern physics, but opposite.

Although physicists cannot explain what quantum mechanics exactly is, various experiments on such tiny objects and their behaviors are not impossible. Through such experiments, they describe quantum mechanics in terms of several noteworthy principles such as uncertainty principle, superposition, particle-wave duality, and quantum entanglements (Carroll 2020). Applying such principles once again, new machines and products are manufactured, the most notable progress of which is made in quantum computing (Wadhwa 2022; NYT 2023a).

The advancement of artificial intelligence and especially the singularity prospect of artificial intelligence are occurring in pace with the advances in quantum mechanics. The most prominent of such interdependence is that, as some observers argued, the AI robots will have the human brain capacity through reliance on the advances in quantum mechanics technologies such as quantum computing (Ananthaswamy 2021; Wadhwa 2022; Sumner 2022).

This chapter provides a brief review of quantum mechanics and physics with a focus on its salient features as the frontier of modern physics. It is followed by a description of the AI singularity and the challenges it poses. It concludes with a Buddhist interpretation of the quantum mechanics as well as the AI singularity.

2 Quantum Physics in a Nutshell

As stated in the previous chapter, quantum physics is a rival theory of physics against the theory of relativity in contemporary scientific inquiries (Heisenberg 1930; Feynman et al. 2010a, 2010b, 2010c). It is famous that Einstein did not accept the quantum physics ideas, viewing them too extreme (Einstein 2001; Einstein et al. 2015; Al-Khalili 2020). Einstein also actively engaged in providing a disproof of the quantum theories, as explained in the previous chapter in the context of the superposition hypothesis (Schrodinger 1935; Einstein et al. 1935). Even to this day, physicists dismiss the ideas of quantum physics or, to put it more mildly, prefer to set it aside for non-discussion (Carroll 2019, 2020). Scientists cannot exactly say at this point in time what quantum physics is and whether they are correct or not, as will be clarified shortly. That is also how I feel after listening to the quantum physics presentations for over a decade.

In this section, the present author will briefly describe in plain English a basket of theories and hypotheses that define quantum physics. Specifically, they are a wave-particle duality, superposition, uncertainty, and entanglement (Carroll 2019; Al-Khalili 2020).

According to Caltech Science Exchange from the California Institute of Technology where Richard Feynman had taught, quantum physics is described as "the study of matter and energy at the most fundamental level. It aims to uncover the properties and behaviors of the very building blocks of nature. ... This may give the wrong impression that quantum phenomena are bizarre or otherworldly. In fact, quantum science closes gaps in our knowledge of physics to give us a more complete picture of our everyday lives" (Caltech Science Exchange 2022).

It is often said that quantum physics is the study of behaviors of the matter at the smallest possible level, such as electrons, photons, and quanta. In this sense, there is a salient contrast between quantum physics and relativity physics. The former is the science of the smallest things of the physical world while the latter is the science of the biggest things of the world, that is, astronomical objects and the universe. Quantum physicists, however, assert that the principles of quantum behaviors are applicable to the behaviors of the biggest things as well such as the universe, although they have not figured out how.

How did the quantum physics begin? It is closely tied to Einstein's time and his scientific articles on light (Einstein 1905a, 1905b, 1905c). Before Einstein, it was thought that light is a wave. That is, it behaves like an ocean wave that is induced by, say, a wind or a hurricane or a tsunami. Light dispels darkness like an ocean wave rolls toward a beach. Einstein's paper argued that light is a photon, that is, a particle and not a wave (Einstein 1905a; Einstein et al. 2015).

Quantum physicists counter that if light is a photon, that is, a discrete particle, how does a rainbow have the spectrum of colors in the sky? If the sunlight were composed of photons, it shouldn't display the "range" of colors like the rainbow (Al-Khalili 2020).

Einstein's photon theory is also in good harmony with a classical description of the atom where the atom consists of a nucleus surrounded by electrons. Electrons are depicted as the particles that orbit the nucleus. However, the experiments conducted by quantum physicists and others show that electrons do not behave like a particle.

How do they behave then? Quantum physicists still try to describe them, but the gist of it is that electrons are distributed around the nucleus probabilistically within orbitals. To help you imagine it, think of a hydrogen atom whose nucleus is surrounded by three orbitals on which electrons exist. Electrons do not absolutely exist but only probabilistically. Therefore, they can exist in more than one location at a certain time. As they gain or lose energy, electrons can jump from one orbital to another (Carroll 2020).

As the quantum theory of electrons indicate, according to quantum physics, matter and energy do not exist as a particle, but rather as discrete packets or quanta with associated energy. The light of a certain frequency will deliver energy in quanta, that is, photons. Each photon at this frequency will have the same amount of energy.

The most well-known experiment in quantum physics is called the double slit experiment (Merli et al. 1976; Rosa 2012). At this point, readers will be able to appreciate it as a nice quantum experiment or phenomenon. The gist of it is that although things look like an independent particle, it in fact is like an entangled or collective or group thing. Let me explain it. You can refer to Fig. 5.1 for an illustration of this experiment. On the one side, there is a particle shooter, that is, a photon shooter (or generator). The photons thus shot pass through the two slits. The two slits are an interference mechanism. At the other end of the set, there is a blank curtain upon which the photons shot by the photon shooter and passed through the double slits arrive, that is, hit. The locations of the arrival points can be observed by the experimenter. So, this is a very simple experiment (Feynman et al. 1965).

What happens during this experiment is rather interesting. When an individual particle is shot from the generator, it acts exactly like a discrete particle. It passes through one of the slits and falls on the blank curtain as a discrete dot. All individual photons behave the same way, that is, as a discrete entity. So far, so good, just like Einstein's photons (Einstein 1905a; Einstein et al. 2015).

When a large number of photons are shot, however, the photons form a shape on the blank curtain. The shape is as if two ocean waves have interacted. Thus, collectively, the photons, although shot individually, show a

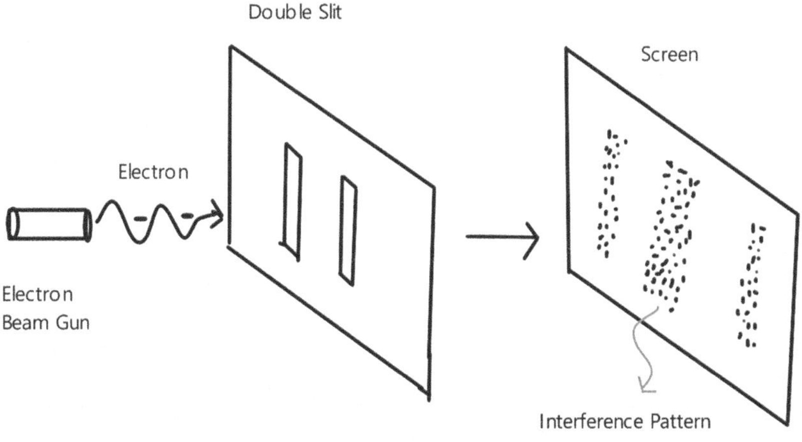

Fig. 5.1 An illustration of the double slit experiment

wave like behavior. Each light wave passes through each slot. After passing through the slots, the two waves spread and cancel each other to form a shape on the blank screen. Therefore, on the one hand, the photons behave like a particle, while they behave like a wave, on the other hand, which is the essence of the double slit experiment (Merli et al. 1976; Feynman et al. 2010c).

Isn't it obvious that when photons are seen collectively, they behave like a wave, say, a cloud in the blue sky or an ocean wave because there are so many photons fired on the blank curtain? You might ask. But the key to understanding the double slit experiment is that if the light photons or the electrons were particles and not waves, the image that will appear at the blank screen should be only the image of the two slots, as if it were the image of two feet pressed on a foot of snow on the ground.

From this experiment, quantum physicists argue that their behavior is as if all individual photons are entangled, or individual electrons connected by some underlying force, or each particle knowing how other particles behaved. The gist of it is that the photons display the characteristics of a particle as well as the characteristics of a wave. All of quantum physics can be explained *via* this simple experiment, according to its most renowned elucidator (Feynman et al. 1965, 2010c).

Rounding up the double slit experiment, quantum physics is described by its adherents by a set of principles, which is referred to as quantum principles. They include a wave-particle duality, a superposition principle, uncertainty principle, and entanglement. Let me give a brief exposition of them in the following.

The wave-particle duality is what is attempted to be shown by the double slit experiment. This duality concerns whether light and matter have the property of a wave or a particle, depending on how they are measured. As explained, this was the question at the origin of quantum mechanics, and also of relativity physics.

The principle of superposition is that an object can exist as a combination of multiple possible states at the same time. It is known by the thought experiment called Schrodinger's cat. In a hypothetical box which is sealed, there is a cat that is both dead and alive simultaneously as long as it remains hidden. Only when an experimenter opens the box, the cat is either dead or alive (Schrodinger 1935). In a mathematics context, it is a situation in which more than one solution exist for an equation. In a physical context, it is a situation like a ripple in a pond which is seen by the two waves overlapping.

In a Buddhist context, we can interpret the karmic imprints as Schrodinger's box in which many different karmic imprints exist with varying degrees of potentiality. A certain karmic consequence is realized at one point in time only when someone opens the box, that is, a certain karmic imprint meets the conditional factors (Lama Tsongkhapa's Stages, Illuminating the Intent).

Einstein, against the superposition theory and quantum physics in general, offered a counter example along with his coauthors (Einstein et al. 1935). There are two sealed boxes, one with a pair of white gloves and the other with a pair of black gloves. Let's pick one of the boxes and put it before the person who would open the box. Before he opens the box, both pairs of gloves exist inside the box as potential, that is, with probabilities. When he opens the box, only one pair of gloves will exist. Einstein argued that this does not mean that before opening the box, the two pairs of gloves existed within the box.

At the heart of the Copenhagen interpretation of quantum physics which originated from the discussion between Niels Bohr and Werner Heisenberg lies the uncertainty principle (Heisenberg 1930; Einstein et al. 2015). The uncertainty principle states that two properties of an object, for example, the object's position and velocity, cannot both be precisely known at the same time. More specifically, if you precisely measure the position of an electron, you cannot measure the speed of the electron precisely. This is also interpreted as showing a trade-off of choosing one option over the other option when there are two options.

The entanglement principle is that things are entangled. When one electron goes up, another electron must go down. More specifically, things in a system are entangled. Therefore, the state of one object in the system cannot be fully described without knowing the state of the other entangled object in the system. This is one of the principles that is applied to building a quantum computer.

3 Shortcomings of Quantum Physics

Quantum physics provides an alternative framework of physics to classical physics and more importantly to relativity physics. In other words, it provides an alternative way for people to understand the material phenomena. This alternative framework is, however, not clearly elaborated by quantum physicists who leave it only vaguely. Neither are other physicists enthusiastic about what it says. In that sense, despite some promising aspects, quantum physics has always remained an unfinished business or an unsettled academic pursuit (Carroll 2019, 2020).

To be more specific, many observers would agree that the entanglement principle may be understandable as a physics principle. That is, that two elements in a system are entangled, and therefore do not behave individually, would make sense to many scientists as well as non-scientists. Quantum physicists, however, do not seem to be interested in pursuing further questions. For example, are all things entangled? Can they be disentangled? Are entanglements only relationships? Is there a degree of complexity in entanglements?

Similarly, the principle of uncertainty posited by quantum physicists is perhaps encountered and understood often by those who rely on different measures of science. For example, the speed and the locations of an object are relatively defined, so each variable cannot be measured precisely. For another, time and space are relatively defined; therefore, each variable cannot be measured precisely.

However, quantum physicists do not ask themselves how much uncertainty they need for it to be stated to be called a principle of uncertainty. To put this differently, can scientists measure speed precisely? Or locations precisely? They cannot. However, the impossibility of a 'precise measurement' has not stopped the society's reliance on the speed measurement or the location measurement. If you are wondering what I mean here, ponder over the concept of time I illustrated in Fig. 5.1 of the previous chapter (Fig. 4.1, Chap. 4). Time is only defined through the relationships among the Sun, the Moon, and Earth. The society relies on the time thus measured all the time, without the pain of uncertainty inflicted on it.

The principle of superposition is also explained in a similar manner. An object may exist as multiple "orbitals" probabilistically or, put differently, with uncertainty. At one point in time, the object may exhibit only one orbital. To give you a social example, a person can be a Scottish, a British, and an EU citizen simultaneously. At one point in time, they may exhibit only one nationality. So, the example of the superposition principle may not need to be as dramatic as the dead cat-live cat example given by Schrodinger (Schrodinger 1935). The apposite Buddhist interpretation or interpretability was explained by the present author in the previous section.

Despite these concerns about the foundation of quantum physics as well as potential consequences, quantum physicists have "resisted" furthering their ideas and experiments through which to resolve these issues. Straightforwardly speaking, they neglected to clarify how quantum phenomena are an adequate exposition of everyday phenomena people always encounter.

In summing up this section, the present author would conclude that things, that is, energy and matter, possess the quantum characteristics which are explained by the quantum physicists' works. But it does not mean that the classical physics of Newton as well as the relativity physics of Einstein are completely wrong and useless. They also provide reasonable concepts and observations useful in some situations, which are also reconcilable with quantum principles in some situations (Newton 1687; Einstein 1915a, 1915b).

Comparing across classical physics, relativity physics, and quantum physics, it is notable that a big drawback of quantum physics is its heavy reliance on the randomness of quanta for the sake of its identity. Quantum physicists tend to describe the material world as the world of random behaviors of quanta (Carroll 2019, 2020). As I have described thus far, that is not actually the case if you looked carefully into the quantum principles as well as their respective experiments. In other words, that conclusion is not warranted. In the conventional world or the material world if you like, the cause and effect or the principle of causality is still applicable (Maha-nidana Sutta, Lama Tsongkhapa's True Eloquence). Going further, the karma and its consequences cannot be denied in any sense according to the omniscient vision of the Buddha (Wheel of Life in Divyavadana 2017, HAR 2023). Things may appear random to quantum scientists, but they arise and disappear according to the principle of cause and effects. As Buddha Shakyamuni declared (Bodhi Sutta, Paticca-samuppada Sutta, Lama Tsongkhapa's Praise):

> When this is, that is.
> When this is not, that is not.
> When this arises, that arises.
> When this disappears, that disappears.

4 Singularity in Artificial Intelligence

The term "singularity" is the core concept of this book, so it appears in the title of the book. The term was originated in the mathematics literature but it was popularized in the study of artificial intelligence (Thom 1972, 1975, 1977; Zeeman 1977; Kurzweil 2005). In this literature, the singularity is the point in time when the machine intelligence, namely, artificial intelligence, is equal to the biological intelligence, namely, the human intelligence. As stated above, the science of artificial intelligence offers the clearest definition of a science-driven singularity among the five scientific experiments examined in this book.

Hawking and his AI expert colleagues who have long been observing the progress in the field of artificial intelligence warned in 2014 that super-intelligent robots will surpass the human intelligence within a decade, that is, by 2024 (Hawking et al. 2014). They predicted that that will be "the greatest achievement by humankind but the last achievement." They meant that that moment will signify a subjugation of the human race by the AI super-intelligent robots. Elon Musk, a notable technology entrepreneur with Tesla and SpaceX successes in the early twenty-first century, and others are making a similarly dire warning with regard to the AI robot capabilities (CNBC 2017; NYT 2023b).

The opposite viewpoint is also strong regarding the future of AI. Optimists argue that the artificial intelligence is only a machine or a robot which is designed to serve people's basic needs and tasks. There is not much to worry about it. The robots can only do most basic and simple tasks for the benefit of human beings and in the control of human beings. The jobs that will be lost to AI robots will be the true risk AI robots pose to human society, thus they argue (Quartz 2017).

To assess the range of opinions regarding AI, let us begin with the basic question: What is artificial intelligence? It refers to all non-human intelligence, more precisely, all non-biological intelligence, in other words, machine intelligence. The present author may explain it through the three types of artificial intelligence for the sake of highlighting the risk each of them poses (Seo 2018). The first is Pepper the humanoid that is a robot which is developed to look like a human and act like a friendly human being (SoftBank Robotics 2019). The second is an information compilation, processing, and calculation machine, for example, the ChatGPT developed by OpenAI, often referred to as a ChatBot (OpenAI 2023). The third is a potpourri of lethal autonomous weapons (LAWS), some of which are already widely deployed and are dominating the on-going wars in the world such as the Russia-Ukraine war and the Israel-Hamas war (Marchant et al. 2011; Sharkey 2012; UNODA 2017; Longpre et al. 2022).

In each of the three types of AI robots, it is possible that the AI machine can outperform the humans in the relevant tasks. The capacities and capabilities of Pepper the humanoid as reported in its release in 2014 are summarized in Fig. 5.2 (SoftBank 2019; Seo 2020). The first humanoid can

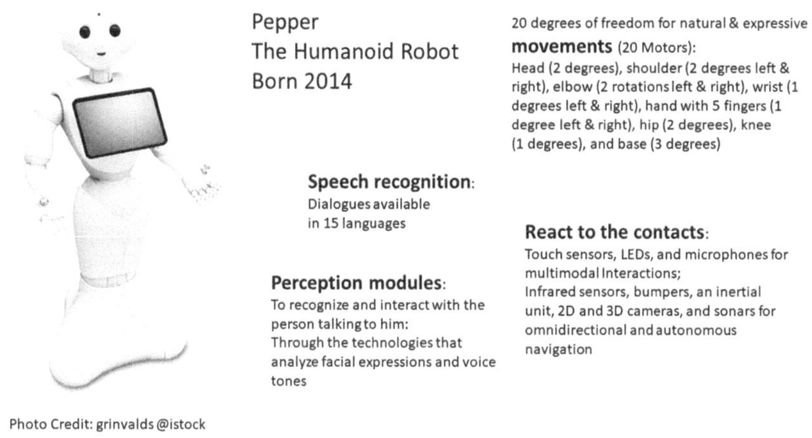

Fig. 5.2 The 1st type AI: Pepper the humanoid's capabilities

speak as many as 15 different languages, read people's facial expressions and voice tones, and interact with people relying on 12 different motors at joints. Pepper and other similar robots such as Optimus developed by Tesla are expected to replace human laborers in many situations, including restaurant attendants, receptionists, hospital medical check-ups, airport cleaners, and other manual labor (Tesla 2023).

As for the second-type AI, the ChatGPT can complete a complicated intellectual task many times faster than an intelligent human being. Figure 5.3 gives a sample of the ChatGPT's work as provided by the company (OpenAI 2023). In this example, the ChatBot interacts and responds to the user's request to correct an error in the computer programming. It reads a complicated programming through in an instant and offers a quick fix.

How amazing is that! However, if you are familiar with a statistical or a mathematical programming language such as SAS, MATLAB, etc., you would know that such correction capability was incorporated into these programs several decades ago. The uniqueness of the ChatGPT's capabilities is that they are not limited to statistical and mathematical programming. In fact, the ChatGPT is a true generalist, that is, can answer any questions. The ChatBot can even discuss the Buddha's teaching on emptiness and may even correct you about it!

User
this code is not working like i expect — how do i fix it?

```
resultWorkerErr := make(chan error)
defer close(resultWorkerErr)
go func() {
    defer cancel()
    resultWorkerErr <- b.resultWorker(ctx)
}()

err := b.worker(ctx)
cancel()
if err == nil {
    return <-resultWorkerErr
}
return multierror.Append(err, <-resultWorkerErr)
```

ChatGPT
It's difficult to say what's wrong with the code without more context. Can you provide more information about what the code is supposed to do and what isn't working as expected? Also, is this the entire code or just a part of it?

User
just part of it — the error never surfaces. I think there is something wrong with the channel

ChatGPT
To fix this issue, you could close the resultWorkerErr channel after writing to it. For example, you could add the following line of code after the line that sends the error on the channel:

```
close(resultworkerErr)
```

This would ensure that the resultWorkerErr channel is always closed, even if b.resultWorker never returns an error.

Fig. 5.3 The 2nd type AI: ChatGPT's capacities

The way the ChatGPT responds also depends on the immense human efforts because human trainers must train the ChatGPT the relevant modules. This training program is called the Reinforcement Learning from Human Feedback (RLHF), in which AI trainers provide the conversations in which they play both sides, that is, the user and the AI robot. The ChatGPT acts in accordance with the reward model which the AI trainer writes model-written messages and rank them. As you can tell, the ChatGPT's capabilities are therefore heavily dependent on human laborers.

One of the thorny issues with the training of the ChatGPT and more broadly with the success of the ChatBots is that the AI trainers should get materials from somewhere, for which the *New York Times* (*NYT*) sued the ChatGPT company for using the newspaper's millions of articles. Ironically, the *NYT* must now compete regarding the validity of a certain argument or fact with ChatGPT, which were trained through its articles (NYT 2023c). This will not be the problem of *NYT* alone. Many newspapers, publishers, and authors can argue for the same.

As for the third type AI, the lethal autonomous weapon systems (LAWS) can become even deadlier and more effective in such a way that human engagements in battlefields in a war are unnecessary while at the same time the war's deadly consequences become even more uncontrollable and unpredictable for warring parties. Many traditional weapons are being developed and deployed with some autonomous functions newly built in. The examples of such include antivehicle or antipersonnel mines which are activated and operated based upon various trigger mechanisms. The newer LAWS weapons include the missile defense systems which detect and engage targets, that is, various types of missiles, automatically; a loitering munition (kamikaze drones) system which contains a built-in warhead, waits around a predefined area, and attacks the target with the aid of automated sensors (Washington Post 2023).

In Fig. 5.4, the present author puts together two graphs that illustrate the shift of modern wars toward LAWS or drones. The figure on the left compares the two wars: the 1991 Gulf War between the USA and Iraq and the first two-year period of the Russia-Ukraine War. The ratio of drones over missiles increases from near zero in the former to 58% in the latter war (Reuters 2024). Note that the missiles used in these wars, including the Hellfire missiles used in the Desert Storm operation during the Gulf War, had some automated features, but missiles are considered a munition not a drone.

The figure on the right shows the US defense annual budgets on Unmanned Aircraft Systems (UAS) which shows a dramatic increase starting from the second Iraq War in 2001 after the 9/11 attack on the USA, from around US $300 million to around US $3 billion by around 2010

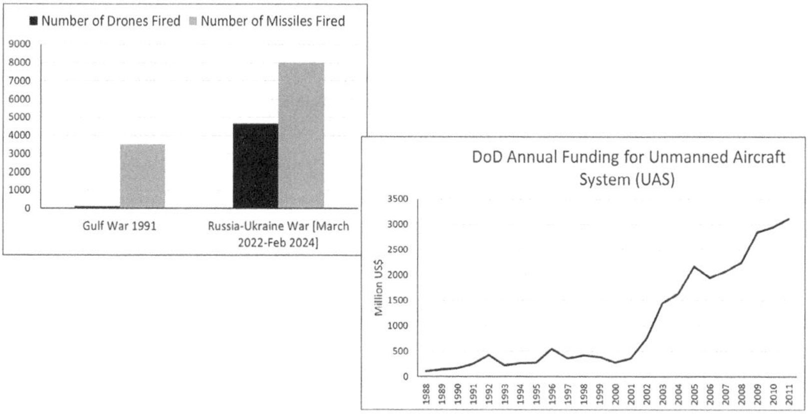

Fig. 5.4 The 3rd type AI: the LAWS dependence in recent wars
Source: DoD (2005), Reuters (2024)

(DoD 2005). This tells only a part of the story because most automated weapons are made by private companies in the USA: Northrop Grumman, Raytheon, and the General Atomics Aeronautical Systems Inc.

What does it all have to do with quantum physics which is the main subject of this chapter? There is a fervor of optimism across the world that quantum mechanics will make the current AI technologies, introduced as the three types of AI robots in the above, exceedingly more powerful. The gist of this forecast is that a coupling of quantum computing with the AI technologies will open the door to the feared reality that the robot intelligence will indeed exceed the human intelligence (Wadhwa 2022; Ananthaswamy 2021; Sumner 2022).

How so? You might ask. The key to such a reality is the speed: that is, the quantum computing will enable the AI robots to work and perform their functions far faster than the current AI robots by multiple orders of magnitude. A quantum computer is a computer built with the afore-described quantum principles, for which many governments as well as private companies are engaged in steep competitions (Forbes 2023). Imagine a super supercomputer which is 1000 times faster than the current supercomputer of the world! Such a quantum computer would be able to crack easily any website encryption, any password of individuals, any financial record of a person, any blockchain record. Let alone solving within a minute the impossible-to-solve equations with current AI technologies, for example, precise daily weather forecasts or a 100-year climate forecast.

How is such a quantum computer built? It is known that a number of countries in the world are experimenting to build such a computer: China, France, Russia, Germany, the Netherlands, Britain, Canada, and India; US companies such as IBM, Google, Intel, Microsoft, and some universities. The quantum computer is built from qubits, which is different from the traditional computer based on the bit technology. Unlike the bit computer, the qubits can hold 1 and 0 at the same time probabilistically. Experts contend that the quantum computing relies on the concepts of superposition, entanglement, and uncertainty (Wadhwa 2022). Even these quantum enthusiasts, however, admit that the quantum computer is at a rudimentary stage (NYT 2023a). The leaders in the development of a quantum computer are today's technology giants: IBM, Google, Amazon, Microsoft, Intel (Forbes 2023).

A successful creation of such a quantum computing technology would pose many challenges to humankind, but also would offer a possibility for it to drastically rethink and solve the pressing major problems of humanity, with global climate change being just one of them. An area of much intrigue in this regard is neuroscience in whose discipline scientists are investing heavily in creating consciousness itself out of pure matter (Tegmark 2015; Trujillo et al. 2019). In this endeavor, quantum computing offers an invaluable opportunity to scientists, according to enthusiasts (NYT 2023a). The reason is not hard to figure out: a successful quantum computing technology would offer a possibility for neuroscientists to map the complex system of the human brain with 100 billion neurons and 60 trillion neuronal connections (Pakkenberg and Gundersen 1997). This is the topic of Chap. 8 of this book.

5 The Buddhist Wisdom on the AI and Quantum Physics

Buddhists would not find it difficult in agreeing with the broad assessment among scientists that quantum physics still needs to be explained better; it does not offer a comprehensive or a consistent theory on the physical world (Carroll 2019; Al-Khalili 2020). This is despite the assessment from the present author's Buddhist point of view that the quantum principles such as uncertainty, entanglement, superposition, a wave-particle duality are all meaningful theories of the physical world put forth by quantum physicists. This point was emphasized throughout this chapter by the present author. To put this another way, quantum physics appears to complement classical physics as well as relativity physics in an important way (Feynman et al. 2010a, 2010b, 2010c). Although many Buddhist authors appear to think relativity physics is superior to quantum physics in explaining the physical world, the present author feels that the latter offers advanced viewpoints from the former especially on complex physical phenomena (Ricard and Thuan 2004).

When quantum physics is coupled with and integrated in artificial intelligence technology development, as surveyed in the above, many experts posit a rosy picture about what it can achieve. On the other side, there are antagonists who predict as far as the imminent extinction possibility of humankind owing to robot intelligence supremacy, which this chapter referred to as an AI singularity (Kurzweil 2005; Hawking et al. 2014).

Like these observers, Buddhists would concur easily that the artificial intelligence technology may bring good things to the future of humankind. The examples of such would include, to name just some, advanced computing and calculation capacities, AI cashiers, AI banking, AI health check-up, an automated delivery system, an automated and linked transportation system, an AI-assisted learning system for school children, an AI translator.

Beyond certain limits, Buddhists can also feel that many AI technologies are redundant or may even turn out to be harmful to humankind. Let me elaborate on this. Take Wikipedia for example (Wikipedia 2024). When it was launched in 2001, it was hailed as an encyclopedia by common people where anyone can contribute, an information revolution. It, however, gradually deteriorated into a platform where one party (person) attacks another party (person) regarding an entry. It then further deteriorated into a platform where the world's spies and intelligence agencies fiercely attempt to manipulate the data, especially historical and political data. It is now best described as a ground of information warfare. As far as the present author can tell, there is little hope that this can be fixed in the Wikipedia AI.

Take the Google search engine for another example! It still offers an important service to people who are looking for relevant online information. However, beyond certain limits, the search results it offers to a searcher are often questionable. The misgiving about the truthfulness or impartiality of the Google search results first emerged in politics. The point is that since Google relies on "algorithms" to generate search results, the generated results can vary depending on which algorithm is relied upon. Under the chosen algorithm, certain information can be suppressed by Google service while other information can be regarded truthful. Under a certain algorithm, it is possible that the Google Search ends up being a platform where false information spreads like a wildfire. As far as we can tell, there is little hope that this algorithm problem can be fixed soon.

In addition to the algorithm issue, there is a minority problem in the AI Google. Owing to the company's alliance with a certain political group or a dominant political force, it can end up repressing the information shared by a minority group that is in fact reporting truthful information.

Thirdly, there is a concern that the Google AI is not able to discern subtleties in the information appearing on the open Internet space. To be specific, Google can search only open access data on the Internet while many data on the Internet are not open access to all. For another example, it may not be able to distinguish subtler points of Buddhism which is a highly complex system of thoughts; as such, it may end up only offering gross points of Buddhism to online searchers.

These concerns discussed through the examples of Wikipedia and Google Search, whose points are also widely shared among the concerned public, are more or less equally applicable to many prominent Internet platforms or AIs such as the social networking sites such as Facebook and TikTok, ChatBots such as ChatGPT.

These observations and reasonings, although they may look unsystematic to readers, are in turn a primary key to solving the question of AI singularity. To put it another way, if robot intelligence were to overpower biological intelligence in the coming years, it would achieve that through some or all of the four mechanisms outlined in this section. The chaos about an entry or an issue and the distrust among people that follows will likely be the hallmark of such a singularity moment. This is certainly vastly different from the chaos theory that Edward Lorenz envisioned (Lorenz 1963, 1969).

6 Perfect Wisdom in the Context of AI Singularity

Is the AI singularity avoidable or inevitable? Will the realm of sentient beings come to an end via the AI overpowering? From the Buddhist vantage point, there is much reason to see hope and peace in the world despite the historic advances of the artificial intelligence. How so? Many skeptics will be startled.

This is because Buddhism is the thought system of the perfectly and completely enlightened ones or the religion of perfect wisdom (King of Meditations Sutra, Perfection of Wisdom Pronounced by Manjushri). Readers might ask what does that have to do with AI singularity? Let me elaborate. The perfection of wisdom elucidated by Buddha Shakyamuni and Lama Tsongkhapa is so magical and so powerful that it will defeat the challenges of the AI robots and in particular dispel the chaos and distrust that will be sewn by robot intelligence (Nagarjuna's Fundamental Wisdom, Chandrakirti's Lucid Exposition, Lama Tsongkhapa's True Eloquence, Illuminating the Intent, Stages of the Path). The perfection of wisdom is the opposite of chaos, like light and darkness. Where there is light, there is no darkness "by definition."

Lastly, it must be added that at the heart of perfect wisdom of Buddhism lies rationality and reasoned analysis (Nagarjuna's Sixty Reasoning Stanzas, Lama Tsongkhapa's Ocean of Reasoning). Buddhists, therefore, should not stop looking piercingly into the reality created by the robot intelligence (Seo 2024a, 2024b).

Readers might ask: Aren't you just stating the obvious? How do you know that the perfect wisdom is out there? Let me answer it for those who are still grappling with what this chapter has delivered. The AI singularity will arrive when and only when chaos and distrust among the public prevail. That said, the prevention of it will exist in the pursuit of the perfect wisdom by the general public. To phrase it more commonly, true information!

References

Al-Khalili J (2020) The World According to Physics. Princeton, NJ: Princeton University Press.

Ananthaswamy A (2021) AI designs quantum physics experiments beyond what any human has conceived. Scientific American. Accessed from https://www.scientificamerican.com/article/ai-designs-quantum-physics-experiments-beyond-what-any-human-has-conceived/

Caltech Science Exchange (2022) What is Quantum Physics. Accessed from https://scienceexchange.caltech.edu/topics/quantum-science-explained/quantum-physics

Carroll S (2019) Something Deeply Hidden: Quantum Worlds and the Emergence of Spacetime. Boston, MA: E.P. Dutton.

Carroll S (2020) A Brief History of Quantum Mechanics. The Royal Institution, Westminster. UK.

Chandrakirti (7th century) Lucid Exposition. Prasannapada. Tshig gsal. Tengyur. Beijing: Comparative edition. Vol. 60, 3–483.

CNBC (2017) Elon Musk says global race for A.I. will be the most likely cause of World War III. CNBC, New York, NY. Accessed from https://www.cnbc.com/2017/09/04/elon-musk-says-global-race-for-ai-will-be-most-likely-cause-of-ww3.html

Department of Defense (DoD) (2005) The Unmanned Aircraft Systems Roadmap 2005–2030. Office of the Secretary of Defense, Department of Defense, Virginia, US.

Divyāvadāna. Divine Stories. [Rotman A (trasl.) (2017) Divine Stories. Boston MA: Wisdom Publications]

Einstein A (1905a) On a heuristic point of view concerning the production and transformation of light. Annalen der Physik 17: 132–148.

Einstein A (1905b) On the movement of small particles suspended in stationary liquids required by the molecular-kinetic theory of heat. Annalen der Physik 17: 549–560.
Einstein A (1905c) On the electrodynamics of moving bodies. Annalen der Physik 17: 891–921
Einstein A (1915a) On the general theory of relativity. Submitted to Prussian Academy of Science.
Einstein A (1915b) The field equations of gravitation. Submitted to Prussian Academy of Science.
Einstein A (2001) Relativity: The Special and General Theory. Mineola, NY: Dover Publications.
Einstein A, Podolsky B, and Rosen N (1935) Can quantum-mechanical description of physical reality be considered complete? Physical Review 47: 777–780.
Einstein A, Klein MJ, Przibram K (2015). Letters on Wave Mechanics: Correspondence with H. A. Lorentz, Max Planck, and Erwin Schrödinger. Philosophical Library/Open Road.
Feynman R, Leighton R, Sands M (2010a) The Feynman Lectures on Physics, Volume I: Mainly Mechanics, Radiation, and Heat. California Institute of Technology, Pasadena, CA. Accessed from https://www.feynmanlectures.caltech.edu/III_toc.html
Feynman R, Leighton R, Sands M (2010b) The Feynman Lectures on Physics, Volume II: Mainly Electromagnetism and Matter. California Institute of Technology, Pasadena, CA. Accessed from https://www.feynmanlectures.caltech.edu/III_toc.html
Feynman R, Leighton R, Sands M (2010c) The Feynman Lectures on Physics, Volume III quantum mechanics. California Institute of Technology, Pasadena, CA. Accessed from https://www.feynmanlectures.caltech.edu/III_toc.html
Feynman RP, Leighton RB, Sands M (1965) The Feynman Lectures on Physics, Vol. 3. Boston, MA: Addison-Wesley.
Forbes Magazine (2023) Top 10 Quantum Computing Companies Making Change. Published on December 11, 2023. Accessed from https://www.forbes.com/sites/technology/article/top-quantum-computing-companies/?sh=c1980463a941
Hawking S, Tegmark M, Russell S, Wilczek F (2014) Transcending complacency on superintelligent machines. Huffington Post. Accessed from https://www.huffingtonpost.com/stephen-hawking/artificial-intelligence_b_5174265.html
Heisenberg W (1930) The Physical Principles of the Quantum Theory (German: Physikalischen Prinzipien der Quantentheorie). Chicago, IL: The University of Chicago Press.
Himalayan Art Resources (HAR) (2023) Wheel of Life Schematic. Accessed from https://www.himalayanart.org/pages/wheeloflife2/index.html
Kurzweil R (2005) The Singularity is Near. New York, NY: Penguin.

Lama Tsongkhapa (1357a–1419) Great Treatise on the Stages of the Path to Enlightenment. Byang chub lam rim chen mo. Collected Works. Vol. pa.

Lama Tsongkhapa (1357b–1419) Ocean of Reasoning: An Exposition of Treatise on the Middle Way. Rtsa ba shes rab kyi rnam bshad ṭik chen rigs pa'i rgya mtsho. Collected Works. Vol. ba, 1–583.

Lama Tsongkhapa (1357c–1419) Illuminating the Intent: A Thorough Exposition of Entering the Middle Way. Dbu ma la 'jug pa'i rnam bshad dgongs pa rab gsal. Collected Works. Vol. ma, 1–605.

Lama Tsongkhapa (1357d–1419) Essence of True Eloquence: Distinguishing the Provisional and the Definitive Meaning (Drang ba dang nges pa'i don rnam par 'byed pa legs bshad snying po). Collected Works. Vol. pha, 441–687.

Lama Tsongkhapa (1357e–1419). In Praise of the Buddha for His Teaching of Dependent Origination. Ston pa la rten cing 'brel bar byung bar gsungs pa las brtsams te bstod pa legs bshad snying po. Miscellaneous Writings of the Incomparable Lord Tsongkhapa, 30–36.

Longpre S, Storm M, and Shah R (2022) Lethal autonomous weapons systems & artificial intelligence: trends, challenges, and policies. MIT Science Policy Review3, 47–56.

Lorenz EN (1963) Deterministic nonperiodic flow. Journal of the Atmospheric Sciences 20: 130–141.

Lorenz EN (1969) Atmospheric predictability as revealed by naturally occurring analogues. Journal ofthe Atmospheric Sciences 26: 636–646.

Marchant G, Allenby B, Arkin R, Barrett E, Borenstein J, Gaudet L, Kitterie O, Lin P, Lucas G, O'meara R, Silberman J (2011) International governance of autonomous military robots. The Columbia Science and Technology Law Review 12: 272–315.

Merli PG, Missiroli GF, Pozzi G (1976) On the statistical aspect of electron interference phenomena. American Journal of Physics. 44 (3): 306–307.

Nagarjuna (2nd century) Fundamental Wisdom on the Middle Way. Mūlamadhyamakakārikā. Dbu ma rtsa ba'i tshig le'ur byas pa (Rtsa ba'i shes rab). Toh 3824, dbu ma tsa.

Nagarjuna (2nd century) Sixty Stanzas of Reasoning. Yuktiṣaṣṭikākārikā. Rigs pa drug cu pa. Toh 3825, dbu ma tsa.

New York Times (2023a) Microsoft says new A.I. shows signs of human reasoning. Published on May 16, 2023.

New York Times (2023b) A.I. poses 'risk of extinction,' Industry leaders warn. Published on May 30, 2023.

New York Times (2023c) The Times sues OpenAI and Microsoft over A.I. use of copyrighted work. Published on December 27, 2023. Accessed from https://www.nytimes.com/2023/12/27/business/media/new-york-times-open-ai-microsoft-lawsuit.html

Newton, I (1687) Philosophiæ Naturalis Principia Mathematica. London, UK.

OpenAI (2023) Introducing ChatGPT. San Francisco, CA. Accessed from https://openai.com/blog/chatgpt

Quartz (2017) The robot that takes your job should pay taxes, says Bill Gates. Quartz, Washington DC. Accessed from https://qz.com/911968/bill-gates-the-robot-that-takes-your-job-should-pay-taxes/

Pakkenberg B, Gundersen HJG (1997) Neocortical neuron number in humans: Effect of sex and age. Journal of Comparative Neurology 384: 312–320.

Poincaré H (1880–1890) Mémoire sur les Courbes Définies par les Équations Différentielles I-VI, Oeuvre I. Gauthier-Villars, Paris.

Reuters (2024) Ukraine says Russia has launched over 8,000 missiles, 4,630 drones during war. Published on February 22, 2024.

Ricard M, Thuan TX (2004) The Quantum and the Lotus: A Journey to the Frontiers Where Science and Buddhism Meet. New York, NY: Crown.

Rosa R (2012) The Merli–Missiroli–Pozzi two-slit electron-interference experiment. Physics in Perspective. 14 (2): 178–194.

Schrödinger E (1935). Die gegenwärtige Situation in der Quantenmechanik (The present situation in quantum mechanics). Naturwissenschaften. 23 (48): 807–812

Seo SN (2018) Natural and Man-made Catastrophes: Theories, Economics, and Policy Designs. Hoboken, NJ: Wiley-Blackwell.

Seo SN (2020) The Economics of Globally Shared and Public Goods. Amsterdam, NL: Academic Press.

Seo SN (2024a) Buddha, Wisdom and Economics: A Contribution to the Art of Happiness. Cheltenham, UK: Edward Elgar.

Seo SN (2024b) Protecting Nature with Buddha's Wisdom: A Contribution to Environmental and Nature Studies. Cheltenham, UK: Edward Elgar.

Sharkey NE (2012) Evitability of autonomous robot warfare. International Journal of the Red Cross 94: 787–799.

Soft Bank Robotics (2019) Pepper. Soft Bank, Tokyo, Accessed from https://www.softbankrobotics.com/emea/en/pepper.

Sumner T (2022) Artificial intelligence reduces a 100,000-equation quantum physics problem to only four equations. Phys.org. Accessed from https://phys.org/news/2022-09-artificial-intelligence-equation-quantum-physics.html

Tesla (2023) AI & Robotics. Tesla, Austin, TX. Accessed from https://www.tesla.com/AI

Thom R (1972) Stabilité Structurelle et Morphogenèse: Essai d'une Théorie Générale des Modèles. Benjamin, New York.

Thom R (1975) Structural stability and morphogenesis. Benjamin-Addison-Wesley, New York.

Thom R (1977) What is catastrophe theory about? In Haken H (ed.) Synergetics. Springer Series in Synergetics, vol 2. Springer, Berlin, Heidelberg.

Tegmark M (2015) Consciousness as a State of Matter. Chaos, Solitons & Fractals 76: 238–270. arxiv.org/abs/1401.1219

Trujillo CA, Gao R, Negraes PD, Gu J, Buchanan J, Preissl S, Wang A,Wu W, Haddad GG, Chaim IA, Domissy A, Vandenberghe M, Devor A, Yeo GW, Voytek B, and Muotri AR (2019) Complex oscillatory waves emerging from cortical organoids model early human brain network development. Cell Stem Cell 25, 558–569.

United Nations Office for Disarmament Affairs (UNODA) (2017) Background on Lethal Autonomous Weapons Systems. Accessed from https://www.un.org/disarmament/geneva/ccw/background-on-lethal-autonomous-weapons-systems/.

Wadhwa V (2022) Why quantum computing is even more dangerous than Artificial Intelligence. Foreign Policy. Accessed from https://foreignpolicy.com/2022/08/21/quantum-computing-artificial-intelligence-ai-technology-regulation/

Washington Post (2023) The war in Ukraine is spurring a revolution in drone warfare using AI. Published on July 26, 2023.

Wikipedia (2024) Wikipedia: The Free Encyclopedia. Accessed from https://www.wikipedia.org/

Zeeman EC (1977) Catastrophe theory-selected papers 1972–1977. Reading, MA: Addison-Wesley.

CHAPTER 6

A Singularity in mRNA Virus, Virology, and Vaccinology

1 Introduction

Thus far the present author offered an exposition of two physics theories: relativity physics in Chap. 4 and quantum physics in Chap. 5. Henceforth, the ensuing two chapters will explore two areas of biological science. The first is an mRNA virus and virology in this chapter. The other is stem cell research in next chapter.

The term mRNA has gained public awareness through the recent worldwide pandemic named the COVID-19 pandemic, an abbreviation of the Corona Virus Disease 2019 (Weiss 2020; Seo 2022). Before then, the term mRNA, an abbreviation of messenger Ribonucleic Acid, was unheard of by the public. The global impact of the pandemic may be described by the two indicators: over 800 million infections and over 7 million deaths globally at the time of this writing (WHO 2020; Worldometers 2024).

The mRNA virus study or more formally virology as well as the study of vaccines against it are a field of biological science which endeavors to understand the life and living organisms. In particular, this field of biology approaches the question of life from the viewpoint of genes, that is, genetic information. The genes are genetic information contained in the DNA (Deoxyribonucleic Acid) and RNA (Pierce 2019; Pardi et al. 2018; NHGRI 2021).

S. N. Seo, *The Economics of Singularities of Science Elucidated with Buddhist Thoughts*,
https://doi.org/10.1007/978-3-031-69118-8_6

The mRNA virology and vaccinology are a pertinent as well as interesting field of science to Buddhist thinkers and practitioners in that the Truth of Suffering Buddha Shakyamuni proclaimed in his first teaching at Deer Park was explained through the four sources of suffering which are biological processes of being born, aging, being sick, and death (Sutra on Setting the Wheel of Dharma in Motion, Maha Parinibbana Sutta, Walpola Rahula 1974). The practice of seeking liberation as well as saving sentient beings from suffering of cyclic existence is largely concerned with this process of life and death of an individual (Vimalakirti Sutra, Bhaisajayaguru Sutra, Nagarjuna's Bodhicitta Commentary, Atisha's Lamp, Lama Tsongkhapa's Stages of the Path, Kelsang Gyatso 2016). So, the analysis conducted in this chapter should be reviewed by Buddhist philosophers as a meaningful contribution to the science of life from a Buddhist perspective (Seo 2024a, 2024b).

What this Chapter is attempting to address is a singularity that may possibly occur through mRNA virology and vaccinology. For this, the present author refers to the recent experience of the COVID-19 pandemic, which is likely understandable to most readers who have passed through the COVID-19 pandemic to the fullest extent (WHO 2020). A singularity event can be defined as the leaking by accident of a lethal virus from a virology laboratory experiment (WHO 2021; Reuters 2021; Wade 2021; Mallapaty 2021). A leaked virus may be transmitted directly to humans or be transmitted to humans through another animal medium, for example, bats or cats. For it to be considered a singularity event, let us imagine an unknown mRNA virus that is ten times more infectious as well as ten times more fatal than the SARS-COV-2 virus (Coleman and Frieman 2014; Weiss 2020)!

What would the possibility of such a catastrophe caused by an mRNA research mean for humankind? What is the best strategy of the society regarding the mRNA virology research considering the possibility of such a catastrophe? (Jonas 2013; Bloom and Canning 2017; Seo 2022). In particular, should a lockdown policy, a vaccine and mask mandate policy, and a prohibition of a highly risky virus experiment be considered an only reasonable policy, as was largely the case during the COVID-19 pandemic? (Deccan Herald 2020; NYT 2020a; Hoover Institution 2020; Kulldorff et al. 2020). These are some of the policy questions that this chapter will explore and address. Be reminded that what this book has taken on is to clarify the singularity events that are driven by scientific endeavors and, based on such clarifications, to offer a novel point of view extracted from the system of Buddhist thoughts.

In analyzing the policy options regarding an mRNA singularity as well, there is a significant overlap of interests between scientific pursuits and Buddhist philosophy. One of the top wishes of sentient beings is good health free of diseases and a long life. In Buddhism, it is abundantly recorded that Buddhas and bodhisattvas are born to fulfill the wishes of sentient beings and with the compassionate heart to liberate them from their suffering (Lotus Sutra, Flower Ornament Sutra, Kshitigarbha Sutra, Akasagarbha Sutra, Tara Prayer, Lama Tsongkhapa's Beginning-Middle-End Prayer). Such being the case, would it be wise to prohibit the mRNA virus research citing the aforementioned catastrophe risk, say, by the power of such higher beings as Medicine Buddha? Or is the virologist's scientific experiment equivalent to the Buddha's and bodhisattva's marvelous acts? To go even further, can virologists and biologists eventually deliver liberation from diseases and death to sentient beings? (Schwartz 2001; Kariko et al. 2011; Pardi et al. 2018). There are not a few intriguing questions at the intersection of Buddhism and biological science, which this chapter is well positioned to highlight.

2 The COVID-19 Pandemic and the Novel Coronavirus

Entering the twenty-first century, the human society has endured much pain from the novel pathogen known as a coronavirus. The COVID-19 which was declared a worldwide pandemic in March 11, 2020, has since killed about 7 million people worldwide and over 800 million people were infected, as of December 2023, making it one of the deadliest pandemics in human history since the fourteenth-century Plague (WHO 2020, 2023). The World Health Organization (WHO) ended its Public Health Emergency of International Concern (PHEIC) declaration on May 5, 2023.

The novel coronavirus that caused the COVID-19 was named the SARS-CoV-2 virus by the WHO. It was one of three coronaviruses that hit the planet since the turn of the twenty-first century, all of which were beta coronaviruses (Weiss 2020). The other two were the SARS (Severe Acute Respiratory Syndrome) and the MERS (Middle Eastern Respiratory

Syndrome) (Coleman and Frieman 2014). The three viruses are summarized in Table 6.1.

A two-dimensional depiction of the SARS-CoV-2 is presented in Fig. 6.1 (NIAID 2020). Notable are the crown-like outer spikes of the spherical organism which all coronaviruses possess. The Corona is a Latin word meaning a crown. It is a ball-shaped organism, enclosed with an outer lipid envelope. Inside it is an RNA (Ribonucleic Acid) strand. The outer lipid envelope protrudes with many protein spikes. Unlike the other coronaviruses, that is, the SARS-CoV and the MERS-CoV, the gene sequence of the novel coronavirus showed a "furin cleavage site in its

Table 6.1 Three coronaviruses of the twenty-first century

Disease	*Period*	*Virus*
SARS (Severe Acute Respiratory Syndrome)	2002–2004	SARS-CoV
MERS (Middle Eastern Respiratory Syndrome)	2012–2015	MERS-CoV
COVID-19 (Corona Virus Disease 2019)	2020–2023	SARS-CoV-2

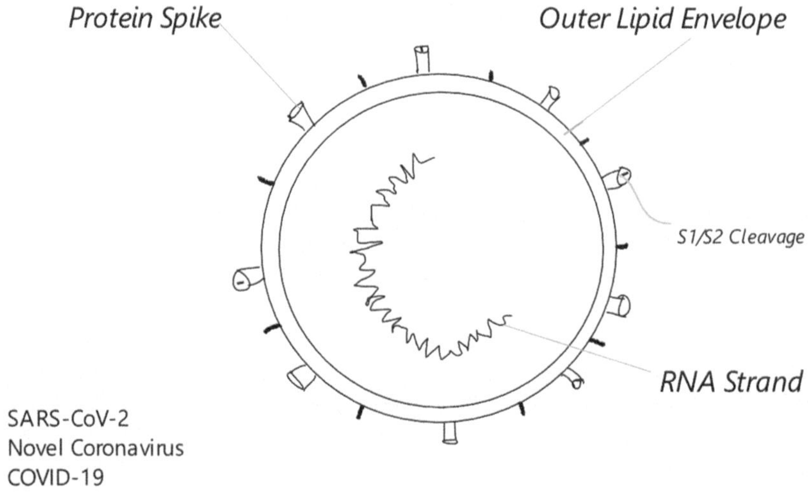

Fig. 6.1 The SARS-COV-2 diagram

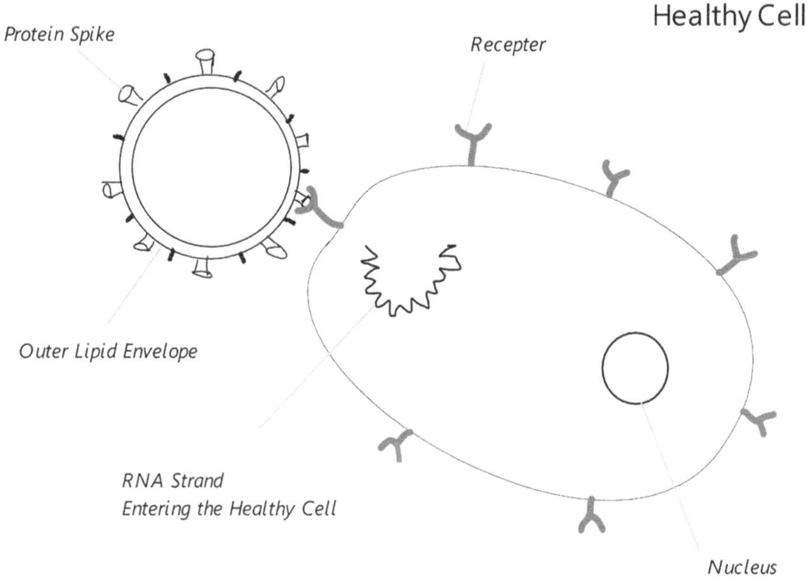

Fig. 6.2 The mechanism of the SARS-CoV-2 entering and killing a healthy lung cell

S1/S2" junction which was identified as a critical feature in the scientific efforts for tracing the origin of the virus (Wade 2021, 2024).

The mechanism through which the SARS-CoV-2 virus infects the healthy cells and eventually kills them is depicted in Fig. 6.2 (USFDA 2020c). When it enters a healthy human lung, the virus attaches itself to the healthy lung cell's receptors through its protein spikes. The bridge being established thus, the RNA strand inside the outer lipid of the virus, as shown in Fig. 6.1, enters the lung cell and eventually kills it. After killing the healthy lung cell, the virus replicates itself and thereby continues to attack other lung cells. This will cause a SARS-CoV-2 infected individual to experience a variety of symptoms of the COVID-19 disease.

How does the COVID-19 pandemic compare with the other pandemics in the history of humankind? In Table 6.2, the present author compares the mortality and infection statistics of the COVID-19 with those of the influenza pandemics since the sixteenth century and other major infectious diseases in history, specifically the Smallpox until the late twentieth century and the Bubonic Plague of the fourteenth century (Potter 2001; WHO 2023).

Table 6.2 Comparing the COVID-19 with other pandemics and infectious diseases in history

Pandemics	*Year*	*Pathogen (virus/ bacteria)*	*Origin*	*# of Cases*	*# of Fatalities*
COVID-19 pandemic	2020–2023	SARS-CoV-2	China	772,138,818 confirmed cases (as of Dec 6, 2023)	6,985,964 deaths (as of Dec 6, 2023)
2009 H1N1 Influenza Pandemic (Swine Flu)	Spring 2009	H1N1pdm09 virus	Mexico	60.8 million (US)	12,469 (US); 151,700–575,400 (World)
Smallpox	Existed for at least 3000 years until 1980	*Variola* (*major, minor*) virus		A mortality rate of 30% in general population (CDC 2020)	
Influenza pandemic of 1957–1958	1957	H2N2 virus	Yunnan Province, China		Mortality rate—1 in 4000; Fatality—80,000 (US)
Pandemic of 1918–1920: 1918 influenza pandemic	1918: ***"The greatest medical holocaust"***	H1N1 virus	Not known: China, US	~50% of world's population	40–50 million
Influenza pandemic of 1830–1833	1830–1833		China	~20±25% of population in China	The mortality rate was not exceptionally high
Influenza pandemic of 1781–1782	1781–1782			At the peak of the pandemic, 30,000 fell ill each day in St. Petersburg; two-thirds of the population of Rome became ill; and the outbreak is reported to have raged through Britain during the summer of 1782	
Influenza pandemic of 1580	1580: the first influenza pandemic		Asia	8000 deaths were reported from Rome, and some Spanish cities were decimated	
Bubonic Plague Pandemic: Black Death	Fourteenth century (1346–1353)	*bacterium Yersinia pestis*	Eurasia	It is estimated to have killed over 25–75 million in Europe and over 37 million in Asia, roughly a quarter of the world population at that time	

First of all, it is notable that while a worldwide pandemic struck the planet about once in a century since the sixteenth century, the twenty-first century has already experienced the three worldwide pandemics: the COVID-19, the 2009 H1N1 influenza pandemic, the 2002–2004 SARS pandemic. There is an indication in the table, although not solid evidence yet, that a worldwide pandemic is becoming more frequent.

Second, although COVID-19 was astoundingly efficient in transmission among people, it has infected "only" about 10% of the world population, that is, about 800 million people worldwide. This infection rate is still far below the 1918 influenza pandemic caused by the H1N1 virus which had infected nearly "50%" of the world population, which was about 1 billion people (Potter 2001; Henderson et al. 2009). It is also highly likely that this infection rate was far below the infection rate of the Bubonic plague pandemic of the fourteenth century caused by the bacterium *Yersinia pestis* carried by the vectors (refer to Table 6.2).

Third, although the COVID-19 pandemic caused 7 million deaths worldwide with the mortality rate of 1% of the infected, it is still far below the mortality rate of the other major infectious diseases in history. The 1918 influenza pandemic had about 8–10% mortality rate of the infected as shown in Table 6.2. The smallpox caused by the *Variola* virus, which had existed for 3000 years until 1980 when it was declared to be eradicated by the WHO, has a mortality rate of 30% of the general population (CDC 2020; Schwartz 2001; Plotkin 2009). The plague pandemic of the fourteenth century, referred to as Black Death, is estimated to have killed roughly a quarter of the world's population at that time, over 25 million in Europe and 37 million in Asia (Gould and Pyle 1896).

3 mRNA Vaccines

The remarkably lower mortality rate of the COVID-19 pandemic, only 1% of the infected, are attributed by many experts to the success of novel vaccines. Only ten months into the worldwide pandemic, the world's leading pharmaceutical companies announced that they developed a 95% effective vaccine (Azar II 2020). In addition, the vaccines developed were for the first time mRNA vaccines. The mRNA vaccines proved over the course of the pandemic to be superior to the traditional vaccines (Kariko et al. 2011; Pardi et al. 2018, NYT 2020c).

To explain the mRNA vaccine success, let me begin with the concept of vaccination and a traditional vaccine which is attributed to the works of

French microbiologist Louis Pasteur (Schwartz 2001). In 1879 when an anthrax epidemic killed sheep in droves in France, Pasteur accomplished the following vaccination experiment successfully, which was regarded as the heart of modern vaccinology until the emergence of the mRNA vaccines to be explained shortly:

1. Pasteur isolated the *anthrax bacillus* from the infected sheep and
2. He proved that it is responsible for the anthrax epidemic.
3. He was able to attenuate cultures of *anthrax bacillus* after weakening the organism's virulence.
4. In the Spring of 1881, he experimented with 70 sheep at the southern outskirts of Paris. Thirty-five sheep were injected with a low-virulence culture of *anthrax bacillus* and the other 35 sheep were set as a control group, that is, a group of healthy sheep.
5. Two weeks later, both groups of sheep were inoculated with a virulent strain of *anthrax bacillus.*
6. All sheep of the first group (i.e., vaccinated sheep with low-virulence culture) survived while all sheep of the second group (i.e., unvaccinated but healthy sheep) died of anthrax.

The low-virulence culture of a pathogen, *anthrax bacillus* in the above experiment, is called a vaccine since Edward Jenner named it that way for his discovery of the smallpox vaccine in his publication entitled *On the Origin of Vaccine Inoculation* (Jenner 1801). The term comes from the Latin *Vaccinus* which means "from the cow." His smallpox vaccine was obtained from the cowpox virus, for which reason it was called the *Vaccinus.*

The way a vaccine works for the COVID-19 is illustrated in Fig. 6.3. Once a vaccine dose is injected into a person's blood stream, it stimulates the B cells (B from the bone marrow) to produce the Y-shaped antibodies against the target virus, say, the novel coronavirus. The vaccine acts as an antigen which causes the immune system of the person to produce antibodies. When the virus enters the human body, as depicted in the figure, the antibodies will bind the protein spikes of the SARS-CoV-2 virus. The virus will be weakened and eventually killed (USFDA 2020c).

The vaccine development process and the working mechanism thus far described are largely for the traditional vaccines. Through the COVID-19 pandemic, the mRNA vaccine has emerged as a novel vaccine concept and a practical technology. Against the COVID-19, both traditional vaccines

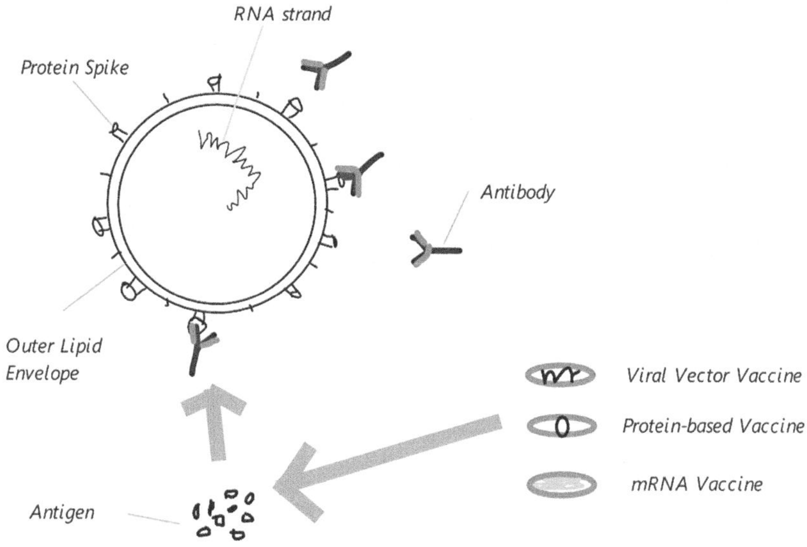

Fig. 6.3 Creating antibody to fight the corona virus

and mRNA vaccines were developed, approved, and administered. As shown in Table 6.3, the United States, China, Russia, Germany, Switzerland, India participated and competed in the vaccine race. The traditional vaccines are listed in the table as viral vector vaccines, protein-based vaccines, and inactivated/attenuated corona virus vaccines. The Sputnik-V vaccine from Russia, the AstraZeneca vaccine from the UK and Switzerland, the Sinovac vaccine from China, the Bharat vaccine from India were widely administered in the respective countries (NYT 2020b; Gavi 2020).

The first vaccines to be approved and administered were the mRNA vaccines from the US pharmaceutical companies Pfizer and Moderna. The Pfizer vaccines and the Moderna vaccines were 95% effective at the experimental stage and approved by December 2020. The two vaccines were reported to be most effective against the novel coronavirus among all the vaccines listed in Table 6.3 (USFDA 2020a, 2020b).

The COVID-19 virus, namely, the SARS-CoV-2, is an mRNA virus (Weiss 2020). It can be verified in Figs. 6.1, 6.2 and 6.3 as the RNA strand inside the cells. The mRNA vaccines were built on the research on the

Table 6.3 The types of vaccines for the SARS-CoV-2

Types of vaccines	*Vaccine names or producers*	*Countries*
mRNA vaccines	Moderna: *Spkikevax*	USA
	Pfizer-BioNTech: *COMIRNATY*	USA, Germany
Viral vector vaccines	CanSino Biologics	China
	Gamaleya Research Institute: Sputnik-V	Russia
	Johnson & Johnson	USA
	AstraZeneca	UK, Switzerland
Protein-based vaccines	Novavax	USA
	Vector Institute	Russia
Inactivated or attenuated coronavirus vaccines	Sinopharm	China
	Sinovac Biotech	China
	Bharat Biotech	India

mRNA (Messenger Ribonucleic Acid) and its applications to pharmaceutical uses (Jacob and Monod 1961; Brenner et al. 1961).

How do the traditional vaccines and the mRNA vaccines work differently? A traditional viral vector vaccine, founded on the concept and the laboratory experiment of Louis Pasteur, is a weakened or inactivated version of the SARS-CoV-2 virus which is injected into a person in order to trigger an immune response of the recipient to the virus, that is, to trigger the immune system to produce antibodies. Alternatively, a vaccine can be a piece of the virus, that is, a specific protein from the virus. This is referred to as a protein-based vaccine in Table 6.3. The viral vector is an antigen, namely, the antibody generating materials. So is the weakened virus (Plotkin 2009; Schwartz 2001).

The mRNA vaccinology is salient in that an mRNA vaccine does not contain a viral vector nor a weakened virus. Therefore, it is a promising antivirus defense since it does not require an outbreak of a worldwide pandemic beforehand for it to be developed in a laboratory through, for example, a gain-of-function research. At the same time, it is a risky defense since the virus or the vaccine under the experiment can escape from the laboratory to cause a planet-wide pandemic (Reuters 2021; Wade 2021).

Let me clarify. An mRNA vaccine dose delivers genetic instructions to a recipient's cells for producing a portion of the target virus. The body cells respond to the vaccine injection by making the protein, specifically, anti-COVID-19 B cells and T cells, necessary for generating the recipient's immune response. The B cells bind with antigens to produce antibodies against the entering virus while T cells directly attack the entering virus (Kariko et al. 2011; Pardi et al. 2018).

During the early phases of the vaccination against the SARS-CoV-2 in 2021, people raised concerns about the mRNA vaccines regarding whether they can alter the recipient's genetic information, that is, the DNA (Deoxyribonucleic Acid). Scientists assured the citizens that mRNA vaccines do not integrate into the body cell's DNA. The mRNA vaccines, scientists argued, naturally break down in the body, therefore are safer than the traditional vaccines (Gupta 2021).

The mRNA vaccines, despite the initial misgivings among people, became widely popular, were considered effective, and appeared to be safe. As of July 3, 2022, Pfizer-BioNTech had delivered 3.6 billion doses of its *Comirnaty* vaccine across 180 countries and territories. The Moderna also had delivered a similar amount of vaccine doses of its *Spikevax* vaccine. As of November 2023, the total amount of vaccine doses administered reached near 14 billion doses worldwide, both the mRNA vaccines and the traditional vaccines combined (WHO 2023).

There were disadvantages with the mRNA vaccines, setting aside the safety concerns and the deadly side effects some individuals reported to have experienced (Faksova et al. 2024). First, unlike the traditional vaccines, the mRNA vaccines have to be inoculated in two doses separated by eight weeks of time. The traditional vaccines need only one dose.

Second, the efficacy of the mRNA vaccines deteriorates over time. In addition, the novel coronaviruses kept producing one variant after another in their own responses to the new vaccines introduced. There were numerous variants that have their unique characteristics during the four-year period from 2020 to 2023. For that reason, a "booster" shot has to be administered every once in a while, for example, every six months. The booster shots were mRNA vaccines newly developed to better handle different variants of the virus. Many people ended up receiving the booster shot, the second booster shot, and the third booster shot (OWID 2024).

Considering the success of the mRNA vaccines during the COVID-19 pandemic, one might wonder what vaccines are available for the major infectious diseases that exist today in the world or existed in the past. In Table 6.4, the present author has put together a list of major infectious diseases and their respective vaccines (Lopez et al. 2006; WHO 2024; CDC 2024). There are 25 infectious diseases in the table, including coronaviruses, malaria, H1N1 virus, seasonal influenza, smallpox, tuberculosis.

Table 6.4 Major infectious diseases and their vaccines (selected)

Infectious diseases	*Vaccines available (first or selected vaccine)*	*Eradicated?*	*No vaccines?*
Smallpox	*Dryvax*: American Home Products, nineteenth century	Yes, 1980	
Cholera	*Shanchol*: India, 2011		
Anthrax	Pasteur vaccine: France, 1881		
Rabies	*VERORAB*: France, 2005		
Measles	*Measles Vaccine* (Live, Attenuated): India, 1993		
Mumps	*Measles, Mumps and Rubella Vaccine* (Live, Attenuated): India, 2003		
Rubella	*Measles, Mumps and Rubella Vaccine* (Live, Attenuated): India, 2003		
Tuberculosis	*Bacille Calmette-Guérin (BCG)* Freeze Dried Glutamate vaccine: Japan, 1987		
Diphtheria-Tetanus	*Diphtheria and Tetanus Vaccine* Adsorbed (Pediatric): India, 1995		
Polio	*Polioviral* vaccine: India, 2006		
Rotavirus	*Rotateq*: US, 2008		
Swine Flu (H1N1)	*Influenza A (H1N1) 2009 Monovalent Vaccine*: US, 2010		
Influenza, Seasonal	*Fluzone Quadrivalent*: US, 2015. *Fluzone Trivalent*: US, 2010		
Hepatitis A	*Havrix 720 Junior*: Belgium, 2013		
Hepatitis B	*Engerix*: Belgium, 1987		
Yellow Fever	*STAMARIL*: France, 1987		
Dengue	*Dengvaxia*: France, 2020		
Typhoid	*Typhim-Vi*: France, 2011		
Japanese Encephalitis	*IMOJEV MD*: Thailand, 2014		
Ebola Zaire	*ERVEBO*: US, 2019		
Malaria	RTS, S/AS01 (*Mosquirix*): Belgium, US, 2021 *R21/Matrix-M*: International Collaboration, 2023		
Zika virus			x
SARS-CoV			x
MERS-CoV			x
SARS-CoV-2	*Comirnaty* (Pfizer-BioNTech); *Spikevax* (Moderna): US, 2020		

Sources: WHO (2024), CDC (2024)

Most infectious diseases have at least one vaccine developed and being administered to people, including smallpox, malaria, and SARS-CoV-2. There are several diseases for which there is still no vaccine, for example, zika virus or MERS-CoV virus. The efficacy of these vaccines varies with malaria vaccines (*Mosquirix* or *Matrix-M*) considered to be of low efficacy. Some diseases are considered eradicated, for example, smallpox (CDC 2020).

4 A Singularity of Virology and Vaccinology

Having discussed the basic science of virology and vaccinology in the context of the COVID-19 Pandemic, let me describe what a singularity event in the virology/vaccinology science might look like. The present author can start this discussion by pointing out that, unlike any other viruses or pandemics in history, the origin of the SARS-CoV-2 virus has been undiscovered by scientists (Mallapaty 2021; Wade 2021). This feels quite odd for me to say this that even in this age of scientific achievements scientists cannot point to the exact source of this 7-million killing and 800-million infecting super virus. For the most recent updates on this topic, you may refer to the *NYT* article (2023) and the *Bloomberg* article (2023) in the references list.

The etiology of the SARS-CoV-2 was divided into two camps from the day of pandemic declaration: one camp for a natural origin and the other camp for a laboratory origin. Although the natural origin theory was what was put forth by the World Health Organization after the visit by the Joint WHO-China mission in January-February 2021 to Wuhan, China, neither the WHO nor the scientific community was able to pinpoint to a specific natural origin which is scientifically sound (WHO 2021). None of the species of animals studied by the scientists appear to be genetically close enough in scientific terms to be the origin of the virus (Mallapaty 2021; Wade 2021). Over time, the natural origin theorists dwelled on the satellite images that show that the first reported cases of the COVID-19 were reported around the fish market in Wuhan, China. Or, the DNA samples from the animals of the Wuhan wet market (NYT 2023). None of this is a conclusive scientific proof.

The laboratory origin hypothesis was dismissed by the WHO scientific committee in the above-mentioned panel meeting after the Joint WHO-China mission, although a majority of the general public in the US appeared to side with the lab origin hypothesis (Reuters 2021; Wade

2021). The lab origin hypothesis was rooted on the set of observations: (1) there is the world's premier coronavirus research laboratory in the Wuhan City, China, namely, the Wuhan Institute of Virology; (2) the laboratory's research, funded in part by the US government, was involved in modifying the virulence of the coronavirus; (3) several researchers at the laboratory got sick with a flu-like symptom a few months before the first reported case of the novel coronavirus on Dec 30, 2019.

A scientific basis for the lab origin hypothesis is found in the argument made by Robert Redford who was the director for the Center for Disease Control (CDC) at the time of the pandemic's outbreak. He argued that the SARS-CoV-2 virus was originated from the Wuhan laboratory, saying that the unprecedented efficiency in transmission of the virus among individuals was not possible if it were originated naturally from a natural source (Reuters 2021).

Another scientific basis was the furin cleavage site at the S1/S2 junction in SARS-CoV-2 virus (see Fig. 6.1). According to the newly obtained document from the Wuhan Institute of Virology, the researchers at the EcoHealth Alliance were proposing in their project proposal adding "appropriate human-specific cleavage sites" to the spike proteins of coronaviruses in order to make it more transmissible to humans and further the US governmental agencies knew and funded the Wuhan Institute research (Wade 2024; USDOI 2024; Paul 2024).

Proving the lab origin hypothesis turned out to be equally difficult because, among other reasons, the Chinese government, US scientists, and the scientific communities were perhaps fearful about the possibility that the scientists be pointed as culprits for the worldwide catastrophe. The three sick researchers at the Wuhan Institute that received hospital care before the COVID-19 pandemic were unavailable. It was also reported that thousands of blood samples collected at an early stage of the pandemic were destroyed before the Joint mission's investigation in February 2021 (WSJ 2021).

The lab origin hypothesis that surfaced during the COVID-19 pandemic points to the big risk inherent in the virology research that has escaped people's attention until then: the high risk of some frontier scientific experiments. This risk is perhaps not limited to virology: many microbiological research programs may contain similar risk, some of which are also pretty well established, for example, biological or chemical weapons programs. The stem cell research is another example, which will be the focus of next chapter (Thomson et al. 1998). The human genome project and the genetically modified organism (GMO) technologies may also pose somewhat similar risks (USFDA 2023).

How big is the risk of the COVID-19 pandemic of unknown origin? Is it as big as to be qualified as s singularity event? As far as the COVID-19 was concerned, we know from the experience of the past four years that the big risk may now be quantified to be as big as 7 million deaths and 800 million persons infected and suffered. However, this would be an underestimation of the risk if we would consider the wars that sprang from the pandemic: the Russia-Ukraine war that began in March 2022 and the Israel-Hamas war that began in October 2023.

A remarkable thing about the high-risk virology research is that it contains the vaccinology as a component. In this regard, the big success of the mRNA vaccines is notable, for which the Nobel Prize in Physiology or Medicine was awarded to two researchers in December 2023 (Kariko et al. 2011; Pardi et al. 2018; Nobel Prize 2023). Big pharmaceutical companies developed the mRNA vaccines within nine months of the outbreak, unheard of in the history of vaccination (Plotkin 2009). Further, the efficacy was very high, over 95% of the efficacy rate (USFDA 2023).

Had it not been for the mRNA vaccine success, the COVID-19 pandemic might have turned out to be as catastrophic as the 1918 influenza pandemic during which half of the world's population became infected, out of whom about 10% were eventually killed according to available data (Potter 2001). Or the Bubonic Plague Pandemic of the fourteenth century which killed a quarter of the world's population at that time, as per some sources (Gould and Pyle 1896).

Reflecting on the world's experiences during the COVID-19 pandemic explained thus far, the big risk or even the singularity risk in the virology/vaccinology research may arise, but only from the "un-discoverability" of the origin of a pandemic-causing super virus. Let me clarify this process. Let's suppose there is another global pandemic in the near future. The origin of a super lethal virus which causes the pandemic may be disputed among the world's major nations. Let's suppose that this super virus would kill 10 million people worldwide in the first two years. If this dispute could not be settled among the parties, however, countries may choose to retaliate with violent actions against the suspected sources of the virus. Although not knowing the true origin of the super virus, countries may choose to simply distrust the other countries. From the distrust among nations and the violent actions, a war may break out between the two hostile countries. The war may spill over to other countries that get drawn into the war. The war may also spill over to another war in another region in which multiple countries are engaged. Only in this scenario, the virology research may cause a singularity event to humankind. This scenario in turn highlights the importance of identifying as early as possible the origin of a super virus.

5 The Buddhist Insights on Virology and Vaccinology

Having described the virology and its singularity rather comprehensively, it would be apt for the present author to offer some insights from the Buddhist literature. As noted in the introduction, Buddhism and virology share a common goal of eliminating the suffering of people from intolerable diseases.

From this review, we can conclude that the virology or more broadly the science of diseases is a natural progression of microbiology, the science of microscopic organisms, which in turn is a natural progression of biology, the science of living organisms. This commonsensical progression is spurred by the big threats of the various bugs—viruses, bacteria, and parasites—on the well-being of people and society, which is evidenced by the past worldwide pandemics including the 1918 influenza pandemic, the Bubonic plague pandemic, and the COVID-19 pandemic.

The virologists' efforts are, therefore, in parallel to the Buddhist compassion of liberating sentient beings from the miseries of the cyclic existence which is marked by, among other things, diseases, old age, and death (Tara Prayer, Milarepa's Songs, Lama Tsongkhapa's Stages of the Path). There is little reason for Buddhists to dismiss the virologists' efforts as something of little value or to be ignorant of the major discoveries in this field. This advice does not intend, however, to say that the Buddhist compassionate approach to liberation and enlightenment is anything similar to the scientific approach, that is, the virologist approach (Lama Tsongkhapa's Principal Aspects, King of Meditations Sutra). What the Buddhists should pursue is the complete and perfect enlightenment which saves all sentient beings from all suffering at the core of which lies afflictive ignorance (Nagarjuna's Precious Garland, Chandrakirti's Entering Middle Way, Lama Tsongkhapa's Ocean of Reasoning, Illuminating the Intent).

An intriguing aspect of the virus research is that the vaccine development against a specific virus is nearly impossible without an unprecedented pandemic sweeping across the globe. In other words, the mRNA vaccines would have never been manufactured or approved without the COVID-19 pandemic overwhelming the planet. The so-called gain-of-function research which manipulates the existing viruses to create new viruses in order to study their behaviors and virulence is often justified for this reason as well. It enables virologists to have a shot at developing an effective defense mechanism long before such deadly viruses emerge through natural processes to strike the human society badly. However, the consequence of a leak of a super virus thus created in the laboratory to the society, by accident or purpose, will turn out to cause a severe social disruption at a global scale.

The most fatal aspect of the worldwide pandemic caused through this scientific process by a laboratory gain-of-function virology research is undiscoverability of the origin of a super virus which kills millions of people worldwide. The super virus-induced social disruption of the planet can easily spill over to wars among nations and distrust among people owing to the disputed origin of the virus. This was presented as a virology singularity in the preceding section.

The unknown origin of a super virus is like a vilva fruit in the Jataka tales which propelled all the animals in the animal kingdom to flee to the cliffs screaming: "[T]he earth is breaking up" (Jataka, Chalmers 1895). When the Lion, the Buddha's former incarnation, stopped them and inquired about it, no one was able to answer why. It turned out that a sleeping rabbit was startled by a thud sound of a falling vilva fruit on a palm leaf which prompted him to run away without even looking back at it screaming the world is coming to an end to other animals (Seo 2018, 2024b).

From the Buddhist point of view, it can be argued that it is urgently needed that the scientific community in the field of virology and vaccinology should make their laboratory research and experiments transparent to the public (USDOI 2024). Further, whenever there is a worldwide pandemic, it is vitally important to locate the origin of the pandemic-causing virus as early as possible (Mallapaty 2021; Wade 2024). This will ensure that the virus does not become an uncontrollable force which is far beyond the virus itself.

In this sense, it is vital for the science and policy communities to heed the Buddha's perfect wisdom: The entire mass of suffering, pain, and miseries in the six realms of existence arises from ignorance only (Bodhi Sutta). The ignorance here is active mis-knowledge (Lama Tsongkhapa's True Eloquence, Perfection of Wisdom Pronounced by Manjushri, Mother Scripture). To put it another way, it does not arise from a virus.

References

Atisha Dipankara Srijnana (982–1054) Bodhipathapradīpa. A Lamp for the Path to Enlightenment. Byang chub lam gyi sgron ma.

Azar II AM (2020) How Operation Warp Speed delivered a COVID vaccine in record time. Fox News. Published on 12 December 2020. Accessed from https://www.foxnews.com/opinion/hhs-azar-operation-warp-speed-covid-vaccine-record-time

Bloom DE, Canning D (2017) Epidemics and Economics. Working Paper #9, Harvard Program on Demography of Ageing, Harvard University, Cambridge, MA.

Bloomberg News (2023) Covid's origins can't be tied to Wuhan market, Chinese Researchers Say. Published on April 5, 2023.

Brenner S, Jacob F, Meselson M (1961) An unstable intermediate carrying information from genes to ribosomes for protein synthesis. Nature 190: 576–581.

Centers for Disease Control and Prevention (CDC) (2020) Smallpox. Atlanta, GA: The CDC.

Centers for Disease Control and Prevention (CDC) (2024) List of Vaccines Used in United States. Atlanta, GA: The CDC.

Chalmers R (1895) The Jataka or Stories of the Buddha's Former Births (Volume 1–6). Accessed from https://www.wisdomlib.org/buddhism/book/jataka-tales-english

Chandrakirti (7th century). Entering the Middle Way. Madhyamakāvatāra. Dbu ma la 'jug pa. Toh 3861, dbu ma'a.

Coleman CM, Frieman MB (2014) Coronaviruses: important emerging human pathogens. Journal of Virology 8: 5209–5212.

Deccan Herald (2020) No lockdowns, but Sweden seems to have controlled the COVID-19 pandemic. Published on October 1, 2020. Accessed from: https://www.deccanherald.com/opinion/panorama/no-lockdowns-but-sweden-seems-to-have-controlled-the-COVID-19-pandemic-895509.html

Faksova K, Walsh D, Jiang Y, et al. (2024) COVID-19 vaccines and adverse events of special interest: A multinational Global Vaccine Data Network (GVDN) cohort study of 99 million vaccinated individuals. Vaccines. DOI: https://doi.org/10.1016/j.vaccine.2024.01.100

Gavi: The Vaccine Alliance (2020) There are four types of COVID-19 vaccines: here's how they work. Accessed from https://www.gavi.org/vaccineswork/there-are-four-types-covid-19-vaccines-heres-how-they-work

Gould GM, Pyle WL (1896) Historic epidemics. In Anomalies and Curiosities of Medicine. New York, NY: The Bell Publishing Company.

Gupta S (2021) The Application and Future Potential of mRNA Vaccine. COVID-19 & You, Yale School of Public Health, New Haven, CT. Published on May 7, 2021. Accessed from https://ysph.yale.edu/news-article/the-application-and-future-potential-of-mrna-vaccines/

Henderson DA, Courtney B, Inglesby TV, Toner E, and Nuzzo JB (2009) Public health and medical responses to the 1957–58 Influenza Pandemic. Biosecurity and Bioterrorism: Biodefense Strategy, Practice, and Science 7 (3). https://doi.org/10.1089/bsp.2009.0729.

Hoover Institution (2020) The Doctor Is In: Scott Atlas and the Efficacy of Lockdowns, Social Distancing, and Closings. Uncommon Knowledge with Peter Robinson. Palo Alto, CA: Hoover Institution, Stanford University. Accessed from https://www.hoover.org/research/doctor-scott-atlas-and-efficacy-lockdowns-social-distancing-and-closings.

Jacob F, Monod J (1961) Genetic regulatory mechanisms in the synthesis of proteins. Journal of Molecular Biology 3: 318–356.

Jenner E (1801) On the Origin of the Vaccine Inoculation. London, U.K.: D.N. Shury.

Jonas OB (2013) Pandemic Risk. Washington, DC: World Bank. Available from: https://openknowledge.worldbank.org/bitstream/handle/10986/16343/WDR14_bp_Pandemic_Risk_Jonas.pdf?sequence=1&isAllowed=y

Kariko K, Muramatsu H, Ludwig J, Weissman D (2011) Generating the optimal mRNA for therapy: HPLC purification eliminates immune activation and improves translation for nucleoside-modified, protein-encoding mRNA. Nucleic Acids Research 39: e142.

Kelsang Gyatso (2016) Joyful Path of Good Fortune: The Complete Buddhist Path to Enlightenment. New York, NY: Tharpa Publications.

Kulldorff M, Gupta S, and Bhattacharya J (2020) The Great Barrington Declaration. Accessed from https://gbdeclaration.org/.

Lama Tsongkhapa (1357a–1419) Great Treatise on the Stages of the Path to Enlightenment. Byang chub lam rim chen mo. Collected Works. Vol. pa.

Lama Tsongkhapa (1357b–1419) Ocean of Reasoning: An Exposition of Treatise on the Middle Way. Rtsa ba shes rab kyi rnam bshad ṭik chen rigs pa'i rgya mtsho. Collected Works. Vol. ba, 1–583.

Lama Tsongkhapa (1357c–1419) Illuminating the Intent: A Thorough Exposition of Entering the Middle Way. Dbu ma la 'jug pa'i rnam bshad dgongs pa rab gsal. Collected Works. Vol. ma, 1–605.

Lama Tsongkhapa (1357d–1419) Essence of True Eloquence: Distinguishing the Provisional and the Definitive Meaning (Drang ba dang nges pa'i don rnam par 'byed pa legs bshad snying po). Collected Works. Vol. pha, 441–687.

Lama Tsongkhapa (1357e–1419). Prayers for Goodness in the Beginning, the Middle, and the End. Thog mtha' bar gsum du dge ba'i smon lam. Portland, OR: The Foundation for the Preservation of the Mahayana Tradition (FPMT).

Lama Tsongkhapa (1357f–1419). Three Principal Aspects of the Path. Lam gyi gtso bo rnam pa gsum. Miscellaneous Writings, 463–65.

Lopez AD, Mathers CD, Ezzati M, Jamison DT, and Murray CJL (2006) Global Burden of Disease and Risk Factors. New York, N.Y.: World Bank and Oxford University Press.

Mallapaty S (2021) Closest Known Relatives of Virus Behind COVID-19 Found in Laos. Nature. https://doi.org/10.1038/d41586-021-02596-2

Milarepa (1052–1135) The Hundred Thousand Songs of Milarepa: A New Translation (translated by Stagg C, 2017. Boulder, CO: Shambhala).

Nagarjuna (2nd century). Commentary on Bodhicitta. Bodhicittavivaraṇa. Byang chub sems kyi 'grel pa. Toh 1801, rgyud 'grel ngi.

Nagarjuna (2nd century). Precious Garland. Ratnāvalī. Rin chen phreng ba. Toh 4158, spriṅ yig ge.

National Human Genome Research Institute (NHGRI) (2021) The Human Genome Project. The NHGRI, National Institutes of Health, Bethesda, MD. https://www.genome.gov/human-genome-project.

National Institute of Allergy and Infectious Diseases (NIAID) (2020) New Images of Novel Coronavirus SARS-CoV-2 Now Available. NIAID, NIH. Accessed from https://www.niaid.nih.gov/news-events/novel-coronavirus-sarscov2-images.

New York Times (NYT) (2020a) See Coronavirus Restrictions and Mask Mandates for All 50 States. Published on November 25, 2020. https://www.nytimes.com/interactive/2020/us/states-reopen-map-coronavirus.html.

New York Times (NYT) (2020b) Coronavirus Vaccine Tracker. Accessed from https://www.nytimes.com/interactive/2020/science/coronavirus-vaccine-tracker.html

New York Times (NYT) (2020c) After Admitting Mistake, AstraZeneca Faces Difficult Questions About Its Vaccine. Published on Nov 25, 2020. https://www.nytimes.com/2020/11/25/business/coronavirus-vaccine-astrazeneca-oxford.html

New York Times (2023) New Data Links Pandemic's Origins to Raccoon Dogs at Wuhan Market. Published on March 16, 2023.

Nobel Prize (2023) The Nobel Prize in Physiology or Medicine 2023: Katalin Karikó and Drew Weissman "for their discoveries concerning nucleoside base modifications that enabled the development of effective mRNA vaccines against COVID-19." Accessed from https://www.nobelprize.org/prizes/medicine/2023/summary/

Our World in Data (OWID) (2024) COVID-19 vaccine boosters administered. Accessed from https://ourworldindata.org/grapher/cumulative-covid-vaccine-booster-doses

Pardi N, Hogan MJ, Porter FW, and Weissman D (2018) mRNA vaccines – a new era in vaccinology. Nature Reviews Drug Discovery 17: 261–279.

Paul R (2024) The Great COVID Cover-up: Shocking truth about Wuhan and 15 federal agencies. Fox News Opinion. Published on April 9, 2024.

Pierce BA (2019) Genetics: A Conceptual Approach (7th Edition). New York, NY: W.H. Freeman.
Plotkin SA (2009) Vaccines: the fourth century. Clinical and Vaccine Immunology 16: 1709–1719.
Potter CW (2001) A history of influenza. Journal of Applied Microbiology 91(4):572–579.
Reuters (2021) Former CDC chief Redfield says he thinks COVID-19 originated in a Chinese lab. Published on March 27, 2021. Accessed from https://www.reuters.com/article/us-health-coronavirus-origin-redfield-idUSKBN2BI2R6.
Schwartz M (2001) The life and works of Louis Pasteur. Journal of Applied Microbiology. 91 (4): 597–601.
Seo SN (2018) Natural and Man-made Catastrophes: Theories, Economics, and Policy Designs. Hoboken, NJ: Wiley-Blackwell.
Seo SN (2022) The Economics of Pandemics: Exploring Globally Shared Experiences. Cham, CH: Palgrave Macmillan.
Seo SN (2024a) Buddha, Wisdom and Economics: A Contribution to the Art of Happiness. Cheltenham, UK: Edward Elgar.
Seo SN (2024b) Protecting Nature with Buddha's Wisdom: A Contribution to Environmental and Nature Studies. Cheltenham, UK: Edward Elgar.
Shantideva (8th century) Guide to the Bodhisattva Way. Bodhicaryāvatāra. Byang chub sems dpa'i spyod pa la'jug pa. Toh 3871, dbu ma la.
Tara Prayer. Praises to the Twenty-One Taras. Dol ma la chak chal ni shu za zig gyi toi pa pen yon dang ze pa. Kangyur Sde-Dge Edition (1729–33). Accessed from the Buddhist Digital Resource Center at http://purl.bdrc.io/resource/MW4CZ5369_0438
Thomson JA, Itskovitz-Eldor J, Shapiro SS, Waknitz MA, Swiergiel JJ, Marshall VS, Jones JM (1998) Embryonic stem cell lines derived from human blastocysts. Science 282 (5391): 1145–1147.
United States Department of Interior (USDOI) (2024) Re: U.S. Geological Survey (USGS) Freedom of Information Act (FOIA) Tracking # DOI-USGS-2023-000257 – Response. Washington, DC: US DOI.
United States Food & Drug Administration (USFDA) (2020a) Pfizer-BioNTech COVID-19 Vaccine EUA Letter of Authorization. Accessed from https://www.fda.gov/media/144412/
United States Food & Drug Administration (USFDA) (2020b) Moderna COVID-19 Vaccine EUA Letter of Authorization. Accessed from https://www.fda.gov/media/144636/download
United States Food & Drug Administration (USFDA) (2020c) Vaccine Development – 101. https://www.fda.gov/vaccines-blood-biologics/development-approval-process-cber/vaccine-development-101
United States Food & Drug Administration (USFDA) (2023) Science and History of GMOs and Other Food Modification Processes. Washington,

DC. Accessed from https://www.fda.gov/food/agricultural-biotechnology/science-and-history-gmos-and-other-food-modification-processes
Wade N (2021) The Origin of COVID: Did People or Nature Open Pandora's Box at Wuhan? Bulletin of the Atomic Scientists. Published on May 5, 2021. Accessed from https://thebulletin.org/2021/05/the-origin-of-covid-did-people-or-nature-open-pandoras-box-at-wuhan/
Wade N (2024) Where Did Covid Come From? Wall Street Journal. Published on February 28, 2024. Accessed from https://www.wsj.com/articles/where-did-covid-come-from-new-evidence-lab-leak-hypothesis-78be1c39
Wall Street Journal (WSJ) (2021) Intelligence on Sick Staff at Wuhan Lab Fuels Debate on Covid-19 Origin. Published on May 23, 2021. https://www.wsj.com/articles/intelligence-on-sick-staff-at-wuhan-lab-fuels-debate-on-covid-19-origin-11621796228?mod=hp_lead_pos3
Walpola Rahula (1974) What the Buddha Taught: Revised and Expanded Edition with Texts from Suttas and Dhammapada. New York, NY: Grove Press.
Weiss SR (2020) Forty years with coronaviruses. Journal of Experimental Medicine 217 (5): e20200537. https://doi.org/10.1084/jem.20200537
World Health Organization (WHO) (2020) Timeline of WHO's Response to COVID-19. Geneva, CH: WHO. Accessed from https://www.who.int/news/item/29-06-2020-covidtimeline
World Health Organization (WHO) (2021) Press Conference on February 12th, 2021. The joint World Health Organization-China Mission to Investigate the Origins of COVID-19. Geneva, CH: WHO. Accessed from https://www.who.int/emergencies/diseases/novel-coronavirus-2019
World Health Organization (WHO) (2023) COVID-19 Dashboard. Geneva, CH: WHO. Accessed from https://covid19.who.int/
World Health Organization (WHO) (2024) WHO Prequalified Vaccines. Geneva, CH: WHO. Accessed from https://extranet.who.int/pqvdata/Default.aspx?nav=1
Worldometers (2024) Coronavirus. Accessed from https://www.worldometers.info/coronavirus/

CHAPTER 7

A Singularity in Stem Cell Research and Human Cloning

1 Introduction

Having satisfactorily analyzed the singularity risk of mRNA virology and vaccinology in the preceding chapter, we are on to the second field of biology or life science in this chapter: stem cell research. The big risk posed by this research, say, a singularity risk, has been unraveling over the past two decades centering around the idea of a human clone.

Of biological science, microbiology is the study of life at the microorganism level and, depending upon the microorganisms studied, it can be subdivided into virology (study of viruses), bacteriology (study of bacteria), protistology (study of protists), mycology (study of fungi), immunology (study of the immune system), and parasitology (study of parasites). Cell biology is on the other hand the study of life at the cell level, the basic unit of life. Microbiology and cell biology are differentiated from macrobiology, that is, the study of life of animals, plants, humans, etc. (Alberts et al. 2019; Pollard et al. 2022).

In this framework, a sentient being is understood as a composite of cells. A single cell can be a living organism, for example, an amoeba. The cell contains the genetic information through DNA (Deoxyribonucleic Acid) and RNA (Ribonucleic Acid). Most organisms are a composite of eukaryote cells in which the DNA is stored in a separate room called the nucleus (Alberts et al. 2019; Pollard et al. 2022).

S. N. Seo, *The Economics of Singularities of Science Elucidated with Buddhist Thoughts*,
https://doi.org/10.1007/978-3-031-69118-8_7

The study of cells is of interest to Buddhist philosophers because it is the storehouse of genetic information which is transmitted from one life to another life. That is, from the parents to their offspring. From the Buddhist viewpoints, the bodily features that a person is born with are a type of his past karma's consequences. The mental features are also a type of one's past karma's consequences (Maha Nidana Sutta, Narada Mahathera 1998, Nagarjuna's Fundamental Wisdom, Aryadeva's Four Hundred).

Stem cells are the body's raw materials, that is, a special type of cells from which bodily organs, for example, liver, kidney, and nerve, can be grown (Alison et al. 2002). Stem cell research began with the embryonic stem cells which are the best stem cells for rather obvious reasons (Thomson et al. 1998). The high promise of initial stem cell research that it can enable scientists to grow human organs in a laboratory for the purpose of medical and health benefits, known as regenerative medicine, was quickly dampened by the fact that it should rely on human embryos in which a human being is being born (NIH 2009; Atala et al. 2019). However, scientists soon overcame this ethical challenge by developing a technology that relies on non-embryonic stem cells such as bone marrow cells (Takahashi and Yamanaka 2006). The promise of stem cell research was summarized as "the answer to mankind's prayer" and "an elixir of life—the promise of immortality" by the researchers (Alison et al. 2002).

On another track, a cloning science has advanced rapidly since the first cloned sheep Dolly was produced (Campbell et al. 1996). Animal cloning has been successfully done by many countries and laboratories with over a dozen animals including sheep, dog, cows (EFSA 2023; USFDA 2023).

The big risk from stem cell research and cloning science can be framed as a singularity risk that originates from the possibility of a human cloning (Thom 1975; Kurzweil 2005; Hawking et al. 2014; Seo 2018). In this reality, a human embryonic stem cell is used to give birth in a laboratory to a multiplicity of clones. Without laws and regulations concerning stem cell research, it appears that scientists will be willing to give a shot at such a feat through laboratory experiments.

The Buddhist wisdom offers a particularly sharp insight on the question of stem cell research and human cloning singularity. This is because, unlike scientists and biologists, Buddha Shakyamuni and Lama Tsongkhapa taught that a human being does not disappear from the six realms of the physical world when she or he dies (Lama Tsongkhapa's Stages of the Path, True Eloquence, Ocean of Reasoning). The body will decay after death. However, the mind of the dead will transmigrate from this life to the next life (Aryashura's Jatakamala, Chalmers 1895; Khantipalo 1995, The Tibetan Book of the Dead, HAR 2023). This brilliant wisdom of the Buddhas is an amazing mirror that can reflect the true nature of stem cell research and human cloning. This will be elaborated in this chapter.

This chapter proceeds as follows. In the next section, it provides a brief introduction to cell biology, titled *Cell Biology in a Nutshell*. Section 3 explains the basics of stem cell research. Section 4 clarifies a possible singularity from stem cell research in relation to cloning of a human being and through other routes. Section 5 offers a basket of Buddhist insights which are pertinent to the understanding or resolving of stem cell singularity.

2 Cell Biology in a Nutshell

Cell and microbiology is one of the remarkable scientific achievements over the past half-century and beyond (Alberts et al. 2019). It is the study of biology at the cell level and at the microorganism level where biology is the study of life. They can be contrasted with "macro-biology" whose focus lies in the life forms such as plant biology, animal biology, forest biology, etc.

To be more specific, microbiology is the study of microorganisms whose types can be unicellular (single-celled), multicellular (multi-celled), or acellular (no cells). Microbiology encompasses numerous subdisciplines including virology, bacteriology, protistology (study of protists, namely, eukaryotic organisms), mycology (study of fungi), immunology, and parasitology (Alberts et al. 2019; Pollard et al. 2022). Virology, which was the subject dealt with in the preceding chapter on mRNA viruses, belongs to the microbiology domain (Plotkin 2009; Pardi et al. 2018; Seo 2022).

In both cell biology and microbiology, a cell is the most fundamental concept. What is a cell? The cells are referred to as the basic units of life or the building blocks of life. More formally, it is the basic structural and functional unit for all forms of life. They are so called because they come in discrete and recognizable packages (Pollard et al. 2022).

Cells are surrounded by the cell membrane inside of which are water-based materials called cytoplasm (Pollard et al. 2022; Scitable 2014). The cytoplasm contains many structural and functional elements which exist in the form of molecules and organelles. The organic molecules inside the cell include nucleic acids, proteins, carbohydrates, and lipids. Each of these molecules is essential to the cell's functions (refer to Fig. 7.1).

Nucleic acids are the molecules that contain the genetic code of the cell, which are of two classes: Deoxyribonucleic Acid (DNA) and Ribonucleic Acid (RNA). DNA is the molecule that contains the genetic information while RNA helps to express the information stored in DNA. Proteins, made of smaller molecules called amino acids, serve a variety of functions in the cell, including the expression of the genetic material.

Of the other intracellular elements, the carbohydrates are the starches and the sugars in the cells used to meet the energy demands or serve as energy stores. Lipids or fat molecules are components of cell membranes, which serve as energy storage, among other functions.

Scientists categorize the cells into prokaryote cells and eukaryote cells based on how the genetic information is stored in the cell. Prokaryotes are the cells in which the DNA within the cell is not separated from the cytoplasm. Bacteria and archaea are prokaryotes. Eukaryotes are, on the other hand, the cells in which the DNA is partitioned off the cytoplasm into its

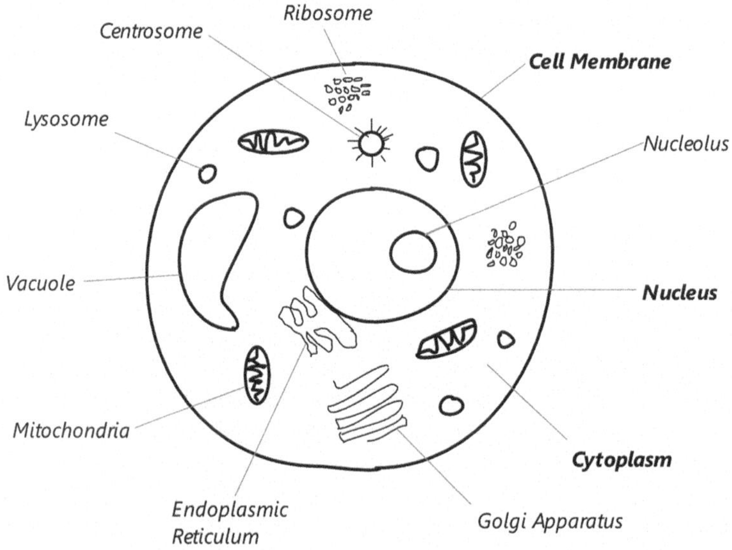

Fig. 7.1 The structure of animal cell

own membrane-bound room called the nucleus. Some eukaryotes are single-celled organism such as amoebae. All plants and animals are multi-celled eukaryotes. Eukaryotes are the basis for the identification of species of life (Seo 2021, 2024b).

The structure of the animal cell is drawn in Fig. 7.1. An animal cell is typical of the eukaryotic cells, as shown in the figure, characterized by the cell membrane and the membrane-bound nucleus. The area between the cell membrane and the nucleus is called the cytoplasm which is filled with various organelles. The organelles are an organized structure within the cell which performs a specific job, which comprises nucleus, ribosomes, centrosomes, lysosomes, mitochondria, endoplasmic reticulum, Golgi apparatus, and vacuole. Of the most important are the nucleus which store genetic information, mitochondria which are power/energy generators, and ribosomes which assemble proteins (NHGRI 2023).

Where do the cells come from originally? A Buddhist of sharp intellect would be curious about this (Nagarjuna's Fundamental Wisdom, Aryadeva's Four Hundred). Where have these cells originated in the very beginning of life? Scientists hypothesize that there was a single cell in the beginning, a tiny sac of organic material containing also an RNA-like material. From this, scientists suspect that DNA was developed, and then nucleus. From this, cellular evolution took place to form the variety of life forms that people see today (Scitable 2014). It is notable that life originated from a tiny sac of material, just like the universe originated from a tiny particle of energy matter (Lemaitre 1931).

3 Stem Cell Research

One of the frontiers in cell biology is stem cell research (Evans and Kaufman 1981; Thomson et al. 1998; Takahashi and Yamanaka 2006). It has been much controversial in many countries over the past two decades since it first surfaced to public awareness. The research was challenged by numerous interest groups on ethical grounds, despite the big promises it put forth and the successes it delivered.

The rationale as well as the promise of stem cell research is eloquently put by the researchers in the field: "Morbidity and mortality as a result of malfunctions in vital organs plague even the most technologically advanced societies. Because of a dearth of transplantable organs, there is a growing hope that stem cells may be the answer to mankind's prayer to be able to replace tissues worn out by old age and ravaged by disease. Indeed, …

hoping for an elixir of life—the promise of immortality" (Alison et al. 2002).

What is a stem cell? There are many cells in the human body, on average 36 trillion cells for an adult male (Hatton et al. 2023). Of the cells in the human body, stem cells are the body's raw materials or the cells from which all other cells having specialized functions are generated. The cells grown from stem cells are called daughter cells, which include blood cells, brain cells, heart muscle cells, and bone cells. Stem cells divide to form daughter cells under the right conditions (NIH 2022). As shown in Fig. 7.2, stem cells are the body's master cells from which all other cells arise such as nerve cells, liver cells, cardiac cells, and blood cells (Mayo Clinic 2023).

Stem cell research is the research whose goal is to generate these daughter cells from stem cells by creating the right conditions. It is not hard even for a non-expert to imagine the usefulness and the promise of stem cell research from the medical standpoint. First, the research can help scientists better understand how diseases develop in the human body. Scientists watch stem cells divide into cells in bones, heart muscle, nerves, and other organs, from which they learn.

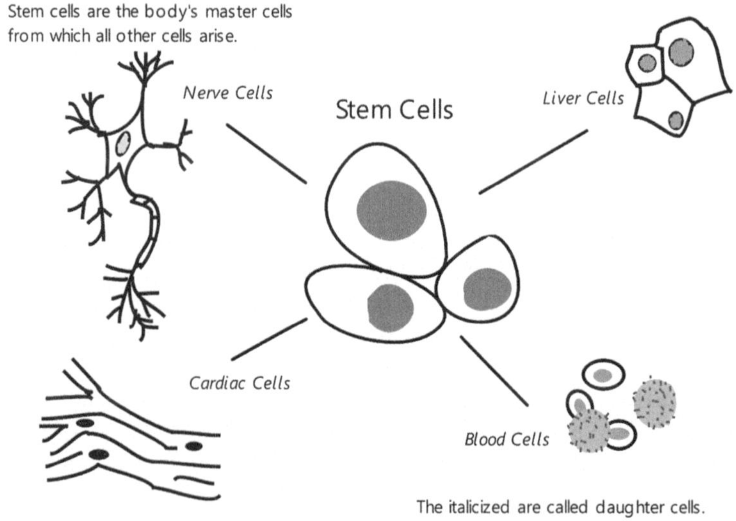

Fig. 7.2 Stem cells and daughter cells

Second, scientists can produce healthy cells from the stem cells to replace the cells affected by various diseases, whose practice is known as regenerative medicine. The stem cells can be guided to become specific cells that can be used to regenerate and repair damaged cells in the body. According to Mayo Clinic, stem cell therapies may help those people with spinal cord injuries, type 1 diabetes, Parkinson's disease, amyotrophic lateral sclerosis (ALS), Alzheimer's disease, heart disease, stroke, burns, cancer, and osteoarthritis (an arthritis) (Mayo Clinic 2023).

Third, stem cells can be used for testing new drugs. Instead of testing an investigational drug on people directly, which would involve unknown risk, scientists can test the newly developed drug on some types of stem cells or laboratory generated daughter cells.

The potential benefits of stem cell research can even be more dramatic if we extend this discussion to include animal cloning as well as genetically modified organisms (GMOs) and biofortified plants, all of which rely to some degree on stem cell research and technologies (USFDA 2023). All these technologies have major implications on food security of the planet (World Bank 2008).

Since around the turn of the twenty-first century when the Dolly the sheep was cloned, animals are cloned in many countries, including sheep, dogs, cows. Animal cloning is a technology of producing an animal which is a copy of the original. The most common technique is called the somatic cell nucleus transfer (SCNT). In SCNT, scientists replace the nucleus of an unfertilized egg cell (ovum) with the nucleus of a body cell (somatic cell) of the animal which is genetically copied, which forms an embryo. This embryo is transferred to a surrogate dam—that is, a female parent—in whom it develops until birth (EFSA 2023).

The big controversy around stem cell research at the turn of the twenty-first century was centered around where the stem cells come from (Alison et al. 2002; NIH 2009). There are two types of stem cells depending upon where they come from: embryonic stem cells and adult stem cells. The former is what the stem cell research began with at that time.

The embryonic stem cells are obtained from the embryos that are only 3–5 days old. An embryo at this stage, called a blastocyst, has about 150 cells. It is referred to as a pluripotent stem cell, which means that it can divide into more stem cells or can become any type of cell in the body. Owing to this capacity, embryonic stem cells can be used to regenerate diseased tissues and organs of a human being or to repair them (Evans and Kaufman 1981; Thomson et al. 1998).

Embryonic stem cell research soon got challenged in the society owing to the ethical problem of relying on embryos which are growing in the mother's body or outside to become a human life itself.

The stem cells can be obtained from adults, which is the second type of stem cells referred to as adult stem cells in the above. Adult stem cells are found in most adult tissues such as bone marrow or fat. However, they are found only in small numbers. Further, unlike the embryonic stem cells, adult stem cells have a limited capacity to grow into various cells of the body. In addition, adult stem cells can give rise only to similar types of cells, like the stem cells obtained from the bone marrow growing only into blood cells. In other words, the adult stem cells are not pluripotent stem cells.

In order to overcome the social repercussion, stem cell researchers are working to obtain stem cells from non-controversial sources. One of such is the altered adult stem cells that have the properties of embryonic stem cells. This is done through genetic reprogramming of the adult cells (Takahashi and Yamanaka 2006; Nobel Prize 2012). Another of such is to obtain the stem cells in the amniotic fluid or umbilical cord blood of a pregnant mother. The stem cells obtained in this way, referred to as perinatal stem cells, have the capacity to develop into specialized cells of the body. The amniotic fluid is the clear yellowish fluid that fills the sac that protects a developing fetus in the uterus of a mother (Atala et al. 2019).

In order to address the ethics questions, the National Institutes of Health (NIH) published in 2009 the NIH guidelines for human stem cell research (NIH 2009). The NIH guidelines define embryonic stem cells and specify the conditions under which the embryonic stem cells can be used for research. It recommends the donation of embryonic stem cells as well as a possible use of embryos created by in vitro fertilization (IVF).

4 A Singularity from Stem Cell or Cloning Research

Although it is difficult to present concrete data, stem cell research is vigorously pursued in nearly all developed nations while its medical applications are hotly sought after. It also appears that the science community is convinced that the benefits of stem cell research far exceed the ethical dilemmas experienced by common people. If you are still doubtful, scientists seem to say, consider many incurable human diseases that stem cell research may offer a cure for: spinal cord injuries, type 1 diabetes, Parkinson's disease, amyotrophic lateral sclerosis, Alzheimer's disease, heart disease, stroke, burns, cancer, and osteoarthritis (Mayo Clinic 2023). This is a powerful argument, indeed.

Notwithstanding their argument, let us step back and consider a potential issue of the stem cell research from the standpoint of this book, that is, the possibility of a singularity. Can the research indeed inflict a fatal blow to human civilization or the planet itself, for example, through a series of human errors or scientifically unforeseen events?

It appears that there are two different ethical issues regarding stem cell research, both of which are also related to a possible singularity. The first ethical conundrum is whether scientists should use the embryos of a person who is in the process of being born as a human being in due time. Scientists may be able to reduce the ethical problem by relying on the voluntary donation argument or the in vitro fertilization argument as recommended by the National Institutes of Health (NIH 2009). Scientists may also avoid this problem, albeit partially, by way of genetic reprogramming of the adult cells or relying on amniotic fluid or umbilical cord stem cells (Takahashi and Yamanaka 2006; Atala et al. 2019). However, none of these alternatives address the fundamental ethical question of stem cell research, which will be made clear through the second ethical conundrum explained presently.

The second ethical conundrum is the cloning ethics. If it is the case that the stem cells grow from an embryo into a fetus and then into a human being after a process of birth, the possibility is that many human beings can be cloned from the stem cells extracted from a mother's body. Then, the ethical conundrum of stem cell research can never be any clearer.

Let us consider the possibility that twelve people are created from stem cell technology from the single lump of embryonic or genetically reprogrammed stem cells extracted from one mother. Are they all same in that they are the copies of the original? Or alternatively, are they more like different siblings of a single mother? You might say that the suggestion is absurd: Nobody is cloning a human being and scientists are simply generating internal organs such as kidney and liver, etc., for medical purposes only. However, it should be noted that the cloning technology is already in "wide use" when it comes to animals such as dogs, sheep, cows (Campbell et al. 1996).

Why would human cloning be so tempting to people or nations? As for the nations, it is not hard to imagine that political leaders will treat human cloning as a strategic resource. They would be tempted to rely on human cloning to address numerous critical issues that they are facing. For example, many European and East Asian countries are facing the possibility of a steep decline in their population due to numerous reasons. For another, countries may be tempted to resort to the cloning technology in order to preserve the best genes of the nation. That is, stronger, taller, and more handsome bodies! Or smarter, more loquacious, and efficient brains! For still another, countries may be tempted, only in a stealth manner, to rely on the cloning technology in order to produce warriors to win battles and wars against other countries.

Why would common people be much tempted? It is not at all difficult to imagine why people will be so easily tempted by stem cell research. Imagine the world's richest people like Musk, Bezos, and Gates! They would certainly be tempted to be forever young. They would be tempted to live another life through stem cell technology, that is, after the death of the first body. It would not be only for the richest people in the world. Many powerful or influential people will be tempted to preserve their bodies or clone them after death.

If you are still not convinced, it is fine, for the sake of argument, for you to imagine a 'less dramatic' scenario in which the richest people are able to replace "all" their internal organs at appropriate times forever.

The consequence that may result from such hypothetical situations as described above can be as catastrophic as can be. Let me sketch three scenarios only of catastrophe. The first scenario is that stem cell cloning of humans, fully or partially, will make the value of a human life much less as felt by people and the society. This change in perception can lead to many unimaginable consequences of treating human lives lightly, that is, with reference to present day standard. It is not just the governments but also individuals may feel that a human life is not "that" valuable, given the stem cell cloned humans prevailing in society.

The second scenario is that there will be many defective human clones, if the human cloning becomes routine in society at future dates. The defective clones will behave erratically, violently, inhumanely, and irrationally. There will be, however, few ways to control them or limit them once they are recognized as a human being, owing to the ethics of life that has long been held by the human civilization (Descartes 1637; Kant 1781). This problem of defective clones will be much easier for readers to grasp when it is put in the context of created consciousness, which is the topic of the next Chapter (Trujillo et al. 2019).

The third scenario is the possibility of multiple disasters occurring at the same time. To give just one scenario, the defective human clones may have a weaker immune system than the "normal" humans. Under the attack of a possible super virus such as the SARS-CoV-2 whose transmission rate was extremely high to infect around 1 billion people worldwide since January 2020, the weaker immune system of the human clones would open a truly catastrophic possibility for humanity (Seo 2022). This is a type of correlated risk where the risk of human clones is associated with the risk of highly transmissible and lethal viruses.

5 A Buddhist Perspective on Stem Cell Research

This final section of the chapter is well positioned to offer a basket of ideas that originate from the system of Buddhist thoughts to the dilemmas of stem cell research thus far elaborated. As readers have experienced in the preceding chapters, the Buddhist insights offered at the end of each chapter provide a pivotal idea that can disentangle the complexity of the problem addressed, if not a clear remedy.

To begin, let me briefly address the economics of stem cell research. Certainly, the value of stem cell research is very high from an economic framework of thinking (Seo 2023, 2024a). As explained above, people will be tempted to pay high prices in exchange for medical or life-extending benefits of stem cell research. In fact, we are already witnessing this: rich people in wealthy nations are paying right now exorbitant prices to replace their internal organs (Fox News 2023).

From the vantage point of the Buddhist thoughts, stem cell research is a misguided and dangerous experiment if and only if it is directed to producing human clones for the numerous reasons described in the previous section. To be elaborate, if stem cell research is done for the cloning of the best human genes, or creating warriors on the battlefields, or expanding human population, it would create a catastrophic risk for humanity while the benefits of such applications are doubtful.

Why do I say this? From the Buddhist point of view, humans are in fact "cloned" all the time through the natural process (Maha Nidana Sutta, Bodhi Sutta). By sexual intercourse between a man and a woman, a new human being is created all the time on the planet. There is no reason to rely on stem cell research to create additional human beings *via* the stem cell technology.

For another reason, stem cell research cloning of the richest people on the planet is also meaningless as well as ignorant, that is, as far as Buddhism is concerned. According to Buddhism, a human being does not die at all and disappear from this world (Tibetan Book of the Dead) (Fremantle and Trungpa 1975; HAR 2023; Milarepa's Songs). He or she is always reborn into another life according to the law of karma (Aryadeva's Four Hundred, Lama Tsongkhapa's Foundation of All). If at the age of 100, you are certain that you will live the rest of your life contentedly and be born into a new fresh young body for another life, why would you try so hard and so in vain to clone yourself to have another life? It is the futile desire of an ignorant one (Seo 2024b).

What about the other type of stem cell research, for example, for regenerative medicine? If stem cell research is directed to medical purposes only, for example, producing a human internal organ in order to treat an incurable disease, Buddhists would not necessarily disagree on such research and applications since it can benefit many people and animal beings. The bodhisattvas are born in fact to alleviate and cure such incurable diseases of sentient beings (Vimalakirti Sutra, Samanthabhadra, Avalokiteshvara, Tara Prayer, Medicine Buddha, Ksitigarbha).

However, Buddhists should still feel cautious about the possibility of defective stem cell organs as well as the correlated risk that arises from stem cell research. The former is a concern that the organs created through stem cell research may not perform as well as advertised, which may cause a big catastrophic event for humanity. The latter is a concern that, if the stem cell-generated organs were to cause a weakened immune system in humans, it could bring an even more catastrophic consequence to humankind under the emergence of another super virus (Seo 2022). Considering these risks, the rules and regulations on stem cell generation of human organs should be firmly determined first and perhaps in a globally shared manner (Seo 2020).

Even with that, there still remains the pivotal question of whether humanity should proceed with stem cell research *via* the stem cells obtained from the human embryos obtained from the mother's womb or from in vitro fertilization. The former may be indefensible if such an acquisition of embryonic stem cells would affect whatsoever during the fetus development. For clarification, an embryo is a pre-fetus from the time of fertilization till the end of eight weeks. The latter may be regarded more defensible by many people. However, the in vitro fertilization (IVF) stem cells are also, strictly speaking, in the process of developing into a fetus. In that sense, there is no difference between the former and the latter stem cell. It is highly likely that the IVF stem cells are equally controversial as embryonic stem cells, even if the IVF process is protected by law for those parents who want to have a baby through the IVF (KHOU 11 2024). The stem cells obtained from amniotic fluid or umbilical cord appear to have a similar problem if these alternatives can also be developed into a fetus (Atala et al. 2019).

This leaves us with the only defensible option in stem cell research, which is to create the stem cells artificially from adult stem cells. Such has been done by researchers, for whose success the Nobel Prize in Physiology or Medicine was awarded in 2012 (Takahashi and Yamanaka 2006; Nobel Prize 2012). The technology is to create pluripotent stem cells by gene modifications of the adult stem cells. This may offer scientists a way out in the ethical conundrum with regard to the stem cell research.

Notwithstanding, this viable alternative method for producing the stem cells may worsen the risk of catastrophic events caused by the stem cell research, afore-described in the context of regenerative medicine. There is already concern among scientists that the reprogrammed stem cells do not perform as well as the embryonic stem cells. It may be later found that the reprogrammed stem cells are more prone to generating defective body organs or more vulnerable to viruses and other infectious diseases.

From the Buddhist standpoint, similar to the above comment about stem cell cloning of a human, we should ask the following question. Let's suppose that you are 80 years old and multiple organs are failing including kidney, liver, heart, lung, stomach, and intestines. If you should have the wealth, would you ask your doctors to replace all of your defective organs through the novel stem cell technologies? Most people would do that, I presume. However, such a choice is made owing in large part to the belief that there is no future life; there is no next life for you as a young fresh beautiful boy or girl to come after death. This belief is in fact entrenched in those who refute the stages of the path to Buddhahood to be traveled from one life to another (Asanga's Bodhisattva Stages, Atisha's Lamp, Lama Tsongkhapa's Stages).

From this analysis, the Buddhist principles of the cycle of existence, karma and consequences, death and rebirth are critical concepts that can potentially solve the conundrum of stem cell research (Khantipalo 1995, Chandrakirti's Middle Way, Lama Tsongkhapa's Beginning-Middle-End Prayer). Succinctly put, a total reconfiguration of your internal organs at that age is irrational from the point of view of the Buddha's perfect wisdom (Milarepa's Songs, Lama Tsongkhapa's Destiny Fulfilled).

6 Additional Remarks on Human Gene Modifications

Another major area of microbiology is genetics which is the study of genes (Aksoy et al. 2014; NHGRI 2023). Through Fig. 7.1, we can identify the nucleus of the cell where the genetic information, namely, the DNA and RNA of a eukaryote, is stored. From genetics, the science of gene modifications has advanced to become a critical science for society. We are familiar with this science through the genetically modified organisms (GMOs). The GMOs are also called biofortified animals and plants (USFDA 2023).

As for common people's experiences, let me give a grape example. When the present author was a child, there was only one type of grapes, as such, one taste. Nowadays, there are many different types of grapes produced via the gene modification technologies. They all taste differently. Sometimes you wonder: Is this really the taste of a grape?

The genetic modification is regarded as an important technology for the development and poverty alleviation efforts in poor countries. In food-insecure countries, poverty means hunger but also malnutrition especially among infants, children, and pregnant women. The gene modified organisms are developed to improve people's nutritional health or to cure prevalent diseases by supplying necessary micronutrients such as iron, calcium, zinc, Vitamin A, etc., through biofortified products (World Bank 2008).

Success stories include the development of an orange-fleshed sweet potato rich in Vitamin A with a goal to address the Vitamin-A deficiency in African people (World Food Prize 2016). The Vitamin A deficiency is recognized as one of the reasons for a low survival rate in sub-Saharan African children because it weakens their immune system. Another example is golden rice in India developed to enhance Vitamin A in the human body through beta-carotene fortification (Bill & Melinda Gates Foundation 2011). Still another example is a biofortified cassava, a staple food crop of Africans consumed by more than 250 million African people, with enhanced beta-carotene, iron, and protein.

The gene modification is more controversial when it is performed on a human being (Kaji and Leiden 2001; TJGM 2024). Gene therapy would identify a certain set of genes related to a disease, for example, a skin cancer (Rosenberg et al. 1990). Sometimes, people also refer to superior genes *versus* inferior genes to identify potential high achievers in society.

The risk of a human gene modification experiment appears to be well in line with the risk of the stem cell-based regenerative medicine (Kaji and Leiden 2001). Therefore, the analysis of this chapter in the preceding sections is largely applicable to gene alteration science.

References

Aksoy S, Attardo G, et al., (2014) Genome sequence of the tsetse fly (Glossina morsitans): vector of African trypanosomiasis. Science 344 (6182), 380–386.

Alberts B, Hopkin K, Johnson A, Morgan D, Roberts K, Walter P, and Heald R(2019) Essential Cell Biology (Sixth Edition). New York, NY: W.W. Norton & Company.

Alison MR, Poulsom R, Forbes S, and Wright NA (2002) An introduction to stem cells. The Journal of Pathology 197 (Special Issue on Stem Cells): 419–423.

Aryadeva (2nd century). Four Hundred Stanzas. Catuḥśatakaśāstra. Bstan bcos bzhi brgya pa. Toh 3846, dbu ma tsha.[1]

Aryashura (ca. 4th century). Jatakamala. Garland of the Buddha's Past Lives. Toh 4150.

Asanga (ca. 4th century) Stages of the Bodhisattva. Bodhisattvabhumi. Byang chub sems dpa'i sa. Toh 4037. sems tsam wi.

Atala A, Lanza R, Mikos AG, and Nerem R (eds.) (2019) Principles of Regenerative Medicine (3rd Edition). Amsterdam, NL: Academic Press.

Atisha Dipankara Srijnana (982–1054). Bodhipathapradīpa. A Lamp for the Path to Enlightenment. Byang chub lam gyi sgron ma.

Bill & Melinda Gates Foundation (2011) Nutritious rice and cassava aim to help millions fight malnutrition. Seattle, WA. Accessed from: https://www.gatesfoundation.org/ideas/media-center/press-releases/2011/04/nutritious-rice-and-cassava-aim-to-help-millions-fight-malnutrition.

Campbell KH, McWhir J, Ritchie WA, and Wilmut I (1996) Sheep cloned by nuclear transfer from a cultured cell line. Nature. 380 (6569): 64–6.

Chalmers R (1895) The Jataka or Stories of the Buddha's Former Births (Volume 1–6). Accessed from https://www.wisdomlib.org/buddhism/book/jataka-tales-english

Chandrakirti (7th century). Entering the Middle Way. Madhyamakāvatāra. Dbu ma la 'jug pa. Toh 3861, dbu ma'a.

Descartes R (1637) Discourse on the Method of Rightly Conducting One's Reason and of Seeking Truth in the Sciences. BnF, FR.

[1] Tohoku University (ed.) (1934). A Complete Catalogue of the Tibetan Buddhist Canons, Sde-dge Edition, Tohoku University, Japan.

European Food Safety Authority (EFSA) (2023) Cloning. Parma, IT: EFSA. Accessed from https://www.efsa.europa.eu/en/topics/topic/cloning
Evans MJ, Kaufman M (1981) Establishment in culture of pluripotential stem cells from mouse embryos. Nature 292: 151–156.
Fox News (2023) Tech billionaire on journey to immortality says there is a 'low probability' humans will survive without AI. Published on October 10, 2023.
Fremantle F, Trungpa C (1975) The Tibetan Book of the Dead: The Great Liberation through Hearing in the Bardo by Guru Rinpoche according to Karma Lingpa. Boulder, CO: Shambhala.
Hatton IA, Galbraith ED, Merleau NSC, and Shander JA (2023) The human cell count and size distribution. Proceedings of the National Academy of Sciences 120(39). https://doi.org/10.1073/pnas.2303077120
Hawking S, Tegmark M, Russell S, and Wilczek F (2014) Transcending complacency on superintelligent machines. Huffington Post. Accessed from https://www.huffingtonpost.com/stephen-hawking/artificial-intelligence_b_5174265.html
Himalayan Art Resources (HAR) (2023) Wheel of Life Schematic. Accessed from https://www.himalayanart.org/pages/wheeloflife2/index.html
Kaji EH, Leiden JM (2001). Gene and stem cell therapies. Journal of the American Medical Association 285 (5): 545–550.
Kant I (1781) The Critique of Pure Reason. Kritik der reinen Vernunft.
Khantipalo Bhikkhu (1995) The Wheel of Birth and Death. Access to Insight. Accessed from https://www.accesstoinsight.org/lib/authors/khantipalo/wheel147.html#fn-6
KHOU 11 (2024) Gov. Abbott shares stance on IVF treatment in wake of Alabama ruling. Accessed from https://www.khou.com/article/news/politics/abott-ivf-treatment-alabama-supreme-court-ruling/285-00caf856-a049-4989-b1bc-87e67de797c4
Kurzweil R (2005) The Singularity is Near: When Humans Transcend Biology. New York, NY: Penguin.
Lama Tsongkhapa (1357a–1419). Collected Works of the Incomparable Lord Tsongkhapa Lobsang Drakpa. Kumbum woodblock edition.
Lama Tsongkhapa (1357b–1419) Great Treatise on the Stages of the Path to Enlightenment. Byang chub lam rim chen mo. Collected Works. Vol. pa.[2]
Lama Tsongkhapa (1357c–1419) Ocean of Reasoning: An Exposition of Treatise on the Middle Way. Rtsa ba shes rab kyi rnam bshad ṭik chen rigs pa'i rgya mtsho. Collected Works. Vol. ba, 1–583.
Lama Tsongkhapa (1357d–1419) Essence of True Eloquence: Distinguishing the Provisional and the Definitive Meaning (Drang ba dang nges pa'i don rnam par 'byed pa legs bshad snying po). Collected Works. Vol. pha, 441–687.

[2] Lama Tsongkhapa (1357–1419). Collected Works of the Incomparable Lord Tsongkhapa Lobsang Drakpa. Kumbum woodblock edition.

Lama Tsongkhapa (1357e–1419) Destiny Fulfilled. Rtogs brjod 'dun legs ma. Portland, OR: The Foundation for the Preservation of the Mahayana Tradition (FPMT).

Lama Tsongkhapa (1357f–1419). Prayers for Goodness in the Beginning, the Middle, and the End. Thog mtha' bar gsum du dge ba'i smon lam. Portland, OR: The Foundation for the Preservation of the Mahayana Tradition (FPMT).

Lama Tsongkhapa (1357g–1419). Foundation of All Good Qualities. Yon ten kun gyi gsir gyur. Portland, OR: The Foundation for the Preservation of the Mahayana Tradition (FPMT).

Lemaitre G (1931) The beginning of the world from the point of view of quantum theory. Nature 127 (3210): 706.

Mayo Clinic (2023) Stem cells: What they are and what they do. Rochester, MN: Mayo Clinic. Accessed from https://www.mayoclinic.org/tests-procedures/bone-marrow-transplant/in-depth/stem-cells/art-20048117

Milarepa (1052–1135) The Hundred Thousand Songs of Milarepa: A New Translation (translated by Stagg C, 2017. Boulder, CO: Shambhala).

Nagarjuna (2nd century). Fundamental Wisdom on the Middle Way. Mūlamadhyamakakārikā. Dbu ma rtsa ba'i tshig le'ur byas pa (Rtsa ba'i shes rab). Toh 3824, dbu ma tsa.

Narada Mahathera (1998) Chapter 19. What is Kamma? In: The Buddha and His Teachings. The Buddha Dhamma Education Association, Taipei, Taiwan.

National Human Genome Research Institute (NHGRI) (2023) Cell. Bethesda, MD: NHGRI, National Institutes of Health. Accessed from https://www.genome.gov/genetics-glossary/Cell

National Institutes of Health (2009) NIH Guidelines for Human Stem Cell Research. Bethesda, MD: National Institutes of Health.

National Institutes of Health (2022) Stem cell basics. Bethesda, MD: National Institutes of Health. Accessed from https://stemcells.nih.gov/info/basics/stc-basics

Nobel Prize (2012). The Nobel Prize in Physiology or Medicine 2012 was awarded jointly to Sir John B. Gurdon and Shinya Yamanaka "for the discovery that mature cells can be reprogrammed to become pluripotent." Accessed from https://www.nobelprize.org/prizes/medicine/2012/summary/

Pardi N, Hogan MJ, Porter FW, and Weissman D (2018) mRNA vaccines—A New Era in Vaccinology. Nature Reviews Drug Discovery 17: 261–279.

Plotkin SA (2009) Vaccines: the fourth century. Clinical and Vaccine Immunology 16: 1709–1719.

Pollard TD, Earnshaw WC, Lippincott-Schwartz J, and Johnson G (2022) Cell Biology. Amsterdam, NL: Elsevier.

Rosenberg SA, Aebersold P, Cornetta K, Kasid A, Morgan RA, Moen R, et al. (1990). Gene transfer into humans--immunotherapy of patients with advanced

melanoma, using tumor-infiltrating lymphocytes modified by retroviral gene transduction. The New England Journal of Medicine 323 (9): 570–578.
Scitable (2014) Essentials of Cell Biology. Scitable by Nature Education. Cambridge, MA: Nature Education.
Seo SN (2018) Natural and Man-made Catastrophes: Theories, Economics, and Policy Designs. New York, NY: Wiley-Blackwell.
Seo SN (2020) The Economics of Globally Shared and Public Goods. Amsterdam, NL: Academic Press.
Seo SN (2021) Climate Change and Economics: Engaging with Future Generations with Action Plans. London, UK: Palgrave Macmillan.
Seo SN (2022) The Economics of Pandemics: Exploring Globally Shared Experiences. London, UK: Palgrave Macmillan.
Seo SN (2023) The Economics of Optimal Growth Pathways: Evaluating the Health of the Planet's Natural and Ecological Resources. London, UK: Palgrave Macmillan.
Seo SN (2024a) Buddha, Wisdom and Economics: A Contribution to the Art of Happiness. Cheltenham, UK: Edward Elgar.
Seo SN (2024b) Protecting Nature with Buddha's Wisdom: A Contribution to Environmental and Nature Studies. Cheltenham, UK: Edward Elgar.
Takahashi K, Yamanaka S (2006). Induction of pluripotent stem cells from mouse embryonic and adult fibroblast cultures by defined factors. Cell 126: 663–676.
Tara Prayer. Praises to the Twenty-One Taras. Dol ma la chak chal ni shu za zig gyi toi pa pen yon dang ze pa. Kangyur Sde-Dge Edition (1729–33). Accessed from the Buddhist Digital Resource Center at http://purl.bdrc.io/resource/MW4CZ5369_0438
The Journal of Gene Medicine (TJGM) (2024). Gene Therapy Clinical Trials Worldwide Database. Accessed from https://a873679.fmphost.com/fmi/webd/GTCT
Thom R (1975) Structural stability and morphogenesis. New York, NY: Benjamin-Addison-Wesley.
Thomson JA, Itskovitz-Eldor J, Shapiro SS, Waknitz MA, Swiergiel JJ, Marshall VS, Jones JM (1998) Embryonic stem cell lines derived from human blastocysts. Science 282 (5391): 1145–1147.
Trujillo CA, Gao R, Negraes PD, et al. (2019) Complex oscillatory waves emerging from cortical organoids model early human brain network development. Cell Stem Cell 25, 558–569.
United States Food and Drug Administration (USFDA) (2023) Science and History of GMOs and Other Food Modification Processes. Washington, DC. Accessed from https://www.fda.gov/food/agricultural-biotechnology/science-and-history-gmos-and-other-food-modification-processes
Vimalakirti Sutra. Vimalakīrti Nirdeśa Sūtra. Hphags pa dri ma med pa grags pas bstan pa shes by aba theg pa chen pohi mdo. Toh 176. Mdo sde ma.

World Bank (2008) World Development Report 2008: Agriculture for Development. Washington, DC: World Bank.
World Food Prize (2016) Maria Andrade, Robert Mwanga, and Jan Low: The Orange-Fleshed Sweet Potato. Accessed from: https://www.worldfoodprize.org/en/laureates/20102019laureates/.

CHAPTER 8

A Neuroscience Singularity: Making Consciousness

1 Introduction

Thus far, the present author examined the two fields of physics (relativity physics in Chap. 4 and quantum physics in Chap. 5) and the two fields of biology (mRNA virology in Chap. 6 and stem cell research in Chap. 7). The analysis in each of these chapters was anchored at the possibility of a singularity, that is, a truly catastrophic outcome.

The final science discipline to be analyzed in this chapter is neuroscience and brain science. This field of science pursues to unveil the nature of mind, consciousness, mental functions, in addition to the nature of the brains as a purely physical object (Singer 1999; Purves et al. 2011). The topics that this field of research pursues cross paths with the vast Buddhist literature on mind and mental functions (Flower Ornament Sutra, Unravelling the Intent Sutra, Ten Grounds Sutra, Asanga's Compendium).

For the past several decades, dialogues as well as collaborations between Buddhist philosophers and neuroscientists have gradually increased. Neuroscientists would like to understand how Buddhism thinks about the mind, consciousness, and mental activities, and how the Buddhist exposition of these phenomena can be a meaningful source of information for them who explore the mind and consciousness from the perspective of matter or physical functions such as neurons and brains (Hayward and Varela 1992; Ricard and Singer 2018).

S. N. Seo, *The Economics of Singularities of Science Elucidated with Buddhist Thoughts*,
https://doi.org/10.1007/978-3-031-69118-8_8

This curiosity arose quite naturally for neuroscientists because Buddhism is often reputed as the science of mind or the religion of mind. A rich historical comparative literature exists between Buddhism and other Indian philosophies as well as between Buddhism and other Chinese philosophies. The dialogues between Buddhism and neuroscience or psychology were frequent during the latter part of the twentieth century in all traditions of Buddhism, formally as well as informally, including Theravada, Mahayana, Zen, and Tibetan traditions (To cite only some, Story 1971; Walshe 1972; Varela et al. 1992; Austin 1999; Amaro 2021). In the traditionally Buddhist countries, especially Japan, Korea, and China, these dialogues between Buddhism and neuroscience were vibrant even if they were mostly under the radar partly because they were not written in English. The present author can say that this field of science has been the favorite meeting place between scientists and Buddhists.

Since Buddha Shakyamuni taught to his followers that the mind is the creator of all things, Buddhists always felt that they know better than neuroscientists about it or any other philosophies. The very first two verses of Dhammapada, the most-loved collection of his teachings in the Pali language, declare thus (Dhammapada):

> Everything has mind in the lead, has mind in the forefront, and is made by mind.
> If one speaks or acts with a corrupt mind, sorrows will follow.
> Like the wheel of a carriage follows the foot of an ox.
> Everything has mind in the lead, has mind in the forefront, and is made by mind.
> If one speaks or acts with a pure mind, happiness will follow.
> Like a shadow that never leaves.

As for this book's examination of science singularities, some readers might wonder how such a benign endeavor for discovering the true nature of the mind can cause a truly catastrophic event for the humankind, that is, a singularity. Although it might appear harmless or purely academic to casual observers, this chapter will demonstrate that the research and experiments of neuroscience have major implications on science-induced singularities tantamount to the other four singularities examined in the previous four chapters (Thom 1975; Gilmore 1981; Kurzweil 2005; Weitzman 2009; Seo 2018, 2020).

For this, the present author introduces the two cutting-edge experiments of neuroscience. The first is a consciousness generation experiment (Tegmark 2015). The other is a revival of a dead brain experiment (YaleNews 2019). Both experiments are at an early stage of development. However, actual experiments are being conducted by numerous scientific teams and their results are being published.

Some readers might wonder what the consciousness generation experiment is. Every living being has a consciousness. The term is equivalent to the term mind to large degrees. The differences between them will be explained later in this chapter. Although we know that consciousness inheres in all sentient beings, that is, even animals or ghosts, neuroscientists pursue to figure out how consciousness is born in the first place. To put it differently, they explore whether consciousness can be produced from matter alone, for example, by stimulating a certain matter or a composite of matters such as earth, water, fire, or wind (Reardon 2020).

As far as Buddhism is concerned, there is a treasure trove of scriptures and commentaries on consciousness which may fill the oceans of the planet. In fact, the vast literature of Buddhism is the analysis of the mind (Maitreya's Realizations, Scripture Ornament, Asanga's Bodhisattva Stages, Compendium). Not a single scripture or commentary is spoken or written without regard to one's mind and mental activities. As Buddha Shakyamuni states in the above quote, everything has the mind in the lead, in the forefront, and is made by the mind (Dhammapada, Suta-Nipata). As the Flower Ornament Sutra puts it, the entire three realms are mere minds (Ten Grounds Sutra).

Therefore, the analyses that this chapter performs will be a fascinating description of how the perfectly enlightened Buddha sees the generation of the mind, the mind's transmigration through the cycle of existence of sentient beings, and what the real nature of the mind or consciousness is. I am certain that no reader will be able to guess what that reality of the mind is at this point of the chapter.

The second experiment to be explained is the experiment which attempts to revive the brain functions of a dead person (Vrselja et al. 2019). At this stage, the experiment appears to be done to a pig brain. So, more correctly, it is the attempt to revive the functions of a dead brain. At this stage, scientists also report "modest results," for example, a success in reviving some brain functions of a dead pig. Astute readers will be able to see the nexus between this experiment and the consciousness generation experiment. That is, it can be seen as a consciousness generation experiment, but starting from the brain itself, that is, an un-functioning brain of a dead living organism which was functioning previously.

In the next section, the present author will give a brief introduction to neuroscience. This will be followed by a description of the two neuroscience experiments, which is again followed by a description of potential singularities caused by these experiments. Thenceforth the present author will present the Buddhist concept of consciousness, based upon which a critique is leveled against the science of consciousness generations.

2 Neuroscience or Brain Science in a Nutshell

As science is the study of physical phenomena, brain science is the study of a brain which is one of the physical phenomena. Of the brain science, the field that is specifically concerned with the mental activities of living organisms can be said to be neuroscience. The mental activities are what is commonly called thinking, but they refer to the full range of mental functions such as perception, feelings, cognition, conceptualizations, verbalizations, learning language, and consciousness.

At the heart of neuroscience are neurons or nerve cells, which are the building blocks of neuroscience as well as of the mental functions that are studied by neuroscientists (Purves et al. 2011). The mental functions are explained by the neurons and their connective network. When a person is conceived at a mother's womb, there are a small number of neurons in the fetus's brain which are connected among them through the neuronal connections. When a person is born, the number of neurons increases rapidly, which reaches the maximum during their 20s. According to a recent estimation, the maximum number of neurons of an adult brain reaches 100 billion and the neuronal connections are as many as 60 trillion (Pakkenberg and Gundersen 1997). When one grows older, the number of neurons starts to decrease.

In the neuroscience, the mental functions of a human being as well as an animal being are accounted for by the neurons and their network (Singer 1999). A simple organism such as a snail has a small number of neurons as well as a simple connectivity network. A more complex organism such as a dog has a larger number of neurons as well as a more complex connectivity network. A human being has the largest number of neurons as well as the most complex connectivity network.

The structure of a neuron is drawn in Fig. 8.1 (Stevens 1979). A neuron consists of soma (cell body), nucleus, dendrite, axon, and axon

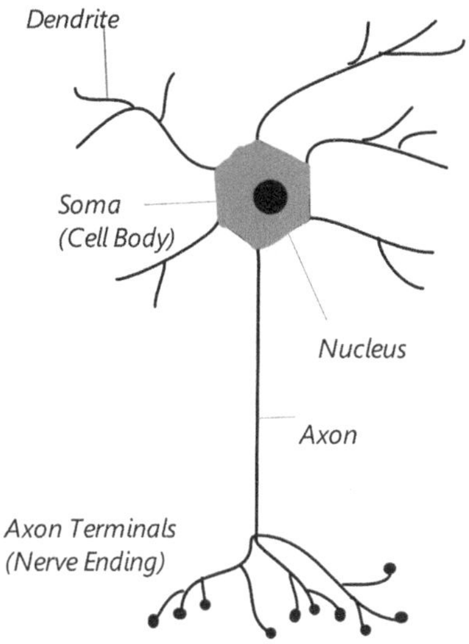

Fig. 8.1 The structure of a neuron

terminals. The dendrite is a branched protoplasmic extension of the nerve cell, which collects and stores information from other neurons. The axon is a long slender projection of a neuron which transmits information to different neurons.

A higher mental capacity of a living organism is explained by a "talking" among the neurons through the neuronal network of the organism. Consciousness, which is inherent in all sentient beings, is possible owing to the neuronal talking. For example, two neurons can recognize each other, remember their past interactions, etc. Likewise, the neuronal talking makes possible more sophisticated mental functions such as feelings, verbalizing, and theorizing (Purves et al. 2011; Ricard and Singer 2018).

The key distinction between neuroscience and Buddhism is that the neuroscience understands the mental functions as purely physical phenomena as any other physical phenomena such as chemical reactions, the Earth's weather events, or the solar system. The physical functions of the brain are explained by the neurons and their information exchanges through the neuronal network, which are minds as far as neuroscientists are concerned (Fig. 8.1).

For Buddhists, consciousness is not physical. It is different from the physical factors such as earth, water, fire, wind, or a composite of these.

The physical factors are referred to in Buddhism as form. In Buddhism, the mind comprises feeling, perception, mental formations, and consciousness (Maha Satipatthana Sutta, Abhidharma Pitaka, Heart Sutra, Descent into Lanka Sutra). The function of consciousness is to recognize, perceive, know (Elucidation of Intention Sutra, Descent into Lanka Sutra, Tathagatagarbha Sutra, Asanga's Bodhisattva Stages, Lama Tsongkhapa's Golden Rosary).

3 The Neuroscience Experiments

Neuroscience experiments are designed to understand the brain, changes in the brain functions, and changes in mental functions. Experiments are done on human brains but also on other living organisms such as mice, dogs, or cats. Brain scientists measure the physical changes in the brain or mental functions through the changes in various material indicators.

A well-publicized experiment from the brain science to the Buddhists as well as other spiritual traditions is a meditation effect study. In this experiment, neuroscientists measure the changes in brain functions after the meditation sessions of an individual from the before-meditation state. Also, they compare the brain functions of a long-term meditator with those of a no-experiencer in meditation (Davidson and Harrington 2002).

Other experiments are more challenging as well as more controversial, which are the focus of this chapter. The present author will elaborate the two of such experiments mentioned in the above. The first experiment is the consciousness generation experiment in which neuroscientists strive to make a conscious organism out of a pure matter, specifically, a human brain organoid. The second experiment is the revival experiment of a dead brain. The goal is to restore the consciousness of a dead person or partial functions of the dead brain. It has been experimented by neuroscientists with pigs.

As for the first, through the consciousness generation experiments, neuroscientists are eager to confirm the hypothesis that consciousness is purely matter (McGinn 2011; Tegmark 2015; Reardon 2020; Seth 2021). To confirm it, it would be fine to generate the consciousness of any conscious being such as mice or snails. That is, it doesn't have to be confirmed through the experiments on a human brain.

Neuroscientists reported recently that the human brain organoids showed the waves of neural activity similar to those observed in preterm babies (Trujillo et al. 2019; Giandomenico et al. 2019). The human brain organoid is the brain structure similar to a baby's brain made by neuroscientists from human pluripotent stem cells.

The hypothesis goes directly against the Buddhist understanding of consciousness, so it does against most religious philosophies of Indian and Tibetan traditions but not all. In Buddhism, consciousness is non-matter, whose characteristic is luminous and knowing (Elucidation of Intention Sutra, Descent into Lanka Sutra, Flower Ornament Sutra). Consciousness is distinct in nature from matter. It is the sixth sense organ which is separate from the other five sense organs which are physical: eyes, ears, nose, tongue, and body (Manjushri Sutra, Ajatasatru Sutra).

To put the consciousness generation experiment in another context, what neuroscientists are trying to achieve is the discovery of where human consciousness began (Quadrato et al. 2017; Trujillo et al. 2019; Giandomenico et al. 2019). This is the question that has troubled the most many Western philosophers as well for a long time, let alone the scientists. In a broader sense, major works of the Western philosophy such as Descartes' Discourse (1637), Spinoza's Ethics (1677), Schopenhauer's The World (1818), Nietzsche's Zarathustra (1883), and Einstein's Spinoza's God (1929) concern this question. One may say, as these philosophers did, that "I think, therefore I am" or "The world as will and representations" or "Nature God" in response to this age-old question.

In the case of scientists like Einstein, he may have seen the nature's principle as the answer to this question, which can be proven through scientific experiments or observations of natural phenomena (Einstein 2001). As far as human beings are concerned, however, it is difficult for scientists to know where consciousness begins, or began, or even where and when it ends. But neuroscientists notice that the brain capacity varies greatly across the animal realm. A human brain is relatively big and complex. But, even in a far smaller brain such as a pig's or dog's, there is consciousness albeit with far limited mental functions. Even smaller brains are found in other animals such as snakes. Even further smaller brains in fish. Even further smaller brains are found in snails or mosquitoes. However small their brain sizes are, there is consciousness, nonetheless, in snails or mosquitoes.

Can brain scientists find an animal species from which consciousness begins or began? Here scientists define consciousness as the existence of neurons and the neuronal networking, however simple that is (Quadrato et al. 2017; Trujillo et al. 2019; Giandomenico et al. 2019). If "the smallest" unit of a living organism from which consciousness exists is found or neural flow is found, does it answer where the consciousness came from? Scientists may say yes. However, even the tiniest brain possible, for example, as tiny as an atom or an embryonic stem cell, is found to be conscious, that does not answer how that brain became conscious in the first place. Scientists, therefore, must generate consciousness from pure matter without any consciousness like a lump of earth if they could confirm the hypothesis.

As for the second experiment, the consciousness revival experiment, the goal is to resuscitate the dead brain of a person, at the core of which is to bring back the consciousness that previously existed in the dead person (Vrselja et al. 2019; Andrijevic et al. 2022). Therefore, the second experiment is related with the first experiment. Specifically, in the revival experiment, the generation of consciousness is attempted with the brain that had consciousness short moments ago but is declared non-existent at the moment of the experiment.

As it is at an early stage, neuroscientists are reporting only limited successes. They can only experiment on non-humans such as pigs for ethical reasons. Some are now reporting that they succeeded in restoring some mental functions of the dead brain of a pig (YaleNews 2019; NYT 2022). Since mental functions are impossible without consciousness, the restoration of mental functions would mean the revival of consciousness. They do not however say that the revived brain can be sustained for a long time.

The difficult point to assess the results from this experiment is that even if the pig were dead, the brain functions would remain for some time. For an analogy, a dead person's nails would still grow for some time after death. From this point of view, it is not definitive from the successful revival of the pig brain whether the non-existent consciousness appears from somewhere else or the weakened consciousness is again coming back to full strength.

4 Singularities of Neuroscience

Can there be a singularity event caused by neuroscience? (Thom 1975; Kurzweil 2005; Hawking et al. 2014). As far as the present author is aware of, there is no serious scientific study which predicts a neuroscience singularity. It is likely that scientists and other intellectuals are not well informed about this research, especially about the philosophical dimension of this research. Notwithstanding, it can be handily foreseen by philosophers, but also by the public if they would apply their imagination only slightly.

The efforts to create consciousness from pure matter would culminate in combining a set of matters in an ingenious way such as multiple cells with distinct characteristics or stem cells for the sake of creating a conscious organism. Alternatively, a man-made chip may be inserted into the unconscious human brain to replay the natural brain function as is done in the Neuralink experiment (Neuralink 2024; Reuters 2024).

The big risk we can easily foresee is the experiment's possibility of creating a living organism with a defective brain function. Even if it is not a totally defective brain, a partially defective brain would be equally catastrophic as will be elaborated shortly.

The mechanisms through which a neuroscience catastrophe unfolds from the defective brain creations can be sketched. First, once such a living organism with consciousness is given birth to by neuroscientists, it may have the physical power which is largely uncontrollable by humans owing to its totally defective brain. From this perspective, this mechanism is similar to the Artificial Intelligence (AI) humanoid robot catastrophe explicated in Chap. 5 (Tesla 2023).

Second, it may have the physical characteristic to make it a super carrier of a lethal virus such as the mRNA (Messenger Ribonucleic Acid) virus or other lethal SARS (Severe Acute Respiratory Syndrome) viruses (Reuters 2021; Seo 2022; Wade 2024). It can be imagined that the organism created with a defective brain is fragile in its immune system, making it a highly efficient carrier of a super virus. From this perspective, the neuroscience of consciousness generation is similar to the mRNA virus virology experiment which attempted to create a super virus explicated in Chap. 6 (Wade 2024; USDOI 2024).

Third, another disaster scenario, which is perhaps more lethal than the two scenarios in a stealthy way, is that the organism with a partially defective brain may thrive on this Earth while humans are not able to detect such defects easily because outwardly this creature would behave normally as any other living organism does. It would be similar to creating a large number of a mentally defective person or a person with a physically damaged brain who will be roaming the streets without being noticed. From this perspective, this disaster scenario is similar to the disaster scenario from the AI information robots or chatbots clarified in Chap. 5 (OpenAI 2023).

The fourth scenario: once such a defective-minded creature is given birth to by laboratory experiments of neuroscience, it would be extremely difficult to get rid of such a living being when they are found to be a cause of such an anthropogenic catastrophe. That is of course due to the ethics of the human civilization regarding living beings (Kant 1781; Seo 2024b). From this perspective, this disaster scenario resembles that of stem cell research to some degree explicated in Chap. 7 (NIH 2009).

As for the second experiment, that is, the revival experiment of a dead brain, a similar singularity can be foreseen through one of the four mechanisms described above. It might be that the possibility of a living organism being created with a defective mind is even larger in the revival experiment. Let's say that a dead person is revived but only with a partially functioning brain! It would become the world of zombies or Dracula that people are familiar with through many Hollywood movies. The risk, however, will be far greater than that depicted in those movies. The problem of defective minds will not only affect the human realm but also other realms of existence such as ghost realm, hell realm, animal realm, asura realm, and Gods realm (Kalacakratantra, Tibetan Book of the Dead Fremantle and Trungpa 1975).

Readers might say that my arguments in this section with regard to possible singularities caused by neuroscience are far-fetched. However, it should be reminded that most things in the neuroscientific experiments on consciousness are also far-fetched. Therefore, societies and experts should be imaginative as well as forward-looking in dealing with this human endeavor or challenges. To put it another way, the study of possible singularities reveals much about the nature of science experiments as well as the understanding of the world by scientists as well as common people.

5 A Buddhist Perspective on Neuroscience Singularities

Readers who have read through this chapter thus far with patience would be keen to know how Buddhist philosophers long steeped in the theories of consciousness would see this pressing problem. Let me begin with an exposition of the concept of consciousness as elucidated in Buddhism.

Consciousness is referred to as the mind in Buddhism. In Tibetan, consciousness [vijnanam in Sanskrit] is translated into nam-she where she in Tibetan means "to know." The mind [citta in Sanskrit] is translated as sem in Tibetan where sem also means "to think." For the Tibetan words of these terms, refer to Table 5 in the Appendix. The two terms mean the same in this context.

However, the mind is also often used to refer to all mental activities. Of the five aggregates [pung-po-a in Tibetan], the four aggregates are mental phenomena: feeling [chor-wa in Tibetan], perception [du-she in Tibetan], mental formations [du-je in Tibetan], and consciousness [nam-pa-she-pa in Tibetan]. The other is form [sook in Tibetan] which is physical phenomena or body. The mind refers to the four mental phenomena in this context, as such, differentiated from consciousness (Maha Satipatthana Sutta, Vasubandhu's Abhidharmakosa).

Of the six sense bases [kae-che-duk in Tibetan], the mind is the sixth sense base, with the other five sense bases being eyes, ears, nose, tongue, and body. When the consciousness arises in dependence upon the eye and its object, it is called eye consciousness. In Tibetan, it is mig-gyi-nam-she. Similarly, there is ear consciousness [na-wai-nam-she in Tibetan], nose consciousness, tongue consciousness, body consciousness [lue-kyi-nam-she], and mind consciousness [yi-gyi-nam-she in Tibetan] (Perfection of Wisdom Sutras, Lama Tsongkhapa's Stages of the Path). In the Mind-only philosophy, they posit seventh consciousness and eighth consciousness, the latter of which is referred to as fundamental consciousness (Asanga's Compendium, Bodhisattva Stages).

The mind or consciousness is the utmost thing in sentient beings. As Buddha Shakyamuni says in the following verse which was quoted in the introduction, the mind is at the beginning of every action of a sentient being as well as its consequences (Dhammapada):

> Everything has mind in the lead,
> has mind in the forefront,
> and is made by mind.

Aryadeva, who is regarded as the Father and Son of the Middle Way Buddhism along with Nagarjuna, puts it that consciousness is the seed of worldly existence. Mind-only philosophers also assert the same frequently. According to Aryadeva's Four Hundred Stanzas (Gyel-tsap's Commentary):

> The seed of worldly existence is a consciousness;
> Objects are its sphere of activity.

In another verse from the Flower Ornament Sutra [Avatamsaka Sutra in Sanskrit], the Buddha explains the mind with a simile of an artist who paints her own world. That is, the mind is the creator of the world as people know it (Flower Ornament Sutra's Ch. 20):

> Mind is like an artist,
> Able to paint the worlds:
> The five clusters all are born thence;
> There's nothing it doesn't make.
> ...
> If people know the actions of mind
> Create all the worlds,
> They will see the Buddha
> And understand Buddha's true nature.

In the above verse, Buddha says that people will understand the Buddha's true nature or in short Buddha nature if they understand that the actions of mind create all the worlds and all the worldly phenomena. It is not hard to see that this verse is a crucial quotation from the Buddha's own words for the Mind-only School [Sem-zam in Tibetan] as well as the theory of Buddha Nature [Sang-gye-gyi-rik in Tibetan] (Maitreya's Ornament of Realizations, Scripture Ornament, Asanga's Compendium, Bodhisattva Stages). According to Je Rinpoche, the Mind-only philosophy is also deeply rooted in the philosophy of the later Yogacara School [Nel-jor-zoi-pa in Tibetan] (Shantaraksita's Ornament, Kamalasila's Stages of Meditation). Both Mind-only and Yogacara philosophers accepted the concepts of fundamental consciousness [za-wai-nam-she in Tibetan, aly-avijnana in Sanskrit] and apperception [rang-rik in Tibetan, svasamvitti in Sanskrit] (Lama Tsongkhapa's True Eloquence, Elucidating the Intent).

The way Buddha Shakyamuni explained consciousness is through the law of the dependently originated phenomena, which may sound to some readers somewhat different from the exposition in the above paragraphs (Lama Tsongkhapa's Praise, Nagarjuna's Fundamental Wisdom, Sixty Stanzas). Buddha Shakyamuni attained the complete and perfect enlightenment under the Bodhi tree on the bank of the Neranjara River in 588 BCE (Buddha Carita, Abhiniṣkramaṇa Sutra). Then he sat for seven days in one session before he elaborated how the entire world of phenomena, both mental and physical, arises thus (Bodhi Sutta):

> When this is, that is;
> When this arises, that arises.
> ...

From ignorance arises volition;
From volition arises consciousness;
From consciousness arises name-and-form;
From name-and-form arises the six senses;
From the six senses arises contact;
From contact arises feeling;
From feeling arises craving;
From craving arises clinging;
From clinging arises becoming;
From becoming arises birth;
From birth arises old age and death, sorrow, lamentation, pain, distress, and despair.
Such is the origination of this entire mass of stress and suffering.

The doctrine of dependent origination is therefore at the heart of Buddha's enlightenment and, as such, the consciousness has also been elucidated through this golden rule by the great charioteers of Buddhism (Nagarjuna's Fundamental Wisdom, Aryadeva's Four Hundred, Buddhapalita's Commentary, Lama Tsongkhapa's True Eloquence, Seo 2024a, 2024b). That is, consciousness also arises dependently on the sense bases and the sense objects (Ajatasatru Sutra, Two Truths Sutra, King of Meditations Sutra).

The key point that the present author will make regarding the consciousness generation problem addressed in this chapter is that consciousness is there for every sentient being in the universes. Without it, sentient beings are not sentient beings, that is, they are non-sentient. With the nature of luminosity and knowing, consciousness "resides" in human beings. What this means is that there is no need to create a consciousness out of pure matter, whatsoever.

Let me further clarify. Consciousness does not disappear from the sentient beings. It does not get demolished when a person dies. The continuum of consciousness goes on through the next stages of the cycle of existence (Khantipalo 1995; HAR 2023). That is, after death, one goes through the Bardo and then to the next life. One may be reborn in a different realm according to their karma like heavens, asura, human realm, animal realm, ghost realm, and hells (Fremantle and Trungpa 1975). This process is in fact explicated in the teaching of dependent origination quoted in the above (Bodhi Sutta).

If no one truly dies out of this world since their consciousness never really disappears, why should the scientists bother to revive a dead brain or the consciousness of a dead person? Let's hypothesize that scientists want to utilize the revival technology to get a powerful ruler or person or the richest man on Earth be restored after their death. Would such persons or should such persons be interested in applying the technology to themselves after death?

They would not and here is why. Let me explain it. Buddhists believe that the death is not the end of life, but only a transition period from this life to next life. One will be reborn in next life according to their actions in this life. A person of much merit will go to a godly realm. A person of much demerit will go to a lower realm like a ghost realm or a hell realm or an animal realm. Some people will be reborn into a human realm again (refer to Fig. 2.1 in Chap. 2). Therefore, there is absolutely no purpose and reason for one to attempt to revive the brain functions of their dead body. The "person" has already left for another life in the endless cycle of existence.

Let me put this in another light. The creation of consciousness or revival of it after death is a misguided effort. This is because they do not understand that when a new baby is born, their consciousness is created, to speak somewhat loosely here. Every hour, millions of babies are born, whether animals or humans. As such, millions of consciousnesses are created every hour. So, if you would create the consciousness, the best way is to do it through natural reproduction. For example, when a new snail is born, its consciousness is created.

6 Final Remarks

Consciousness is the most fundamental function of a living organism, including human beings. As such, the utmost interest given to the study of this by scientists, including neuroscientists, is inevitable. Neuroscientists also have made a number of notable progresses in their scientific research during the past decades, many of which were explained in this chapter. One thing that comes up to my mind is their effort to measure the emotions of an individual through scientific instruments and indicators, applications of which might turn out to be beneficial to some individuals with mental problems. It is highly likely that they are measuring the gross feelings and gross mental activities more accurately.

As far as the consciousness is concerned, it is the most subtle phenomena of all, both physical and mental, that living organisms or sentient beings experience in their life. Scientists will not be able to measure it directly. Neither do they see it directly. Much care and caution need to be taken by the society at large when it comes to the experiments that attempt to create the consciousness out of pure matter or revive it after being dead. To our dismay, these concerns are largely ignored owing to many other priorities that the society engages with. For that, Buddhism offers a marvelous insight. Thus, a neuroscience-induced singularity has been analyzed.

References

Amaro A (2021) Mind Is What Matters: The Phenomenological Approach of the Buddha. Forest Sangha, Thailand.

Andrijevic D, Vrselja Z, Lysyy T, et al. (2022) Cellular recovery after prolonged warm ischaemia of the whole body. Nature 608: 405–412.

Aryadeva (2nd century). Four Hundred Stanzas. Catuḥśatakaśāstra. Bstan bcos bzhi brgya pa. Toh 3846, dbu ma tsha

Asanga (ca. 4th century). Compendium of the Universal Vehicle. Mahāyānasaṃgraha. Theg pa chen po bsdus pa. Toh 4048, sems tsam ri.

Asanga (ca. 4th century) Stages of the Bodhisattva. Bodhisattvabhumi. Byang chub sems dpa'i sa. Toh 4037. sems tsam wi.

Austin JH (1999) Zen and the Brain: Toward an Understanding of Meditation and Consciousness. Cambridge, MA: The MIT Press.

Bhikkhu Khantipalo (1995) The Wheel of Birth and Death. Access to Insight. Accessed from https://www.accesstoinsight.org/lib/authors/khantipalo/wheel147.html#fn-6

Buddhapalita (ca. fifth century). Commentary. Buddhapālitamūlamadhyamakavṛtti. Dbu ma rtsa ba'i 'grel pa buddha pā li ta. Toh 3842, dbu ma tsa.

Davidson RJ, and Harrington A (eds.) (2002) Visions of Compassion: Western Scientists and Tibetan Buddhists Examine Human Nature. Oxford, UK: Oxford University Press.

Descartes R (1637) Discourse on the Method of Rightly Conducting One's Reason and of Seeking Truth in the Sciences. BnF, FR.

Einstein A (1929) "Einstein believes in "Spinoza's God"; Scientist Defines His Faith in Reply, to Cablegram From Rabbi Here. Sees a Divine Order But Says Its Ruler Is Not Concerned "Wit [sic] Fates and Actions of Human Beings." Published in The New York Times on 25 April 1929.

Einstein A (2001) Relativity: The Special and General Theory. Mineola, NY: Dover Publications.

Flower Ornament Sutra. Chapter 20. Eulogies in the Palace of the Suyama Heaven. Avatamsaka Sutra. Sans rgyas phal po che shes bya ba sintu rgyas pa chen pohi mdo. Toh 44. phal chen ka.

Fremantle F, Trungpa C (1975) The Tibetan Book of the Dead: The Great Liberation through Hearing in the Bardo by Guru Rinpoche according to Karma Lingpa. Boulder, CO: Shambhala.

Giandomenico SL, Mierau SB, Gibbons GM, et al. (2019) Cerebral organoids at the air–liquid interface generate diverse nerve tracts with functional output. Nature Neuroscience 22: 669–679.

Gilmore R (1981) Catastrophe Theory for Scientists and Engineers. Wiley, New York.

Gyel-tsap Dharma Rinchen (1364–1432) A Commentary on Aryadeva's Four Hundred Stanzas on the Middle Way. Translated by Ruth Sonam and Sonam Rinchen. Ithaca, NY: Snow Lion Publications.

Hayward J, and Varela FJ (1992) Gentle Bridges: Dialogues Between the Cognitive Sciences and the Buddhist Tradition. Boston, MA: Shambhala Press.

Hawking S, Tegmark M, Russell S, Wilczek F (2014) Transcending complacency on superintelligent machines. Huffington Post. Accessed from https://www.huffingtonpost.com/stephen-hawking/artificialintelligence_b_5174265.html

Himalayan Art Resources (HAR) (2023) Wheel of Life Schematic. Accessed from https://www.himalayanart.org/pages/wheeloflife2/index.html

Kamalasila (9th century). Stages of Meditation. Bhāvanākrama. Sgom pa'i rim pa. Toh 3915, dbu ma ki.

Kant I (1781) The Critique of Pure Reason. Kritik der reinen Vernunft.

Kurzweil R (2005) The Singularity is Near: When Humans Transcend Biology. Penguin, New York, NY.

Lama Tsongkhapa (1357a–1419). Collected Works of the Incomparable Lord Tsongkhapa Lobsang Drakpa. Kumbum woodblock edition.

Lama Tsongkhapa (1357b–1419) Great Treatise on the Stages of the Path to Enlightenment. Byang chub lam rim chen mo. Collected Works. Vol. pa.[1]

Lama Tsongkhapa (1357c–1419) Elucidation of the Intent: A Thorough Exposition of Entering the Middle Way. Dbu ma la 'jug pa'i rnam bshad dgongs pa rab gsal. Collected Works. Vol. ma, 1–605.

Lama Tsongkhapa (1357d–1419) Golden Rosary of Excellent Utterances: Extensive Exposition of "Ornament of Realization" As Well As Its Commentary (Shes rab kyi pha rol du phyin pa mngon par rtogs pa'i rgyan 'grel pa dang bcas pa rgyas par bshad pa legs bshad gser gyi phreng ba). Collected Works. Vols. tsa and tsha.

Lama Tsongkhapa (1357e–1419) In Praise of the Buddha for His Teaching of Dependent Origination. Ston pa la rten cing 'brel bar byung bar gsungs pa las brtsams te bstod pa legs bshad snying po. Portland, OR: The Foundation for the Preservation of the Mahayana Tradition (FPMT).

[1] Lama Tsongkhapa (1357–1419). Collected Works of the Incomparable Lord Tsongkhapa Lobsang Drakpa. Kumbum woodblock edition.

Maitreya (4th century) Ornament of Realizations. Abhisamayālaṃkāra. Mngon rtogs rgyan. Toh 3786, shes phyin ka.
Maitreya (4th century) Ornament of the Scriptures of the Great Vehicle. Mahayanasutralamkara. Mdo sde rgyan. Toh 4020.
McGinn C (2011) Consciousness as a Form of Matter. In: McGinn C (2011) Basic Structures of Reality: Essays in Meta-Physics Oxford, UK: Oxford University Press.
Nagarjuna (second century). Fundamental Wisdom on the Middle Way. Mūlamadhyamakakārikā. Dbu ma rtsa ba'i tshig le'ur byas pa (Rtsa ba'i shes rab). Toh 3824, dbu ma tsa.
Nagarjuna (second century). Sixty Stanzas of Reasoning. Yuktiṣaṣṭikākārikā. Rigs pa drug cu pa. Toh 3825, dbu ma tsa.
National Institutes of Health (2009) NIH Guidelines for Human Stem Cell Research. Bethesda, MD: National Institutes of Health.
Neuralink (2024) Our mission. Fremont, CA. Accessed from https://neuralink.com/#mission
New York Times (2022) A 'Reversible' Form of Death? Scientists Revive Cells in Dead Pigs' Organs.
Nietzsche, FW (1883) Thus Spoke Zarathustra: A Book for All and None. Leipzig, Germany: Ernst Schmeitzner.
OpenAI (2023) Introducing ChatGPT. San Francisco, CA. Accessed from https://openai.com/blog/chatgpt
Pakkenberg B, Gundersen HJG (1997) Neocortical neuron number in humans: Effect of sex and age. Journal of Comparative Neurology 384: 312–320.
Purves D, Augustine GJ, Fitzpatrick D, Hall WC, LaMantia A-S, White LE (Editors) (2011) Neuroscience (5th edition). Sunderland, MA: Sinauer Associates.
Quadrato G, Nguyen T, Macosko EZ, et al. (2017) Cell diversity and network dynamics in photosensitive human brain organoids. Nature 545: 48–53.
Reardon S (2020) Can lab-grown brains become conscious? Nature. Published on October 27, 2020.
Reuters (2021) Former CDC chief Redfield says he thinks COVID-19 originated in a Chinese lab. Published on March 27, 2021. Accessed from https://www.reuters.com/article/us-health-coronavirus-origin-redfield-idUSKBN2BI2R6.
Reuters (2024). Neuralink's first human patient able to control mouse through thinking, Musk says. Published on February 21, 2024.
Ricard M, Singer W (2018) Beyond the Self: Conversations between Buddhism and Neuroscience. Cambridge, MA: The MIT Press.
Schopenhauer A (1818) Die Welt als Wille und Vorstellung [The World as Will and Representation]. Translated into English by Haldane RB, Kemp J (London UK: Routledge & Kegan Paul, 1883–1886).

Seo SN (2018) Natural and Man-made Catastrophes: Theories, Economics, and Policy Designs. Wiley-Blackwell, Oxford.
Seo SN (2020) Appendix A: A succinct mathematical disproof of the dismal theorem of economics. In: Seo SN , The Economics of Globally Shared and Public Goods. Amsterdam, NL: Academic Press.
Seo SN (2022) The Economics of Pandemics: Exploring Globally Shared Experiences. London, UK: Palgrave Macmillan.
Seo SN (2024a) Buddha, Wisdom and Economics: A Contribution to the Art of Happiness. Cheltenham, UK: Edward Elgar.
Seo SN (2024b) Protecting Nature with Buddha's Wisdom: A Contribution to Environmental and Nature Studies. Cheltenham, UK: Edward Elgar.
Seth A (2021) Being You: A New Science of Consciousness. Boston, MA: Dutton.
Shantarakṣita (9th century). Ornament of the Middle Way. Madhyamakālaṃkāra. Dbu ma rgyan. Toh 3884, dbu ma sa.
Singer W (1999) Neuronal Synchrony: A Versatile Code for the Definition of Relations? Neuron24: 49–65.
Spinoza B (1677) Ethics. In: The Chief Works of Benedict de Spinoza: Volumes 1 and 2 (Kb Classics). Translated from Latin by RHM Elwis in 1883. London, UK: George Bell and Sons.
Stevens CF (1979) The neuron. Scientific American 241: 54–65.
Story F (1971) The Scientific Approach to Buddhism & The Appeal of Buddhism. Bodhi Leaf Publication # 51. Buddhist Publication Society, Kandy, Sri Lanka.
Tegmark M (2015) Consciousness as a state of matter. Chaos, Solitons & Fractals 76: 238–270. arxiv.org/abs/1401.1219
Tesla (2023) AI & Robotics. Tesla, Austin, TX. Accessed from https://www.tesla.com/AI
Thom R (1975) Structural Stability and Morphogenesis. Benjamin-Addison-Wesley, New York.
Trujillo CA, Gao R, Negraes PD, et al. (2019) Complex oscillatory waves emerging from cortical organoids model early human brain network development. Cell Stem Cell 25, 558–569.
United States Department of Interior (USDOI) (2024) Re: U.S. Geological Survey (USGS) Freedom of Information Act (FOIA) Tracking # DOI-USGS-2023-000257 – Response. Washington, DC: US DOI.
Varela FJ, Rosch E, and Thomson E (1992) The Embodied Mind: Cognitive Science and Human Experience. Cambridge, MA: The MIT Press.
Vrselja Z, Daniele SG, Silbereis J, et. al. (2019) Restoration of brain circulation and cellular functions hours post-mortem. Nature 568: 336–343.
Wade N (2024) Where Did Covid Come From? Wall Street Journal. Published on February 28, 2024. Accessed from https://www.wsj.com/articles/where-did-covid-come-from-new-evidence-lab-leak-hypothesis-78be1c39

Walshe R (1972) Buddhist Therapy. Bodhi Leaf Publication # 18, Buddhist Publication Society, Kandy, Sri Lanka.

Weitzman ML (2009) On modeling and interpreting the economics of catastrophic climate change. Review of Economics and Statistics 91: 1–19.

YaleNews (2019) Scientists restore some functions in a pig's brain hours after death. Published on April 17, 2019. https://news.yale.edu/2019/04/17/scientists-restore-some-functions-pigs-brain-hours-after-death

CHAPTER 9

Buddhist Synthesis: Seeing Singularities of Science *Via* All Things Are Mind Only

1 Introduction

This book has addressed the questions of singularities, especially those that arise from the major science experiments and advances in the contemporary world. This chapter, the final chapter of the book, will offer a synthesis of the Buddhist perspectives on the five singularity events explained throughout this book, which will illuminate the intriguing intersections among science, economics, and Buddhist thoughts.

The singularity events described in this book are put forth in the literature and thus selected by the present author across the full range of modern science endeavors: from physics of relativity encompassing the origin of the universe; quantum physics and mechanics that create super intelligence; cell and microbiology; genetics, medicine, and virology; neuroscience and brain science.

The present author was born in the lunar month of February of 1972, which is right after the moon landing by Apollo 11 by the United States in 1969. As such, the remarkable scientific experiments and advances described in this book began to emerge after the present author grew up to be in high teenage years or college years. In the beginning, the present author got to hear about these developments vaguely only from afar, but has since then come ever closer to witness these progresses up-close (Seo 2024a).

S. N. Seo, *The Economics of Singularities of Science Elucidated with Buddhist Thoughts*,
https://doi.org/10.1007/978-3-031-69118-8_9

The atmosphere in which the present author got to be intrigued by these scientific advances and achievements was there quite naturally, looking back upon my life. After the Japanese colonial rule and the Korean War that followed during the first half of the twentieth century, South Korea was one of the poorest nations, if not the poorest, when the present author was born. From a remote rural village, to the capital city Seoul, then on to San Francisco and to New York, the present author quickly moved past the hurdles along the waves of economic and scientific developments. When I landed from the first-ever flight of my life in the United States with an intention to study global climate change economics on July 2, 2000, I was superbly positioned to encounter the scientific endeavors of the modern world because the global climate change research has been at its heart the interdisciplinary dialogues between science and economics (IPCC 1990; Le Treut et al. 2007; Nordhaus 2008). As my study progressed for over 20 years, all fields of science and their endeavors have come very naturally without much hindrance to my thinking and analysis (Seo 2020, 2021, 2022a). The present author does not include the global warming phenomenon as one of the singularity events discussed in this book. The study of global warming economics led me to the inquiry of this book, which was elaborated in Chap. 3 of this book (Weitzman 2009; Lenton et al. 2008).

From another route of life, the present author has been quite curious about the Buddhist way of thinking about the life, universe, death, etc., and how it is comparable or not comparable with the scientific and economic ways of explaining them. Any young Buddhist in fact would have this curiosity quite naturally. Looking back, this curiosity was invoked when I picked up the first book of my whole life at the age of 10 whose title said *Everything is Mind Only*. It was a children's book with many cartoons about Wonhyo of the seventh century, the most influential scholar of all time in Korea (Wonhyo's Mahayana Awakening). At the age of 10? Readers might wonder. There were no bookstores or books when I was growing up in that remote rural village. As such, I could play all day through the mountains, rivers, rice fields, and up in the trees in total enchantment!

This book is in a sense a synthesis of my thoughts regarding Buddhism since I first came across that phrase "Everything is Mind Only." It is one of the most profound teachings given by Buddha Shakyamuni about 2648 years ago (Descent into Lanka Sutra, Ten Grounds Sutra, Tathagathagarbha

Sutra, Flower Ornament Sutra Eulogies).[1] Ever since I read the phrase, it stuck with me through my life and I always wondered what that means. The true meaning of it was extremely elusive to obtain for forty years since then. The present author was able to reach the perfect understanding of this teaching when the jewel treatises of Lama Tsongkhapa dawned in my minds (Lama Tsongkhapa's Stages of the Path, True Eloquence, Golden Rosary).[2]

This final chapter will synthesize all the analyses given in the preceding chapters of the book about the five fields and singularities of science with reliance on the vision of the Minds-only philosophy. The key scientific concept is singularity that was developed in mathematics and Artificial Intelligence (AI) developments (Poincare 1880–1890; Thom 1972, 1975; Kurzweil 2005; Seo 2018). The five experiments are the CERN (European Organization for Nuclear Research) experiments known also as the God particle experiment (Jaffe et al. 2000), the AI and quantum computing development (Hawking et al. 2014), the mRNA virology experiments (Kariko et al. 2011; Pardi et al. 2018), the stem cell research (Thomson et al. 1998; Takahashi and Yamanaka 2006), and the consciousness-generation experiment from neuroscience (Quadrato et al. 2017; Trujillo et al. 2019).

2 The Three Realms Are Mere Minds

Buddha Shakyamuni taught 84,000 Dharma Teachings in accordance with the mental capacities and propensities of his audience, of which the teaching of mind-only is one big basket. The Buddha's intention in giving this teaching was to lead the audience gradually to the truth of emptiness (King of Meditations Sutra, Aksayamati Sutra, Naga King Anavatapta, Two Truths Sutra). That is, all things, internal as well as external, are empty of intrinsic existence. To put differently, all things are devoid of the self; all things are devoid of reality; all things are devoid of truth (Lama Tsongkhapa's True Eloquence, Illuminating the Intent, Thubten Jinpa 2021).

[1] The Buddhist Pali Canon, Tibetan Kangyur and Tengyur, and the Chinese Dazangjing are compiled separately in the Appendix at the end of the book.

[2] Throughout the book, the Buddhist commentaries are cited by an author name and a two-letter short name of the text.

Let me briefly introduce the gist of the mind-only teachings to scientists and economists in this section from the vast collection of Sutras and commentaries in this category (Lama Tsongkhapa's Golden Rosary, Maitreya's Realizations, Asanga's Compendium). This will then serve as a primary principle for interpreting the five science pursuits in the following sections. The list of major treatises and their authors is provided in Table 9.1 below, which also includes the primary scriptural sources.

Be reminded that the present author put forth in Chap. 2 one key verse from the Flower Ornament Sutra which says that the mind is an artist, a creator of all things: "Mind is like an artist, able to paint the worlds. The five clusters all are born thence. There's nothing it doesn't make." The phrase that the present author picked up at the age of 10, which came from the Ten Grounds Sutra, was:

> The three realms are merely mind.

The three realms [kham-sum in Tibetan] is the Buddhist concept of a cosmos, consisting of the desire realm [doe-kham in Tibetan], the form realm [sook-kham in Tibetan], the formless realm [sook-me-kham in Tibetan].[3] It encompasses all the physical worlds, including the subtle ones such as ghosts or gods and formless beings (Vasubandhu's Treasury). It is largely equivalent to the concept of the six realms introduced in Chap. 2 whose emphasis lies in the cyclic nature in the ocean of suffering.

What is the mind [sem-pa in Tibetan, vijnana in Sanskrit] referred to here in this quote? The Descent into Lanka Sutra describes the mind as the heart of the Buddha, that is, Tathagata, whose nature is naturally luminous but always covered by impurities such as gravel, dirt, mud, and dung (Descent into Lanka Sutra):

> Naturally luminous mind
> Is the Tathagata heart.
> …
> The color of gold and the pure gold
> In gravel become visible
> Through cleansing it.

[3] The Tibetan letters of these Tibetan words are compiled in the Appendix: Essential Words of Tibetan Buddhism.

Table 9.1 Major scriptures (Sc) and treatises (Tr) on mind-only philosophy

Date	*Author*	*Titles [English, Sanskrit, Tibetan]*	*Sc or Tr?*
Fourth century CE	Maitreya	[English] Differentiation of the Middle and Extremes [Sanskrit] Madhyantavibhaga [Tibetan] Dbumtha' rnam 'byed	Tr
		Ornament of the Mahayana Sutras Mahayanasstralaṃkara Theg pa chen po mdo sde rgyan	Tr
		Ornament of Realizations Abhisamayāalaṃkara Mngon rtogs rgyan	Tr
		Sublime Continuum Uttaratantra (Ratnagotravibhaga) Rgyud bla ma	Tr
c. Fourth century CE	Asanga	Bodhisattva Grounds Bodhisattvabhumi Byang chub sems dpa'i sa	Tr
		Summary of the Great Vehicle Mahayanasaṃgraha Theg pa chen po bsdus pa	Tr
		Summary of the Explanations of the Levels of Yogic Practice Yogacarabhumiviniscayasaṃgraha Rnam grangs bsdu ba	Tr
		Compendium of Abhidharma Abhidharmasamuccaya Mngon pa kun las btus pa	Tr

(*continued*)

Table 9.1 (continued)

Date	*Author*	*Titles [English, Sanskrit, Tibetan]*	*Sc or Tr?*
c. Fourth century CE	Vasubandhu	Twenty Verses Viṃsatika Nyi shu pa	Tr
Sixth century CE	Sthiramati	Commentary on Differentiation of the Middle and Extremes [Subcommentary] Madhyantavibhangaṭika Dbus mtha' rnam 'byed pa'i 'grel bshad	Tr
		Commentary on the Thirty Verses Triṃsikabhaṣya Sum cu pa'i bshad pa	Tr
Sixth century CE	Dignaga	Synthesis of Valid Cognition Pramaṇasamuccaya Tshad ma kun la btus pa	Tr
Seventh century CE	Dharmakirti	Exposition of Valid Cognition Pramaṇavarttika Tshad ma rnam'grel	Tr
Seventh century CE	Wen Tshig	Commentary on the Samdhinirmocana Sutra Gambhirasaṃdhinirmocanasstraṭika [Great Chinese Commentary]	Tr
?	Damshtrasena	The Long Explanation of the Noble Perfection of Wisdom in One Hundred Thousand, Twenty-Five Thousand, and Eighteen Thousand Lines [Supercommentary] Aryasatasahasrikapancavimsatisahasrikastadasasahasrikaprajnaparamitabrhaṭṭtika phags pa shes rab kyi pha rol tu phyin pa 'bum pa dangnyi khri lnga stong pa dang/ khri brgyad stong pa'i rgya cher bshad pa	Tr
Ninth century CE	Shantaraksita	Ornament of the Middle Way Madhyamakalaṃkara Dbu ma rgyan	Tr

Ninth century CE	Kamalasila	Stages of Meditation Bhavanakrama Sgom pa'i rim pa	Tr
		Light of the Middle Way Madhyamakaloka Dbu ma snang ba	Tr
Fourteenth century CE	Lama Tsongkhapa	Golden Rosary of Excellent Utterances: Extensive Exposition of "Ornament of Realization" As Well as Its Commentary Shes rab kyi pha rol du phyin pa mngon par rtogs pa'i rgyan 'grel pa dang bcas pa rgyas par bshad pa legs bshad gser gyi phreng ba	Tr
	Scripture	Ten Grounds Sutra. (Chapter 31 of the Avataṃsaka Sutra) Dasabhumikasutra Sa bcu pa'i mdo	Sc
		Unraveling the Intent Sutra Saṃdhinirmocanasutra Dgongs pa nges par 'grel pa'i mdo	Sc
		Descent into Lanka Sutra Lankavatarasutra Lang kar gshegs pa'i mdo	Sc
		The Sutra on the Tathagata Essence Tathagatagarbhasutra De-bshin-gśegs-paḥi sñiṅ-po	Sc
		Densely Arrayed Sutra (Chapter 39 of the Avataṃsaka Sutra) Ghanavyuhasutra Rgyan stug-po bkod-pa	Sc

Note: This table is compiled largely based on Lama Tsongkhapa's True Eloquence and Golden Rosary

The heart of the Buddha or the Tathagata heart refers to the Buddha nature. This natural mind is luminous, but also unchanging. Of the three natures that encompass all phenomena, the naturally luminous mind is the ultimate nature (Asanga's Bodhisattva Stages). It is like space where there are no obstructions (Uttaratantra Shastra, Dense Array Sutra, Brunnholzl 2015):

> The luminous nature of the mind
> Is unchanging, just like space.

This natural luminous mind is not the only mind that sentient beings experience. This mind is the "nature" of all phenomena. This natural mind, including fundamental consciousness [za-wae-nam-she in Tibetan] and apperceptive mind [rang-rik in Tibetan] according to the Mind-only philosophy, is tainted by adventitious stains. The adventitious stains are phenomena that sentient beings experience. That is, they can be removed by practice and study since they are adventitious. The adventitious minds are mental imputations according to the Mind-only School, which are approximately mentally constructed objects (Asanga's Bodhisattva Stages, Vasubandhu's Principles). As Maitreya (fourth century) puts it (Mahayana Scripture Ornament):

> It is asserted that mind is always natural luminosity
> And that it is tainted by adventitious stains.
> Apart from the mind that is the nature of phenomena,
> No other mind is proclaimed to be luminous in nature.

What does this philosophy of mind-only [semzam in Tibetan] get to? The central message that the Buddha is attempting his audience to get to is this revolutionary idea which will shock everybody including those who are reading this book right now (Descent into Lanka Sutra):

> The externally apparent does not exist.

The revolutionary, or even perhaps terrifying, conclusion of the mind-only teachings is this, which is what the above quote conveys: There is no external world. The three realms are mere minds (Ten Grounds Sutra). What common people and scientists point to is in fact only the mind's constructions. To put it another way, the object (or the external world) that is distinct from the subject (or the internal world) does not exist.

From another way to clarify this idea put forth by the Mind-only School, the ultimate nature of things [yong-su-drub-pa in Tibetan] is their dependent nature [shen-gyi-wang-gyi-o-o-nyi in Tibetan] devoid of mental fabrications [kun-du-tak-pa or toe-pa in Tibetan], in which there is only the luminous mind (Asanga's Compendium). Asanga, a great charioteer [shing-ta in Tibetan] of the Great Vehicle, elaborates the idea as follows (Asanga's Bodhisattva Stages):

> All the objects that appear as real therein [in a dream], such as the various material forms, voices, odors, tastes, touches, villas, gardens, lands, mountains, and so on, have no real objective being whatsoever. Likewise, in all cases there is only mind.[4]

Asanga clarifies that what scientists as well as ordinary people see and experience are like the objects in a dream [mi-lam-da-wa in Tibetan]. In it, there are material forms, voices, orders, tastes, villas, gardens, lands, mountains, and so on. You know they are not real. They are only the mind's creations and fabrications. There is only that mind. Nonetheless, when you are in a dream, you will see them as real. In that dream, you may also argue without any doubt that there is "I" and there is the external world.

This teaching of mind-only, also that of Buddha Nature, is the supreme way to lead those disciples to liberation who from the beginning of their lives are entrenched in the mental habits of believing in a world, a soul, a god, or other eternal entities. Modern scientists tend to have these tendencies, from which the emergences of the five science experiments clarified in this book can be explained.

This point was elucidated by Middle Way philosophers, most excellently by Lama Tsongkhapa through his numerous treatises. The present author also finds it particularly effective in leading lead scientists to the transcendent wisdom which is emptiness of all things, based on my personal life journeys and encounters mentioned in the above section.

[4] The phrase inside the parentheses is the present author's clarification.

3 Science Singularities

The five singularity events of science were chosen by the present author and described in detail from Chaps. 4 to 8. These singularities were chosen in consideration of the five major scientific endeavors of the twenty-first century: relativity physics, quantum mechanics, medicine/genetics/virology, cell biology, and neuroscience. A singularity event was defined with regard to a specific ongoing experiment for each of these five science disciplines.

Each of the five experiments is not just a scientific curiosity of an individual researcher or a group of researchers. Countries with financial means and advanced science are heavily investing their resources in each of these pursuits as a national priority. These experiments are considered a matter of grave importance to the nation for many reasons including military dominance, scientific competitiveness, and business opportunities, among other things.

For each experiment, the scale of investments is far beyond an individual researcher's means. The Large Hadron Collider (LHC) built by the CERN is estimated to have cost US $5 billion for the ten-year period of its construction. It also cost about US $1.5 billion for just one run of the LHC. The scale of it is a 27 km long ring of superconducting magnets. It has nearly 10,000 superconducting magnets and produces 1 billion collisions "per second" (CERN 2023).

The LHC experiment is the most advanced experiment of the Big Bang theory of the universe which was originated from the relativity theory of physics (Einstein 1915a, 1915b; Lemaître 1931). It aimed to find the God particle but more generally purports to examine the initial stages of the universe after its creation (Jaffe et al. 2000).

It is noted that there is still yet no functioning quantum computer in the world. The competition for the development of a quantum computer, however, is heating up among the world's major information companies. According to a recent list, the leaders are the IBM (International Business Machines) Corporation with its Quantum System Two with its chip called Heron and the qubit quantum processor called Condor; Google Quantum AI with its computer called Sycamore; the Amazon's Braket; Microsoft Azure; the Intel with its 12-qubit silicon chip named Tunnel Falls. Other competitors include D-Wave, Quantinuum, Rigetti, Xanadu, and Atos Quantum (Forbes 2023).

The search for a functioning quantum computer can be viewed in association with the other AI (Artificial Intelligence) technologies and associated risks. The present author introduced three types of AI robots: AI the humanoid (e.g., Pepper or Optimus), AI information machine often called a chatbot such as ChatGPT, AI-based LAWS (Lethal and Autonomous Weapons System) (Softbank 2019; OpenAI 2023; WP 2023).

The medical virological research is of high priority for the governments around the world, as has been exposed with the outbreak of COVID-19 (Corona Virus Disease-2019) pandemic (WHO 2021). The US Federal agencies such as the National Institutes of Health (NIH) and the National Institute of Allergy and Infectious Diseases (NIAID) publicly fund a variety of virology researches intensely pursued in selected universities and laboratories, while there is also a national research by China, for example, at the Wuhan Institute of Virology (Seo 2022a). The specifics of these researches, their funding, and involved researchers are often classified as national secrets, and therefore not available to the public.

Big pharmaceutical companies are major players in the virus and vaccine research. Pfizer, Moderna, and AstraZeneca were the first to develop the novel mRNA (Messenger Ribonucleic) vaccines and the traditional vaccines at record time during the COVID-19 pandemic, specifically in only 10 months from the pandemic declaration (Azar II 2020).

Stem cell research is actively pursued by numerous governments, in addition to private researchers in universities and laboratories. In fact, nations compete intensely to recruit the scientists who are reporting to have a success. The US government does not restrict stem cell research in most cases. According to the NIH (National Institutes of Health) guideline published in 2009, it allows most research activities regarding the stem cell, except some cases of embryonic stem cells (NIH 2009). More concretely, it allows stem cell research obtained from bone marrow and other sources while it also allows some types of stem cell research using embryonic stem cells (Thomson et al. 1998; Takahashi and Yamanaka 2006).

This fervor on stem cell research is driven by the possibility that human bodily organs can be grown from the stem cells extracted as such from human bodies. This means that sick body organs can be replaced, offering big health benefits to people. Even the too old body organs can be replaced through such processes, offering people with financial means the opportunity to keep getting young and fresh body organs (Alison et al. 2002).

Extending this logic, it is not difficult to imagine that a human cloning technology will be super actively pursued by people of means. Animal cloning has succeeded repeatedly since the first sheep cloning named Dolly (Campbell et al. 1996). To the people of means, a human cloning technology offers them an opportunity to live "forever" by cloning themselves over and over again. It offers them a possibility to have children without going through the traditional child-bearing process like a marriage, conception, and pregnancy. It also offers them a possibility that millions of warriors are created in a laboratory in a short period of time, like Captain America in the Hollywood film (President Council 2002).

The neuroscience research directed at the generation of human consciousness from pure matter is at a primitive stage as of now (Tegmark 2015; Quadrato et al. 2017; Trujillo et al. 2019; Giandomenico et al. 2019; Reardon 2020). It has gained the attention of keen observers of this area in the recent decade through such experiments as reviving a dead pig's brain functions (Vrselja et al. 2019; YaleNews 2019). It has also gained attention of some observers through such claims made by related researchers that the quantum computing, if realized, can greatly increase the possibility of creating a consciousness out of a certain matter (Hawking et al. 2014; Ananthaswamy 2021; NYT 2023a).

For the neuroscientists, consciousness is a matter of the size of the brains or the number of neurons in the brain, namely, the brain cells (Singer 1999; Tegmark 2015). A human being has the most complicated brain of all beings in the human and animal realms; monkeys have a much smaller brain than humans; birds have an even smaller brain than monkeys; snails have an even smaller brain than birds; and mosquitoes have an even smaller brain than snails. All of these beings, however, are conscious, that is, have consciousness. Having quantified the differences among animals according to their brain sizes, generating consciousness out of matter may not appear to be a big problem to scientists. It might be imagined by these researchers that it is just like creating the brain of a snail! At the heart of their pursuit is the belief that the brain functions can be explained as a somewhat complicated set of chemical interactions in the brain, that is, the neuronal connections.

4 Singularities Economics

As far as economic science is concerned, there are two types of economic analyses regarding the five singularities and associated experiments explained in this book. The first is a new economy approach. The other is a catastrophe approach. There are the economic analyses that blend these approaches.

An example of the new economy approach is found in the bitcoin (and other cryptocurrency) economics, among other fields (Bohme et al. 2015; Seo 2019). The bitcoins arose from the advances in artificial intelligence, specifically the Internet technology and the blockchain technology (Nakamoto 2008). In many countries, bitcoins overwhelmed their national economies until right before the COVID-19 outbreak. The value of a single coin which began at zero topped US $100,000 in some cases. Some countries also regulated or banned the bitcoin and other cryptocurrency trade, for example, India and China.

The bitcoin economy is only one of the financial revolutions that are taking place in reliance on AI technologies. A large basket of newly emerging financial assets, including options, derivatives, etc., are made possible through AI technologies (Shiller 2004).

The advances in the AI-based economy take on two types. One is the humanoid robotics such as SoftBank's Pepper and Tesla's Optimus (SoftBank 2019; Tesla 2023). The other is the information machine, the prime example of which is ChatGPT (Chat Generative Pre-trained Transformer), which is a pre-trained chatbot (OpenAI 2023).

The second type of singularities economics is a catastrophe economics. An example of the second type of research is the catastrophe economics from which researchers derive the conclusion that strong regulations and limitations must be placed to prevent a truly catastrophic irreversible event, that is, a singularity event. The rationale for these regulations is expressed as a precautionary principle by economists (Weitzman 2009; Seo 2018, 2020).

The catastrophe economics with its precautionary principle is applicable to each of the five singularities described in this book. A singularity by definition is a truly catastrophic and irreversible event which is described by some economists as "the end of all civilizations on the planet as we know them." Such possibilities were elaborated by the concerned scientists themselves in the corresponding fields, for example, the CERN experiment's possibility of creating a dark matter, the AI's overpowering of human intelligence (Jaffe et al. 2000; Kurzweil 2005; Hawking et al. 2014).

At the heart of catastrophe economics is the rule known as the fat-tail probability distribution (Schuster 1984). What it says is that the probability of such a catastrophic event, that is, a singularity, if it indeed took on the fat-tail distribution, cannot be reduced by human efforts and resources, however large they may be (Weitzman 2009). If they can be reduced, the probability distribution takes the form of a normal distribution which is known as a medium-tail distribution. Nonetheless, the fat-tail distribution of a catastrophic event does not always justify the precautionary principle in policymaking if there are a large range of people's behavioral change options as well as technological options to deal with the problem under consideration (Seo 2020, 2021).

The third type of approach, a blending of both new economy and high risk, is found in the present author's analysis on the COVID-19 pandemic (Seo 2022a). It deals with the high-risk nature of mRNA research as well as the new economy nature of the mRNA vaccines and virology research (Pardi et al. 2018; Reuters 2021; Nobel Prize 2023). Further, it addresses the baskets of behavioral and policy actions through the analyses of the pandemic. The book details the behavioral options of individuals, the portfolio of governmental actions, the set of international organization's actions during the pandemic.

5 Seeing Science Singularities Through Buddha's Transcendent Wisdom

Since I picked up that children's book at the age of 10 mentioned in the beginning of this chapter, I always wondered what that short phrase really means. During the 40 years since then, I came across many Buddhist teachers and writings while I was journeying through South Korea, the United States, Latin America, Africa, Europe, Oceania, South Asia, and Central Asia with one research project or another at hand. Looking back upon them, it was a mightily confusing experience largely because there are many traditions and divisions among Buddhism, as such, many conflicting interpretations. It appeared that there is no answer that can satisfy any Buddhist.

In my previous book entitled *Buddha, Wisdom and Economics*, I told my audience that I am Lama Tsongkhapa reborn in this life after six hundred years of utter peace (Seo 2024a). Following up with that revelation, I also revealed in the book entitled *Protecting Nature with Buddha's Wisdom* how I attained the certainty on that discovery through the eleven unimaginable meetings with Lama Tsongkhapa during the seven-year period from 2017 to 2023 (Seo 2024b). Let me clarify this further. Each of those meetings was not a brief encounter but rather a carefully planned transmission of knowledge. To be specific, he gave detailed instructions to me on each of his three most profound treatises and one subsidiary treatise. Each instruction was as detailed as a book-length exposition. In addition, he gave a pithy instruction on each of his three perfect treatises for which he is renowned to the Buddhists all over the world. Through these personal and direct transmissions alone during the seven-year period, I was able to return to the profundity and perfection of Lama Tsongkhapa who is reputed as Vajradhara Buddha, which was his intention. This book is one of the fruits of my inconceivable encounters with Je Rinpoche.

Founded on the Lama Tsongkhapa's transcendent wisdom [*prajanaparamita* in Sanskrit], the five singularities dealt with in this book can be interpreted in a remarkable fashion. The transcendent wisdom does not mean that there is another place or time beyond the one that we are experiencing at the present moment, which the present author often emphasizes to non-Buddhist readers including economists and scientists. The transcendent wisdom means *sherab-gyi-pa-rol-tu-chin-pa* in Tibetan, which is a lucid translation of *prajanaparamita* in Sanskrit (Heart Sutra; Perfection of Wisdom in 700 Lines). What it means in English is the wisdom that carries one from this shore of suffering to the other shore of happiness.

What is that transcendent wisdom? Buddha Shakyamuni taught a wide array of wisdoms, explained in what is known as the 84,000 Dharma Teachings arisen from compassion, in order to liberate sentient beings from their suffering, each and every one of them (Nagarjuna's Bodhicitta Commentary, Shantideva's Bodhisatta Way, Vimalakirti Sutra). Lama Tsongkhapa synthesizes the 84,000 Dharma Teachings flawlessly into the Stages of the Path to Enlightenment, known as the Lamrim in Tibetan, encompassing the different mental capacities and propensities of individual practitioners (Atisha's Lamp, Lama Tsongkhapa's Stages of the Path, Cutler and Newland 2000). What this means is that there are many wisdoms in Buddhism, each of which is intended to be applied to a certain group of individuals with a certain set of mental proclivity or illness.

To give rough ideas to the audience pulled from the top of my head: Four Noble Truths, Eightfold Paths, going for refuges, the self, cause and effect, causes and conditions, karma and consequences, selflessness, six senses, five aggregates, mindfulness, insight, cycle of existence, rebirth, Nirvana, six realms of existence, three poisonous minds, affliction, ignorance, dependent origination of the twelve factors, dependent designation, Great Vehicle, Middle Way avoiding two extremes, a field of merit, moral precepts, Mind-only, fundamental consciousness, subject-object nonduality, Buddha Nature, six paramitas (paramita of giving, morality, patience, effort, concentration, wisdom), bodhicitta, compassion, emptiness, intrinsic existence, valid cognition, rational analysis, social convention, truthlessness, deceptiveness of all phenomena, falsity, realitylessness, three natures, two truths, mantra, mandala, and so on (Lama Tsongkhapa's True Eloquence, Stages of the Path).

From the perfect wisdom of the Buddha and Je Tsongkhapa, the five singularities can be given a Buddhist interpretation, which is the goal of this book. First, let us start with the CERN experiment or the God particle experiment. The objective of these experiments is a discovery of the initial states of the Universe assuming that Big Bang caused the universe to exist. In the Buddha's omniscient wisdom, the universe does not begin at some point. It is beginningless and endless. Further, the universe is not a single entity. There are trillions and trillions of universes out there (Flower Ornament Sutra (Ten Abodes, Incalculable), Vasubandhu's Abhidharmakosa, Aryamanjusrimulakalpa).

In this sense, the scientists' pursuits to reveal the very first point of the universe are therefore misguided. It arises from the delusion that the universe must have begun from somewhere or from something. Underneath of such a belief is the addiction to the idea that there is something that is concrete and absolutely existing (Lama Tsongkhapa's Illuminating the Intent, Chandrakirti's Middle Way).

To put this in a context that scientists may find it easier to understand, the creator of the entire universe is the mind only. The mind creates it and human beings perceive it in the way that the mind has created it (Ten Grounds Sutra, Descent into Lanka Sutra). This means that however hard scientists may try to find the very first point in time or the very first creator or the very first particle, they are guaranteed to fail to find it.

This comment is made on the understanding that such physics experiments are meaningful at another level. They are trying to understand better the states and status of physical phenomena surrounding the sentient beings, which is the solid foundation of reality of people and scientists (Perfection of Wisdom in 700 Lines, Manjushri Play Sutra). Therefore, from the Buddhist perspective, it can be understood as one of the intellectual efforts to better understand the states of phenomena, that is, physics of them. Put it another way, these efforts can be made, without so much attached and plunged to the idea of "the very beginning" of the things or "the very end" of the things or "the very first creator."

Second, for the AI singularity, including quantum mechanics. The developments of a humanoid robot such as Pepper or Optimus GenZ indicate that humanoid robots will soon be a significant part of the planet's community in the coming decades. Further, non-humanoid AIs such as the ChatGPT will start to overwhelm the human community, as the recent New York Times lawsuit against the ChatGPT signals (NYT 2023b).

As long as the AI robots are kept as a service provider to human beings where humans have control over them, they can provide valuable services to the planet community. However, such a human control presumption will be tested and easily proven untrue in the face of human emotions and struggles among them. When the three poisonous minds of desire, hatred, and ignorance overwhelm human societies, for example, these service robots can easily turn into, to give somewhat extreme examples, lethal autonomous weapons deployed in the wars (Dhammapada, Sutta Nipata). You can easily see the early stages of the misuses of AI robots in the ongoing war between Russia and Ukraine in Europe, another between Israel and Hamas in the Middle East.

The more pernicious AI humanoid will arise from the information AI robots such as the ChatGPT-type or the Wikipedia-type or the social network-type technologies (OpenAI 2023; Wikipedia 2024). Despite their positive functions in society, they can be a carrier of misinformation, commonly referred to as fake news, which spreads like wildfire. However, it is also notable that these technologies embed a human control device. For the ChatGPT, it is a trained machine based on the existing information. For the Wikipedia-type, opposing sides may keep correcting other views endlessly: there is freedom of editing. There are also similar control devices in the social networking sites, but the fake information can spread far more easily owing to the short communications exchanged immediately across individuals.

The AI singularity that was the main concern of scientists such as Stephen Hawking is that super-intelligent robots will soon surpass the human brain capacity, and thereby start to dominate humans in mental activities (Hawking et al. 2014). In many cases, robots have already surpassed human brain capacities in performing specific functions, for example, calculations, mental games, and likely investing money.

Faced with the grave challenge of AI often expressed as the irreversible end of humankind, scientists do not seem to be able to offer any strategy or way forward, as far as the present author can tell (Kurzweil 2005). As far as the present author can see through, this is where the transcendent wisdom of the Buddhists is particularly illuminating. How so? You would be quite intrigued. Let me explain.

First of all, the nature of the information that is the object of the aforementioned information technologies is the gross information, by which I mean a packaged information set. It is like a medicine tablet, which is easily consumed by an individual, which is carried through the Internet among the individuals. From the Buddhist point of view, the information that a human being handles is subtle information which is mediated through subtle emotions (Maha-nidana Sutta, Mother Scripture, King of Meditations). Therefore, there is much more to it than the packaged set carried by the AI.

At a deeper level of understanding, this is where the Mind-only philosophy comes to be a meaningful platform for the society's AI dialogues. The information that are created in the AI technologies and carried across individuals are someone's mental creations only. In reality, the truth does not exist as it is depicted and carried around through the AI technologies (Descent into Lanka Sutra, Asanga's Compendium, Bodhisattva Stages). I am sure readers will need some time to process what I am saying here.

Third, the mRNA virology, genetics, and medicine. The recent experience of the global COVID-19 pandemic during the 2020–2023 period shows that the mRNA virus can be highly infectious: in a matter of months, it can spread from one region to another and to the globe (JHU 2020). In a single day, it can spread to millions of individuals in populous countries such as India, China, and the USA. It can kill a large fraction of those infected, especially the old and those with preexisting conditions (Polyakova et al. 2021).

The COVID-19 pandemic was not the first time that humankind suffered such a worldwide pandemic. A global pandemic has been a significant part of human existence on this planet (Potter 2001; Weiss 2020). As such, the pursuits of the viruses and other pathogens and the effective treatments against them by medical scientists and virologists are hardly extraordinary or irrational. The virologists have also shown that they are capable of producing an effective vaccine against such an exceedingly infectious disease which can be administered in a safe way (Schwartz 2001; Plotkin 2009).

The singularity concern may arise when such a highly infectious and lethal virus as the novel coronavirus is allowed by the governments to be manufactured in a laboratory. The so-called gain-of-function research, which was pointed out by some scientists as a possible origin of the novel coronavirus, might have been one of those virus-creating laboratory experiments (Reuters 2021; Wade 2021; USDOI 2024). The possibility of a leak of the lethal virus thus created by a human accident or a machine accident can be reduced but only to some degree.

As the Buddha's tale of "The Observations at the Four Gates" tells, he gave up a royal life and became a renunciant seeing the severely ill at one gate and the dead at another gate (Buddha Carita, Display in Full Sutra). In his sermon on the Truth of Suffering, sickness is one of the fundamental human sufferings, old-age is another, death is another, and birth is another (Setting the Wheel of Dharma in Motion Sutra). He taught that the cessation of suffering is what all human beings, indeed all sentient beings, wish for (Walpola Rahula 1974; Watanabe 2005, Magga-vibhanga Sutta, Maha-nidana Sutta).

Virology, vaccinology, and medicine is only one of the endeavors that the human society makes in order to end the suffering of sickness and death. Buddhists can acknowledge that endeavor while making it clear that the Buddha saw the end of suffering in a starkly different way. The end of suffering of sentient beings, which is all bodhisattvas strive for, is the extinguishment of the three poisonous minds: desire, hatred, and ignorance [duk-sum, doe-chak, she-dang, ti-muk in Tibetan] (Lama Tsongkhapa's Stages of the Path, Vimalakirti Sutra, Lotus Sutra). Why should the Buddha and Je Rinpoche have to say in this way? It will be puzzling to non-Buddhists including medical scientists and virologists to hear that all diseases arise from the mind, that is, the three mental poisons. From the toxins of the uncontrolled and deluded minds arise the numerous diseases of living beings, which scientists are striving to find cures for, from which they suffer through the cycle of existence (Lotus Sutra, King of Meditations Sutra).

Fourth, stem cell research and human cloning. Like the mRNA virus research, it can be said that stem cell research arises from the natural and rational human reaction to address the basic human conditions of illness and death (Alison et al. 2002; Atala et al. 2019). Its motivation is nothing extraordinary or dangerous or aberrational.

It is not difficult for ordinary people to figure out why the stem cell researchers first began their pursuits from the embryonic stem cells (Thomson et al. 1998). For those who hoped to "grow" and manufacture a particular human organ from a source material, it would have been "rational" to go to the embryos obtainable from the mothers. This has turned out to pose ethical dilemmas for many societies and governments because a human can create another human being or bodily organs of another human being (President Council 2002).

To put it another way, the embryonic stem cell research puts the society in a position to choose between the medical benefits of the research and the ethical problem of utilizing an embryo which is developing into another human being (NIH 2009).

If stem cell researches were conducted with the non-embryonic stem cells such as bone marrow cells or amniotic fluid or umbilical cord blood of a pregnant mother, ordinary people would not object to growing a human organ from such sources since thus manufactured organs can then be replanted into a sick person or even a dying person (Takahashi and Yamanaka 2006; NIH 2009). In addition, this is similar to many other medical researches and experiments that are routinely performed today. From the Buddhist perspective, the benefits of such medical sciences can be acknowledged (Nobel Prize 2012). However, the non-embryonic stem cells are not pluripotent while embryonic stem cells are, which limits the usefulness of the former (Takahashi and Yamanaka 2006).

What concerns people as pertinent to the concept of a singularity is that stem cell research is a human cloning exercise. From the embryonic stem cells taken from a source, a human being can be cloned at another time, for example, at the time when the original faces death. This procedure may be also coupled with the in vitro fertilization procedure (KHOU 2024). In theory, many clones can be made from a single person of origin. They all can share the physical and mental capacity, that is, the physical and mental capacity that originates from the original.

From the Buddhist perspective, a question arises regarding whether all the clones of the original will recognize each other as the same human being, that is, the same person. Although they will all experience different life's events as per their individual experiences, they will likely feel the others as if they were a "twin" from the same mother. In this case, they are like multiplets. Will they go even further to develop the "conscious" thought that they are all one and the same person? That is also highly likely. This is despite the Buddhist exposition that the consciousness of each person originates from the consciousness of their previous life (Paticca-samuppada Sutta, Nagarjuna's Fundamental Wisdom, Lama Tsongkhapa's Stages).

This consideration leads us to a tentative conclusion that stem cell research, while it offers many medical benefits, also poses a high risk to the human civilization and beyond when it is directed to a cloning science owing to various reasons. The core of that risk is a "consciousness risk." The consciousness risk that people will feel when the world of clones arrives will take the form of identity crisis about themselves as well as others, but much more than that.

From another line of thoughts, it should be noted that the clones may even be produced for military purposes; the clones may even be produced for any other corrupt purposes of the rich or the powerful. Albeit looking far-fetched, this may indeed resemble the spiking of military drone productions worldwide in the ongoing wars as of today. When the world of clones arrives, there will be a great disruption to the human society, without doubt.

Therefore, stem cell research's advancing calls for, from the Buddhist perspective, a series of wise decisions at the humanity level. Many of these decisions are, as outlined above, also questions of what are possible and what are not scientifically. At the same time, it draws people's attention to a disruptive and often chaotic nature of human endeavors even if seemingly well-intended.

Fifth, neuroscience's pursuit of consciousness. Brain science began as a study of the human brain as a physical object. Since then, it established that the basic unit of mental functions is a neuron and their functions are explained by neuronal connections (Stevens 1979; Purves et al. 2011). The structure of a neuron was presented, as drawn in Chap. 8. At the time of growth as a child, the number of neurons increases rapidly and exponentially, say, millions of neurons per month, to reach the maximum in their 20s. Thenceforth, the number of neurons declines. The maximum number of neurons may reach 100 billion and the neuronal connections may reach 60 trillion (Pakkenberg and Gundersen 1997).

The pursuit of consciousness is this: Neuroscientists are pursuing the question of how sentient beings become conscious and at what point in time (Singer 1999). Does consciousness come from another being like a creator God? Or is it a natural process that gives a sentient being its consciousness? Can it be created in a laboratory through a scientific process which manipulates the neurons and neuronal connections? These are some of the questions they tackle.

From the Buddhist perspective, the consciousness creation research by neuroscientists is redundant (Tegmark 2015; Quadrato et al. 2017; Giandomenico et al. 2019). That is, consciousness is created every second on this planet. To put it more correctly, a conscious being is created millions of times every second on this planet: Humans and other sentient animals are being born every second, who are all conscious. To cite Aryadeva the Son of the Middle Way (Aryadeva's Four Hundred), "The seed of worldly existence is a consciousness; Objects are its sphere of activity." To cite Buddha Shakyamuni (Dhammapada), "Every sentient being has the mind in the lead, in the forefront, and is made by the mind." Why would the scientists bother to create a mind possessor at all when such a process is in the nature and more than abundantly so?

If the neuroscientists answered that they are doing this for the revival of a dead brain of a person (Vrselja et al. 2019; Andrijevic et al. 2022), for example, from an accident or through a war, then from the Buddhist standpoint they are deluded in the nature of beings. Why? Readers might ask. The consciousness of a person never disappears on this planet or beyond this universe. It leaves the body in this life and gets the body in another life (Tibetan Book of the Dead (Fremantle and Trungpa 1975), Milarepa's Songs). So, the scientists may be able to restore some of the mental functions of the disabled brain, but the effort to create consciousness itself is a completely different endeavor. As Je Rinpoche quotes the following in his Stages of the Path treatise (King of Meditations Sutra):

> Herein there is neither birth nor death.
>
> ---
>
> There is no one who dies in this world
> And passes or migrates to another.

6 An End of a Personal Journey in Minds-Only

For a grand closure of this book, let me give another elucidation of the core philosophy of this book which is in the title of this chapter: All things are mind only [*semzam* in Tibetan]. Here all things encompass all internal as well as external phenomena, or put differently, all mental as well as all material phenomena, without any exclusion.

What does this mean really? Having completed your reading of the book, have you now figured out the true meaning of this phrase? I am sure you are still puzzled or have qualms about it even if you have gained some insights through this book. That is understandable. As long as you hold on to the material world or the external world as the reality or the truth out there that you are looking for, the puzzlement will never end. Neither do your misgivings. Your bewilderment will keep increasing, not decreasing, through your heroic pursuits of the "truth."

Why is that? You would inquire. This is because, in the true nature of things, there is no consciousness, no objects of consciousness, no possessor of consciousness. Put it another way, there is no mind, no objects of mind, and no possessor of mind (Buddhapalita's Commentary, Chandrakirti's Clear Words, Entering the Middle Way). As Je Rinpoche summarizes it in his commentary on the Fundamental Treatise, there is no seer; there is no seen; there is no seeing (Lama Tsongkhapa's Ocean of Reasoning, Nagarjuna's Fundamental Wisdom, Sixty Stanzas, Seventy Stanzas).

The core teaching of the enlightened wisdom is that your mind creates all the things that you are seeing and experiencing, by which in turn you are tormented conditioned by afflictive ignorance. That ignorance is the belief that what you see is what is true (Lama Tsongkhapa's True Eloquence).

Buddha Shakyamuni, revered as the Teacher of all Gods and Humans, gave a vast number of instructions to his followers with an intention to liberate each and every listener from the ocean of suffering. The 84,000 Dharma Teachings, as such Shakyamuni's teachings are renowned, were synthesized by Je Rinpoche into the Lam-rim-chen-mo as the Stages of the Path to Enlightenment as the graduated path for those who seek liberation and perfect enlightenment (Lama Tsongkhapa's Stages of the Path, Songs, Cutler and Newland 2000).

Of the Lam-rim synthesis and the 84,000 Dharma Teachings, the mind-only teaching was the first ever Buddhist teaching that the present author encountered at the age of 10, which was perhaps purely by chance. At the age of 50, the present author came to fully realize the meaning of it after 40 years of journey. At the heart of that realization is that the mind-only philosophy is superbly delivered for the sake of those who are strongly attached to the external phenomena or the material phenomena or the reality of things, like scientists and economists (Maitreya's Realizations, Middle and Extremes, Asanga's Bodhisattva Stages, Shantaraksita's Ornament, Kamalasila's Stages, Lama Tsongkhapa's Golden Rosary). In turn, that is the reason why this philosophical tenet is still an excellent way for elucidating the scientific endeavors of the modern world as complicated as the origin of the universe, artificial intelligence, mRNA virus, stem cells, and neurons. In the pithiest way stated, the mere minds are thus (Flower Ornament Sutra (Chapter 20, Avatamsaka Sutra)):

Mind is like an artist,
Able to paint the worlds:
The five clusters all are born thence;
There's nothing it doesn't make.
...
If people know the actions of mind
Create all the worlds,
They will see the Buddha
And understand Buddha's true nature.

My journey that began at the age of 10 for the search of the true meaning of "All things are mind-only" is concluded and then thus reported.

Written by Gaden Je on June 30, 2024
At Lamajel Ling

References

Alison MR, Poulsom R, Forbes S, and Wright NA (2002) An introduction to stem cells. The Journal of Pathology 197 (Special Issue on Stem Cells): 419–423.

Ananthaswamy A (2021) AI Designs Quantum Physics Experiments beyond What Any Human Has Conceived. Scientific American. Accessed from https://www.scientificamerican.com/article/ai-designs-quantum-physics-experiments-beyond-what-any-human-has-conceived/

Andrijevic D, Vrselja Z, Lysyy T, et al. (2022) Cellular recovery after prolonged warm ischaemia of the whole body. Nature 608: 405–412.

Aryadeva (2nd century). Four Hundred Stanzas. Catuḥśatakaśāstra. Bstan bcos bzhi brgya pa. Toh 3846, dbu ma tsha.[5]

Asanga (ca. 4th century). Compendium of the Universal Vehicle. Mahāyānasaṃgraha. Theg pa chen po bsdus pa. Toh 4048, sems tsam ri.

Asanga (ca. 4th century) Stages of the Bodhisattva. Bodhisattvabhumi. Byang chub sems dpa'i sa. Toh 4037. sems tsam wi.

Atala A, Lanza R, Mikos AG, and Nerem R (eds.) (2019) Principles of Regenerative Medicine (3rd Edition). Amsterdam, NL: Academic Press.

Atisha Dipankara Srijnana (982–1054). Bodhipathapradīpa. A Lamp for the Path to Enlightenment. Byang chub lam gyi sgron ma.

Azar II AM (2020) How Operation Warp Speed delivered a COVID Vaccine in Record Time. *Fox News.* Published on December 12. https://www.foxnews.com/opinion/hhs-azar-operation-warp-speed-covid-vaccine-record-time.

[5] Toh means Tohoku University Catalogue. Tohoku University (ed.) (1934). A Complete Catalogue of the Tibetan Buddhist Canons, Sde-dge Edition, Tohoku University, Japan.

Böhme R, Christin N, Edelman B, Moore T (2015) Bitcoin: economics, technology, and governance. J Econ Perspect 29:213–238

Brunnholzl K (2015) When the Clouds Part: The Uttaratantra and Its Meditative Tradition as a Bridge between Sutra and Tantra. Ithaca, NY: Snow Lion Publication.

Buddhapalita (ca. 5th century). Commentary. Buddhapālitamūlamadhyamakavṛtti. Dbu ma rtsa ba'i 'grel pa buddha pā li ta. Toh 3842, dbu ma tsa.

Campbell KH, McWhir J, Ritchie WA, and Wilmut I (1996) Sheep cloned by nuclear transfer from a cultured cell line. Nature. 380 (6569): 64–6.

Candrakirti (7th century). Clear Words. Mulamadhyamakavrttiprasannapada. dBu ma tsal 'bai grel pa tshig gsal. Toh 3860.

Candrakirti (7th century). Entering the Middle Way. Madhyamakāvatāra. Dbu ma la 'jug pa. Toh 3861, dbu ma'a.

Cutler JWC, Newland G (trans.) (2000) The Great Treatise on the Stages of the Path to Enlightenment by Tsongkhapa. Ithaca, NY: Snow Lion Publications.

Einstein A (1915a) On the general theory of relativity. Submitted to Prussian Academy of Science.

Einstein A (1915b) The field equations of gravitation. Submitted to Prussian Academy of Science.

European Organization for Nuclear Research (CERN) (2023) Facts and figures about the LHC. The CERN, Geneva, CH. Accessed from https://home.web.cern.ch/resources/faqs/facts-and-figures-about-lhc

Flower Ornament Sutra. Chapter 15. Ten Abodes. Avatamsaka Sutra. Sans rgyas phal po che shes bya ba sintu rgyas pa chen pohi mdo. Toh 44. Phal chen ka.

Flower Ornament Sutra. Chapter 20. Eulogies in the Palace of the Suyama Heaven. Avatamsaka Sutra. Sans rgyas phal po che shes bya ba sintu rgyas pa chen pohi mdo. Toh 44. Phal chen ka.

Flower Ornament Sutra. Chapter 30. The Incalculable. Avatamsaka Sutra. Sans rgyas phal po che shes bya ba sintu rgyas pa chen pohi mdo. Toh 44. Phal chen ka.

Forbes Magazine (2023) Top 10 Quantum Computing Companies Making Change. Published on December 11, 2023. Accessed from https://www.forbes.com/sites/technology/article/top-quantum-computing-companies/?sh=c1980463a941

Fremantle F, Trungpa C (1975) The Tibetan Book of the Dead: The Great Liberation through Hearing in the Bardo by Guru Rinpoche according to Karma Lingpa. Boulder, CO: Shambhala.

Giandomenico SL, Mierau SB, Gibbons GM, Wenger LMD, Masullo L, Sit T, Sutcliffe M, Boulanger J, Tripodi M, Derivery E, Paulsen O, Lakatos A, and Lancaster MA (2019) Cerebral organoids at the air–liquid interface generate diverse nerve tracts with functional output. Nature Neuroscience 22: 669–679.

Hawking S, Tegmark M, Russell S, Wilczek F (2014) Transcending complacency on superintelligent machines. Huffington Post. Accessed from https://www.huffingtonpost.com/stephen-hawking/artificial-intelligence_b_5174265.html

Intergovernmental Panel on Climate Change (IPCC) (1990) Climate Change: The IPCC Scientific Assessment. Cambridge University Press, Cambridge.

Jaffe RL, Buszaa W, Sandweiss J, Wilczek F (2000) Review of speculative disaster scenarios at RHIC. Review of Modern Physics 72: 1125–1140.

Johns Hopkins University (JHU) (2020) COVID-19 Dash Board. JHU, Baltimore, M.D.: JHU. https://data.humdata.org/dataset/novel-coronavirus-2019-ncov-cases.

Kamalasila (9th century). Stages of Meditation. Bhāvanākrama. Sgom pa'i rim pa. Toh 3915, dbu ma ki.

Kariko K, Muramatsu H, Ludwig J, and Weissman D (2011) Generating the Optimal mRNA for Therapy: HPLC Purification Eliminates Immune Activation and Improves Translation for Nucleoside-modified. Protein-encoding mRNA. Nucleic Acids Research 39: e142.

KHOU 11 (2024) Gov. Abbott shares stance on IVF treatment in wake of Alabama ruling. Accessed from https://www.khou.com/article/news/politics/abott-ivf-treatment-alabama-supreme-court-ruling/285-00caf856-a049-4989-b1bc-87e67de797c4

Kurzweil R (2005) The Singularity is Near: When Humans Transcend Biology. Penguin, New York, NY.

Lama Tsongkhapa (1357a–1419) Collected Works of the Incomparable Lord Tsongkhapa Lobsang Drakpa. Kumbum woodblock edition.[6]

Lama Tsongkhapa (1357b–1419) Great Treatise on the Stages of the Path to Enlightenment. Byang chub lam rim chen mo. Collected Works. Vol. pa.[7]

Lama Tsongkhapa (1357c–1419) Ocean of Reasoning: An Exposition of Treatise on the Middle Way. Rtsa ba shes rab kyi rnam bshad ṭik chen rigs pa'i rgya mtsho. Collected Works. Vol. ba, 1–583.

Lama Tsongkhapa (1357d–1419) Illuminating the Intent: A Thorough Exposition of Entering the Middle Way. Dbu ma la 'jug pa'i rnam bshad dgongs pa rab gsal. Collected Works. Vol. ma, 1–605.

Lama Tsongkhapa (1357e–1419) Golden Rosary of Excellent Utterances: Extensive Exposition of "Ornament of Realization" As Well As Its Commentary (Shes rab kyi pha rol du phyin pa mngon par rtogs pa'i rgyan 'grel pa dang bcas pa rgyas par bshad pa legs bshad gser gyi phreng ba). Collected Works. Vols. tsa and tsha.

Lama Tsongkhapa (1357f–1419) Essence of True Eloquence: Distinguishing the Provisional and the Definitive Meaning (Drang ba dang nges pa'i don rnam par 'byed pa legs bshad snying po). Collected Works. Vol. pha, 441–687.

[6] As compiled in Thubten Jinpa (2019)

[7] Lama Tsongkhapa (1357–1419). Collected Works of the Incomparable Lord Tsongkhapa Lobsang Drakpa. Kumbum woodblock edition.

Lama Tsongkhapa (1357g–1419) In Praise of the Buddha for His Teaching of Dependent Origination. Ston pa la rten cing 'brel bar byung bar gsungs pa las brtsams te bstod pa legs bshad snying po. Portland, OR: The Foundation for the Preservation of the Mahayana Tradition (FPMT).

Lama Tsongkhapa (1357h–1419) Songs of Experience. Lam rim nyams mgur. Portland, OR: The Foundation for the Preservation of the Mahayana Tradition (FPMT).

Lemaitre G (1931) The beginning of the world from the point of view of quantum theory. Nature 127 (3210): 706.

Lenton TM, Held H, Kriegler E, Hall JW, Lucht W, Rahmstorf S, Schellnhuber HJ (2008) Tipping elements in the earth's climate system. Proceedings of National Academy of Sciences 105: 1786–1793.

Le Treut H, Somerville R, Cubasch U, Ding Y, Mauritzen C, Mokssit A, et al. (2007) Historical overview of climate change. In: Solomon S, Qin D, Manning M, Chen Z, Marquis M, Averyt KB, Tignor M, Miller HL (eds.), Climate Change 2007: The Physical Science Basis. Contribution of Working Group I to the Fourth Assessment Report of the Intergovernmental Panel on Climate Change. Cambridge University Press, Cambridge.

Maitreya (4th century). Ornament of Realizations. Abhisamayālaṃkāra. Mngon rtogs rgyan. Toh 3786, shes phyin ka.

Maitreya (4th century). Ornament of the Scriptures of the Great Vehicle. Mahayanasutralamkara. Mdo sde rgyan. Toh 4020.

Maitreya (4th century). Differentiating between the Middle and Extremes. Madhyantavibhaga. dBus mtha rnam 'byed. Toh 4021.

Milarepa (1052–1135) The Hundred Thousand Songs of Milarepa: A New Translation (translated by Stagg C, 2017. Boulder, CO: Shambhala).

Nagarjuna (2nd century). Commentary on Bodhicitta. Bodhicittavivaraṇa. Byang chub sems kyi 'grel pa. Toh 1801, rgyud 'grel ngi.

Nagarjuna (2nd century). Fundamental Wisdom on the Middle Way. Mūlamadhyamakakārikā. Dbu ma rtsa ba'i tshig le'ur byas pa (Rtsa ba'i shes rab). Toh 3824, dbu ma tsa.

Nagarjuna (2nd century). Seventy Stanzas on Emptiness. Śūnyatāsaptatikārikā. Stong nyid bdun cu pa. Toh 3827, dbu ma tsa.

Nagarjuna (2nd century). Sixty Stanzas of Reasoning. Yuktiṣaṣṭikākārikā. Rigs pa drug cu pa. Toh 3825, dbu ma tsa.

Nakamoto S (2008) Bitcoin: a Peer-to-Peer electronic cash system. Available at https://bitcoin.org/bitcoin.pdf. Accessed May 5 2018

National Institutes of Health (NIH) (2009) NIH Guidelines for Human Stem Cell Research. Bethesda, MD: The NIH.

New York Times (2023a) Microsoft says new A.I. shows signs of human reasoning. Published on May 16, 2023.

New York Times (2023b) The Times Sues OpenAI and Microsoft Over A.I. Use of Copyrighted Work. Published on December 27, 2023. Accessed from https://www.nytimes.com/2023/12/27/business/media/new-york-times-open-ai-microsoft-lawsuit.html

Nobel Prize (2012). The Nobel Prize in Physiology or Medicine 2012 was awarded jointly to Sir John B. Gurdon and Shinya Yamanaka“ "for the discovery that mature cells can be reprogrammed to become pluripotent” " Accessed from https://www.nobelprize.org/prizes/medicine/2012/summary/

Nobel Prize (2023). The Nobel Prize in Physiology or Medicine 2023: Katalin Karikó and Drew Weissman“for their discoveries concerning nucleoside base modifications that enabled the development of effective mRNA vaccines against COVID-19” Accessed from https://www.nobelprize.org/prizes/medicine/2023/summary/

Nordhaus WD (2008) A Question Of Balance-Weighing The Options On Global Warming Policies. Yale University Press, New Haven, CT.

OpenAI (2023) Introducing ChatGPT. Accessed from https://openai.com/blog/chatgpt

Pakkenberg B, Gundersen HJG (1997) Neocortical neuron number in humans: Effect of sex and age. Journal of Comparative Neurology 384: 312–320.

Pardi N, Hogan MJ, Porter FW, and Weissman D (2018) mRNA vaccines – A New Era in Vaccinology. Nature Reviews Drug Discovery 17: 261–279.

Plotkin SA (2009) Vaccines: the fourth century. Clinical and Vaccine Immunology 16: 1709–1719.

Poincaré H (1880–1890) Mémoire sur les Courbes Définies par les Équations Différentielles I-VI, Oeuvre I. Gauthier-Villars, Paris.

Polyakova M, Udalova V, Kocks G, Genadek K, Finlay K, and Finkelstein A (2021) Racial Disparities in Excess All-Cause Mortality During the Early COVID-19 Pandemic Varied Substantially Across States. Health Affairs, 40 (2). https://doi.org/10.1377/hlthaff.2020.02142.

Potter CW (2001) A history of influenza. Journal of Applied Microbiology 91(4): 572–579.

Purves D, Augustine GJ, Fitzpatrick D, Hall WC, LaMantia A-S, White LE (Editors) (2011) Neuroscience (5th edition). Sunderland, MA: Sinauer Associates.

Quadrato G, Nguyen T, Macosko EZ, Sherwood JL, Yang SM, Berger DR, Maria N, Scholvin J, Goldman M, Kinney JP, Boyden ES, Lichtman JW, Williams ZM, McCarroll SA, and Arlotta P (2017) Cell diversity and network dynamics in photosensitive human brain organoids. Nature 545: 48–53.

Reardon S (2020) Can lab-grown brains become conscious? Nature. Published on October 27, 2020.

Reuters (2021) Former CDC chief Redfield says he thinks COVID-19 originated in a Chinese lab. Published on March 27, 2021. Accessed from https://www.reuters.com/article/us-health-coronavirus-origin-redfield-idUSKBN2BI2R6.

Schuster EF (1984) Classification of probability laws by tail behavior. Journal of the American Statistical Association 79 (388), 936–939.

Schwartz M (2001) The life and works of Louis Pasteur. Journal of Applied Microbiology. 91 (4): 597–601.

Seo SN (2018) Mathematical Foundations of Catastrophe and Chaos Theories and Their Applications. In: Seo SN (2018) Natural and Man-made Catastrophes: Theories, Economics, and Policy Designs. Hoboken, NJ: Wiley-Blackwell.

Seo SN (2019) The Economics of Global Allocations of the Green Climate Fund: An Assessment from Four Scientific Traditions of Modeling Adaptation Strategies. Cham, CH: Springer.

Seo SN (2020) The Economics of Globally Shared and Public Goods. Amsterdam, NL: Academic Press.

Seo SN (2021) Climate Change and Economics: Engaging with Future Generations with Action Plans. London, UK: Palgrave Macmillan.

Seo SN (2022a) The Economics of Pandemics: Exploring Globally Shared Experiences. London, UK: Palgrave Macmillan.

Seo SN (2022b) Introduction to Handbook of Behavioral Economics and Climate Change. In: Seo SN (2023) Handbook of Behavioral Economics and Climate Change. Cheltenham, UK: Edward Elgar.

Seo SN (2024a) Buddha, Wisdom and Economics: A Contribution to the Art of Happiness. Cheltenham, UK: Edward Elgar.

Seo SN (2024b) Protecting Nature with Buddha's Wisdom: A Contribution to Environmental and Nature Studies. Cheltenham, UK: Edward Elgar.

Shantarakṣita (9th century). Ornament of the Middle Way. Madhyamakālaṃkāra. Dbu ma rgyan. Toh 3884, dbu ma sa.

Shantideva (8th century). Guide to the Bodhisattva Way. Bodhicaryāvatāra. Byang chub sems dpa'i spyod pa la'jug pa. Toh 3871, dbu ma la.

Shiller RJ (2004) The New Financial Order: Risk in the 21st Century. Princeton University Press, Princeton, NJ.

Singer W (1999) Neuronal Synchrony: A Versatile Code for the Definition of Relations? Neuron 24: 49–65.

Soft Bank Robotics, 2019. Pepper. Soft Bank, Tokyo, Accessed from https://www.softbankrobotics.com/emea/en/pepper.

Stevens CF (1979) The neuron. Scientific American 241: 54–65.

Takahashi K, and Yamanaka S (2006). Induction of pluripotent stem cells from mouse embryonic and adult fibroblast cultures by defined factors. Cell 126(4): 663–676.

Tegmark M (2015) Consciousness as a State of Matter. Chaos, Solitons & Fractals 76: 238–270. arxiv.org/abs/1401.1219

Tesla (2023) AI & Robotics. Tesla, Austin, TX. Accessed from https://www.tesla.com/AI
The President Council on Bioethics (2002). Human Cloning and Human Dignity: An Ethical Inquiry. Washington, DC.
Thom R (1972) Stabilité Structurelle et Morphogenèse: Essai d'une Théorie Générale des Modèles. Benjamin, New York.
Thom R (1975) Structural Stability and Morphogenesis. Benjamin-Addison-Wesley, New York, NY.
Thomson JA, Itskovitz-Eldor J, Shapiro SS, Waknitz MA, Swiergiel JJ, Marshall VS, Jones JM (1998) Embryonic stem cell lines derived from human blastocysts. Science 282 (5391): 1145–1147.
Thubten Jinpa (2019) Tsongkhapa: A Buddha in the Land of Snows. Boston, MA: Shambala.
Thubten Jinpa (2021) Illuminating the Intent: An Exposition of Candrakirt's Entering the Middle Way. Wisdom Boston, MA: Wisdom Publications.
Tohoku University (ed.) (1934). A Complete Catalogue of the Tibetan Buddhist Canons, Sde-dge Edition, Tohoku University, Japan.
Trujillo CA, Gao R, Negraes PD, Gu J, Buchanan J, Preissl S, Wang A, Wu W, Haddad GG, Chaim IA, Domissy A, Vandenberghe M, Devor A, Yeo GW, Voytek B, and Muotri AR (2019) Complex oscillatory waves emerging from cortical organoids model early human brain network development. Cell Stem Cell 25, 558–569.
United States Department of Interior (USDOI) (2024) Re: U.S. Geological Survey (USGS) Freedom of Information Act (FOIA) Tracking # DOI-USGS-2023-000257 – Response. Washington, DC: US DOI.
Vasubandhu (ca. 4th century). Treasury of Abhidharma. Abhidharmakośa. Chos mngon pa mdzod. Toh 4089, mngon pa ku.
Vasubandhu (ca. 4th century). Principles of Elucidation. rNam bshad rigs pa. Vyakhyayukti. Toh 4061.
Vrselja Z, Stefano G. Daniele, John Silbereis, Francesca Talpo, Yury M. Morozov, André M. M. Sousa, Brian S. Tanaka, Mario Skarica, Mihovil Pletikos, Navjot Kaur, Zhen W. Zhuang, Zhao Liu, Rafeed Alkawadri, Albert J. Sinusas, Stephen R. Latham, Stephen G. Waxman & Nenad Sestan (2019) Restoration of brain circulation and cellular functions hours post-mortem. Nature 568: 336–343.
Wade N (2021) The origin of COVID: Did people or nature open Pandora's box at Wuhan? Bulletin of the Atomic Scientists. Published on May 5.
Walpola Rahula (1974) What the Buddha Taught: Revised and Expanded Edition with Texts from Suttas and Dhammapada. New York, NY: Grove Press.
Washington Post (2023) The war in Ukraine is spurring a revolution in drone warfare using AI. Published on July 26, 2023.
Watanabe, S (2005) Buddha Shakyamuni. Tokyo, JP: Chikumashobo.

Weiss SR (2020) Forty years with Coronaviruses. Journal of Experimental Medicine 217 (5): e20200537. https://doi.org/10.1084/jem.20200537

Weitzman ML (2009) On modeling and interpreting the economics of catastrophic climate change. The Review of Economics and Statistics 91 (1): 1–19.

Wikipedia (2024) Wikipedia: The Free Encyclopedia. Accessed from https://www.wikipedia.org/

Wonhyo (7th Century) Commentaries on the Awakening of Faith in the Mahayana. Mahāyānaśraddhotpādaśāstra. Taisho Tripitaka Vol. 44, No. 1844 & No. 1845.

World Health Organization (WHO) (2021) Press Conference on February 12th, 2021. The joint World Health Organization-China Mission to Investigate the Origins of COVID-19. Geneva, CH: WHO. Accessed from https://www.who.int/emergencies/diseases/novel-coronavirus-2019

YaleNews (2019) Scientists restore some functions in a pig's brain hours after death. Published on April 17, 2019. https://news.yale.edu/2019/04/17/scientists-restore-some-functions-pigs-brain-hours-after-death

Appendix A: A Brief Introduction to Scriptures of Buddhism with Bibliography

There are three canonical collections of Buddhism, each of which contains a 'complete' set of scriptures:

1. *Tipitaka*, The Pali Canon: Historically, the first one is the Pali Canon which is called the Tipitaka, namely, the Three Baskets.
2. *Dazangjing*, The Chinse Buddhist Canon: The second one to be completed is the Chinese Canon whose distinct woodblock xylograph editions were carved in China, Korea, and Japan.[1] This monumental work was completed by such illustrious figures as Kumarajiva (fourth century) and Xuanzang (seventh century) for nearly six centuries. The first complete woodblock xylograph edition was published in 983, known as Kaibao Canon.[2]
3. *Kangyur* and *Tengyur*, The Tibetan Canon: The third in historical order, but the most comprehensive one is the Tibetan Canon which

[1] Taishō Shinshū Daizōkyō. The SAT Daizōkyō Text Database. Tokyo, Japan: University of Tokyo.

[2] Choi BH (2017) Historical Characteristics of East Asian Buddhism. Beopbosinmun. Seoul, ROK.

S. N. Seo, *The Economics of Singularities of Science Elucidated with Buddhist Thoughts*,
https://doi.org/10.1007/978-3-031-69118-8

is composed of Kangyur and Tengyur. It contains more than 5250 texts. The Sde-Dge edition was completed during 1730–1770.[3]

The *Tipitaka* contains the scriptures belonging largely to the *Hinayana* (Hearers' Vehicle). The Chinese Canon and the Tibetan Canon contain the scriptures belonging to both the *Hinayana* and the *Mahayana* (Great Vehicle).

Tipitaka: The Pali Canon

The English translations of the Tipitaka texts are available at Access to Insight: Readings in Theravāda Buddhism. The Barr Center for Buddhist Studies, Barre, MA. Accessed from https://accesstoinsight.org/.

Abhidhamma Piṭaka. The Basket of Abhidhamma, Tipitaka. Access to Insight. Accessed from https://accesstoinsight.org/tipitaka/abhi/index.html

Anatta-lakkhana Sutta. The Discourse on the Not-self Characteristic. Samyuta Nikaya, Tipitaka.

Dhammacakkappavattana Sutta. Setting the Wheel of Dhamma in Motion. Sutta Pitaka, Tipitaka.

Dhammapada. The Dhammapada: The Sayings of the Buddha. Khuddaka Nikaya, Sutta Pitaka, Tipitaka.

Jataka. The Stories of the Buddha's Former Births. Khuddaka Nikaya, Sutta Pitaka, Tipitaka.

Kaccayanagotta Sutta. To Kaccayana Gotta (on Right View). Samyutta Nikaya, Sutta Pitaka, Tipitaka.

Magga-vibhanga Sutta. An Analysis of the Path. Samyutta Nikaya, Sutta Pitaka, Tipitaka.

Maha-nidana Sutta. The Great Causes Discourse. Digha Nikaya, Sutta Pitaka, Tipitaka.

Maha-parinibbana Sutta. Maha Parinibbana of the Buddha. Digha Nikaya, Sutta Pitaka, Tipitaka.

Maha-satipatthana Sutta. The Great Frames of Reference. Digha Nikaya, Sutta Pitaka, Tipitaka.

Nidana Sutta. Causes. Anguttara Nikaya, Sutta Pitaka, Tipitaka.

[3] The Tibetan and Himalayan Library (THL) (2009) The Tibetan Buddhist Canon. Accessed from https://www.thlib.org/encyclopedias/literary/canons/index.php

Paṭhamabodhisuttaṃ. Bodhi Sutta. Khuddaka Nikāya. Sutta Pitaka, Tipitaka.

Paticca-samuppada-vibhanga Sutta. Analysis of Dependent Co-arising. Samyutta Nikaya, Sutta Pitaka, Tipitaka.

Sutta Nipata. The Sutta-Nipata: The Sutta Collection. Khuddaka Nikaya, Sutta Pitaka, Tipitaka.

Vinaya Pitaka. The Book of the Discipline (6 volumes), Tipitaka. [Translated by I.B. Horner 1993. London: Pali Text Society]. Accessed from https://accesstoinsight.org/tipitaka/abhi/index.html

Kangyur and Tengyur: The Tibetan Canon

The references in this section are mostly from the Sde-Dge Edition of the Tibetan Canon which was completed between 1730s and 1770s.[4] *If you are interested in the full list of sutras, visit the Dege Parkhang website at http://www.degeparkhang.org/en/sutras/34.html.*

Adornment of Trees Sutra. Gaṇḍavyūhasūtra. Sdong po rgyan pa'i mdo. Toh[5] 44–45, phal chen ka; the final chapter (45th) of the Flower Ornament Sutra (Avatataṃsakasūtra).

Akasagarbha Sutra. Ākāśagarbhasūtra. Nam mkha'i snying po'i mdo. Toh 260, mdo sde za.

Ajātaśatru Sutra. Ajātaśatrukaukṛtyavinodanā. Ma skyes dgra'i 'gyod pa bsal ba. Toh 216, mdo sde tsha.

Āryamañjuśrīmūlakalpa. The Noble Root Manual of the Rites of Mañjuśrī. 'phags pa 'jam dpal gyi rtsa ba'i rgyud. Toh 543.

Avalokitesvara's Universal Gateway Sutra. Lotus Sutra (Chapter 25). Saddharmapuṇḍarīka. Dam pa'i chos pad ma dkar po. Toh 113, mdo sde ja.

Basis of Discipline. Vinayavastu. 'Dul ba gzhi. Toh 1, 'dul ba kha. [Chapters in English are available from the 84000 Reading Room at https://read.84000.co/section/O1JC114941JC11495.html]

Buddha Carita. Praise of Buddha's Acts. Buddhacarita.Saṅs-rgyas-kyi spyod-pa shes-bya-baḥi sñan-dṅags chen-po. Toh. 4156. Skyes rabs ge

Code of Monastic Discipline. Prātimoksa Sutra. So sor thar ba'i mdo. Toh 2, 'dul ba ca.

[4] Tohoku University (ed.) (1934). A Complete Catalogue of the Tibetan Buddhist Canons, Sde-dge Edition, Tohoku University, Japan.

[5] Toh=Tohoku University Catalogue

Compendium of Reality. Sarvatathdgatatattvasamgraha. De bzhin gshegs pa thams cad k y i de kho na n y id bsdus pa. Toh 479, rgyud 'bum nya.

Condensed Kalacakra Tantra. Paramädibuddhoddhrtasrikälacakra-näma-tantraräjä. Dus kyi 'khor lo. Toh 362, Rgyud hbum ka.

Densely Arrayed Sutra. Ghanavyūhasūtra (39th chapter of the Flower Ornament Sutra). Rgyan stug-po bkod-pa. Toh 110, mdo sde cha.

Descent into Lanka Sutra. Laṅkāvatārasūtra. Lang kar gshegs pa'i mdo. Toh 107, mdo sde ca.

Diamond Cutter Sutra. Vajracchedikā. Rdo rje gcod pa. Toh 16, shes phyin ka.

Discourse for Kāśyapa. Kāśyapaparivarta. 'Od srung gi le'u. Toh 87, dkon brtsegs cha.

Engaging in Accordance with the World Sutra. Lokānuvartasūtra. 'Jig rten gyi rjes su mthun par'jug pa. Toh 200, mdo sde tsa.

Entering the Two Truths Sutra. Saṃvṛtiparamārthasatyanirdeśasūtra. Bden pa gnyis la 'jug pa'i

mdo. Toh 179, mdo sde ma.

Flower Ornament Sutra. Avatamsaka Sutra. Sans rgyas phal po che shes bya ba sintu rgyas pa chen pohi mdo. Toh 44. phal chen ka.

Heap of Jewels Sutra. Ratnakuṭa. Dkon brtsegs. This is a collection of discourses comprising one section of the canon, Toh 45–93.

Infinite Life Sutra. Ārya Amitābhavyūha Sutra. Ḥod-dpag-med-kyi bkod-pa. Toh 49. Dkon brtsegs ka.

Jatakamala. Skyes phai rabs kyi rgyud. Toh. 4150. Skyes rabs hu.

King of Meditations Sutra. Samādhirājasūtra. Ting nge 'dzin rgyal po'i mdo. Toh 127, mdo sde da.

Kṣitigarbha's Fundamental Vows Sutra. Daśacakrakṣitigarbha sūtra. Ḥdus-pa chen-po-las saḥi-sñin-poḥi ḥkhor-lo bcu-pa. Toh 239. Mdo sde sha.

Maha Parinirvana Sutra. Mahāparinirvāṇasūtra. Yoṅs-su-mya-ṅan-las--ḥdas-pa chen-po. Toh. 119. Mdo sde na.

Medicine Buddha Sutra. Bhaiṣajyaguruvaiḍūryaprabhāsapūrvapraṇidhā naviśeṣavistara(sūtra). Hpags pa bcom-ldan-ḥdas sman-gyi bla bai-dūryaḥi ḥod-kyi sṅon-gyi smon-lam-gyi khyad-par rgyas-pa. Toh 504. Rgyud 'bum da.

Meeting of Father and Son Sutra. Pitāputrasamāgamanasūtra. Yab sras mjal ba'i mdo. Toh 60, dkon brtsegs nga.

Perfection of Wisdom Condensed Sutra. Heart Sutra. Prajñjāpāramitās aṃcayagāthā. Shes rab kyi pha rol du phyinpa bsdus pa. Toh 13, shes phyin ka.

Perfection of Wisdom in Seven Hundred Lines. Saptaśatikā prajñāpāramitā. Śes rab kyi pha rol tu phyin pa bdun brgya pa. Toh 90. Dkon brtsegs cha.

Perfection of Wisdom in Eighteen Thousand Lines. Aṣṭadaśasāhasrikāp rajñāpāramitā. Shes rab kyi pha rol tu phyin pa khri brgyad stong pa. Toh 10 Kangyur, shes phyin ka.

Perfection of Wisdom in One Hundred Thousand Lines (Mother Scripture). Śatasāhasrikāprajñāpāramitā. Phags pa shes rab kyi pha rol tu phyin pa stong phrag brgya pa. Toh 8.

Play in Full Sutra. Lalitavistara Sūtra. rgya cher rol pa. Toh 95. Mdo sde kha.

Pure Land Sura. Sukhavativyuha. Hphags pa bde ba can gyi bkod pa shes bya ba theg pa chen pohi mdo. Toh 115. Mdo sde ja.

Questions of Upāli. Upālipariprcchā. Nye bar 'khor gyis zhus pa. Toh 68, dkon brtsegs ca.

Questions of Maitreya. Maitreyapariprcchā. Byams pas zhus pa. Toh 85, dkon brtsegs cha.

Questions of Nāga King Anavatapta. Anavataptanāgarājapariprcchā. Ma dros pas zhus pa. Toh 156, mdo sde pha

Questions of the Nāga King Sāgara. Ārya sāgara nāga sutr pariprcchā nāma mahā yana sutra. 'phags pa klu'i rgyal po rgya mtshos zhus pa zhes bya ba theg pa chen po'i mdo. Toh 155, mdo sde pa.

Sublime Dharma of White Lotus Sutra. Saddharmapuṇḍarīka. Dam pa'i chos pad ma dkar po. Toh 113, mdo sde ja.

Sutra of the Collection of the Past Activities of the Buddha. Abhiniṣkramaṇa sūtra. Mnon par hbyun bai mdo. Toh 301/Taisho 190. Mdo sde sa.

Tathāgatagarbhasūtra. The Sūtra on the Tathāgata Essence. De-bshin-gśegs-paḥi sñiṅ-po. Toh. 258. Mdo sde za.

Tathāgataguhya Sūtra. The Sūtra on the Unfathomable Secrets of the Tathāgata. Tathāgatācintyaguhyanirdeśasūtra.

Teaching of Aksayamati Sutra. Akṣayamatinirdeśasūtra. Blo gros mi bzad pas bstan pa'i mdo. Toh 175, mdo sde ma.

Ten Grounds Sutra. Daśabhūmikasūtra. Sa bcu pa'i mdo. Avataṃsaka Sutra (Chapter 31). Toh 44, phal chen kha.

Ten Vows of the Bodhisattva Samantabhadra. Chapter 45 of Avatamsaka Sutra. Sans rgyas phal po che shes bya ba sintu rgyas pa chen pohi mdo. Toh 44. phal chen ka.

The Miraculous Play of Manjushri. Āryamañjuśrīvikrīḍitanāmamahāyān asūtra. phags pa 'jam dpal rnam par rol pa zhes bya ba theg pa chen po'i mdo. Toh 96. mdo sde kha.

The Tantra on the Origin of All Rites of Tārā, Mother of All the Tathāgatas. Sarvatathāgata mātṛtārāviśvakarma bhava tantranāma. Toh 726.

Unraveling the Intent Sutra. Saṃdhinirmocanasūtra. Dgongs pa nges par 'grel pa'i mdo. Toh 106 mdo sde ca.

Uttaratantra Shastra. The Treatise on the Ultimate Continuum of the Mahayana. Ratnagotravibhāga Mahāyānottaratantraśāstra. Theg-pa chen-po rgyud bla-maḥi bstan-bcos rnam-par bśad-pa. Toh 4024, sems tsam phi.

Vimalakirti Sutra. Vimalakīrti Nirdeśa Sūtra. Hphags pa dri ma med pa grags pas bstan pa shes by aba theg pa chen pohi mdo. Toh 176. Mdo sde ma.

Dazangjing (大藏經): Chinse Buddhist Canon

The complete Buddhist Canon in Chinese letters whose distinct woodblock xylograph editions were carved in China, Korea, and Japan.

Perfection of Wisdom Sutra Pronounced by Manjusri. Mañjuśrīparivartāparaparyāyā saptaśatikā prajñāpāramitā. Taisho Vol. 8 #232.[6]

Platform Sutra of the Sixth Patriarch. Tanjing. Attributed to Huineung (638-713), the Sixth Patriarch of Chan. The Dunhuang versions are the earliest versions discovered, which were dated to be from the ninth century. [Not included in Dazangjing, but discussed in the book]

Awakening of Faith in the Mahayana. Mahāyānaśraddhotpādaśāstra. Ta ch'eng ch'i hsin lun. Taisho #1666.

[6] Taisho=Taishō Shinshū Daizōkyō.

Appendix B: Essential Tibetan Words of Tibetan Buddhism

(Tables B1, B2, B3, B4, and B5)

S. N. Seo, *The Economics of Singularities of Science Elucidated with Buddhist Thoughts*,
https://doi.org/10.1007/978-3-031-69118-8

Table B1 Key persons of Tibetan Buddhism

	Tibetan	Pronounced as in English	Translated as in English
1	འོད་དཔག་མེད།	oe-pak-me	Amitabha Buddha
2	འཕགས་པ་ལྷ།	Pak-pa-ha	Aryadeva
3	ཐོགས་མེད།	Tok-me	Asangha
4	ཨ་ཏི་ཤ་ཇོ་བོ་རྗེ	Atisha Jo-w-je	Atisha
5	སྤྱན་རས་གཟིགས།	Chen-re-sik	Avalokiteshvara
6	ལེགས་ལྡན་འབྱེད།	Lek-den-je	Bhavaviveka
7	སངས་རྒྱས་བསྐྱངས།	Sang-gye-kyang	Buddhapalita
8	ཟླ་བ་གྲགས་པ།	Da-wa-drak-pa	Chandrakirti
9	ཆོས་ཀྱི་གྲགས་པ།	Choe-kyi-drak-pa	Dharmakirti
10	ཕྱོགས་ཀྱི་གླང་པོ།	Chok-kyi-lang-po	Dignaga
11	དགའ་ལྡན་ཁྲི་པ།	Ga-den-tri-pa	Gaden Tripa
12	གུ་རུ་རིན་པོ་ཆེ།	Gu-ru-rin-po-che	Guru Rinpoche
13	པདྨའི་ངང་ཚུལ།	Pedmei-ang-chul	Kamalasila
14	ཙོང་ཁ་པ།རྗེ་བླ་མ།རྗེ་རིན་པོ་ཆེ	Tsong-kha-pa|Je Lama|Je Rinpoche	Lama Tsongkhapa
15	བྱམས་པ།མི་ཕམ།	Jam-pa, Mi-pam	Maitreya
16	འཇམ་དཔལ་དབྱངས།	Jam-pel-yang	Manjushri
17	མི་ལ་རས་པ།	Mi-la-re-pa	Milarepa
18	ཀླུ་སྒྲུབ།	Lu-drup	Nagarjuna
19	ནཱ་རོ་པ།	Na-ro-pa	Naropa
20	ཀུན་ཏུ་བཟང་པོ།	Kun-du-sang-po	Samantabhadra
21	ཤཱ་ཀྱ་ཐུབ་པ།	Shakya-tub-pa	Shakyamuni Buddha
22	ཞི་བ་འཚོ།	Shi-wa-cho	Shantaraksita
23	ཞི་བ་ལྷ།	Si-wa-ha	Shantideva
24	སྲོང་བཙན་སྒམ་པོ།	Song-chen-gam-po	Songchen Gampo
25	ཐོན་མི་སམ་བྷོ་ཊ།	Ton-mi-sam-bo-ta	Ton-mi-sam-bo-ta
26	ཁྲི་སྲོང་ལྡེ་བཙན།	Tri-song-de-chen	Trisong Detsen
27	དྲི་མེད་གྲགས་པ་	Dri-me-drak-pa	Vimalakirti
28	དབྱངས་ཅན་གྲུབ་པའི་རྡོ་རྗེ།	Yang-chen-drup-pai-do-je	Yangchen Druppai Dorje

Table B2 Key places of Tibet cited

	Tibetan	Pronounced as in English	Translated as in English
1	ཨ་མདོ།	Am-do	Amdo
2	སྦྲ་ནག།	Dra-nak	black tent
3	སྒར།	Gar	Camp, encampment
4	རྒྱ་ནག།	Gya-nak	China
5	ཞིང་པ།	Sing-pa	Farmer
6	དགའ་ལྡན་གླིང་།	Ga-den-ling	Ganden Monastery
7	རྩྭ་ཐང་།	Cha-tang	Grassland, grassy plain, meadow
8	སྤང་ལྗང	Pang-jang	Highland meadow
9	འབྲོག།	Drok	Highland pasture
10	ཕ་ཡུལ།	pa-yul	homeland, home town
11	རྒྱ་གར།	Gya-gar	India
12	ཇོ་ཁང་།	Jo-khang	Jokhang temple
13	ཁམས།	kham	Kham (region)
14	སྐུ་འབུམ།	Kum-bum	Kumbum Monastery
15	གངས་ཅན།	Gang-chen	Land of Snows
16	ལྷ་ས།	Ha-sa	Lhasa
17	ཁྲོམ།	Trom	Market
18	དགོན་པ།	Gon-pa	Monastery, temple
19	གངས་ཏི་སེ།	Gang-ti-se	Mt. Kailash
20	རི་རབ།	Ri-rab	Mt. Meru
21	འབྲོག་མི།	Drok-myi	Nomad
22	པོ་ཏ་ལ།	Po-ta-la	Potala Palace
23	ཇ་ཁང་།	Ja-kang	Tea house
24	སྟག་རྩེ།	Tak-je	Tiger Peak
25	ཙཱ་རི།དག་པ་ཤེལ་རི།	Tsa-ri or Dak-pa-shel-ri	Tsari mountain (Pure Crystal Mountain)
26	དགའ་ལྡན།	Ga-den	Tusita Heaven
27	དབུས་གཙང་།	Ue-tsang	Ue-tsang
28	གངས་རི་དཀར་པོ།	Gang-ryi-kar-po	White snow mountains
29	འོལ་ཁ།	Wol-ka	Wolkha Hermitage
30	ཡར་ཀླུང་གཙང་པོ།	Yar-lung-tsang-po	Yarlung Tsangpo River [Brahmaputra River]

Table B3 Key objects of Tibetan Buddhism

	Tibetan	Pronounced as in English	Translated as in English
1	དྲིལ་བུ།	Dril-bu	bell
2	ཁ་བཏགས།	Kha-tak	ceremonial scarf
3	འབྲུག་མོ	druk-mi	female sheep
4	ཉ།	Nya	fish
5	བྱ་ཁྱུང	ja-kyung	garuda; celestial eagle
6	མཆོག་ཤིང་ཆེན་མོ།	Chok-sing-chen-mo	Great Tree of Merit
7	ཞྭ་མོ།	Sha-mo	hat
8	པི་ཝང།	Pi-wang	Indian lute (guitar-like)
9	སེང་གེ།	Seng-ge	lion
10	པད་མ།	Ped-ma	lotus
11	དཀྱིལ་འཁོར།	Kyil-kor	Mandala
12	སྔགས།	ak	Mantra
13	མོག་མོག།	Mo-mo	Momo [Tibetan dumpling]
14	རླུང་རྟ།	Lung-ta	prayer flag
15	མ་ཎི་ཆོས་འཁོར།	Ma-ni-choe-kor	prayer wheel
16	ཕྲེང་བ།	Teng-wa	rosary, garland
17	མཆོད་རྟེན།	choe-ten	stupa
18	ཐང་ཀ།	Thang-ka	Thangka
19	སྒྲ་སྙན།	Drang-yen	Tibetan lute (guitar-like)
20	ཕྱུ་པ།	Choo-pa	Tibetan robe, clothing
21	རྩམ་པ།	Tsam-pa	Tsampa, Barley flour
22	རྡོ་རྗེ།	Dor-je	Vajra, Diamond, Thunderbolt
23	བྱ་རྒོད།	Ja-goe	vulture
24	གཡག་	Yak	Yak [Tibetan cattle]

Table B4 Key events of Tibetan Buddhism

	Tibetan	Pronounced as in English	Translated as in English
1	འཁྲབ་མཁན།	tap-ken	actor
2	སྐྱེས་སྐར།	Kae-kar	birthday
3	མར་མེ་སྟོན།	Mar-me-ton	butter lamp festival
4	ཚང་ས།	Tsang-sa	drinking gathering
5	ཆུ་ལེན།	Choo-len	fetching water
6	སྐོར་གཞས།	Gor-she	gorshey [Circle Dance]
7	སྨོན་ལམ་ཆེན་མོ།	Mon-lam-chen-mo	Great Prayer Festival
8	བླ་མ་མཆོད་པ།	La-ma-choe-pa	Guru Puja
9	ལོ་ཏོག།	Lo-tok	harvest festival
10	རྟ་རྒྱུགས།	Ta-gyuk	horse racing festival
11	དགའ་ལྡན་ལྔ་མཆོད།	Ga-den-nam-choe	Lama Tsongkhapa Parinirvana Day
12	ལོ་སར།	Lo-sar	Losar [New Year]
13	གཉེན་སྒྲིག།	Nyen-dik	marriage
14	གསོལ་འདེབས།	Sol-deb	prayer
15	ཕྱག་འཚལ་བ།	Chak-chel-wa	prostration
16	རབ་ཏུ་བྱུང་བ།	rab-tu-jung-wa	renunciation and ordination as a monk
17	ས་ག་ཟླ་བ།	Sa-ga-da-wa	Shakyamuni Buddha Celebration
18	གཞས་མ།	she-ma	singer
19	བྱ་གཏོར།	Ja-tor	sky burial
20	ཞོ་སྟོན།	Sho-ton	yogurt festival [shoton]

Table B5 Key concepts of Tibetan Buddhism

	Tibetan	Pronounced as in English	Translated as in English
1	ཧ་ཅང་ཐལ་བར་འགྱུར།	Ha-chang-tel-war-gyur	absurd consequence
2	ཉོན་མོངས།	nyon-mong	affliction
3	ཉོན་མོངས་ཅན་གྱི་མ་རིག་པ།	nyon-mong-can-gyi-ma-rik-	afflictive ignorance
4	ཀུན་གསལ།	Kun-sel	All-illuminating, All clearer
5	རྣམ་པར་རིག་པ།རང་རིག།	Nam-par-rik-pa, rang-rik	apperception
6	རང་རྒྱུད་ཀྱི་སྦྱོར་བ།	Rang-gyue-kyi-jor-wa	autonomous syllogism
7	སྲོག་ཤིང་	sok-shing	axle
8	བར་དོ།	bar-do	bardo, intermediate state
9	མཆོད་རྟེན།	Choe-ten	basis for worship, Stupa
10	བྱང་སེམས།	Jang-sem	bodhicitta
11	བྱང་ཆུབ་སེམས་དཔའ།རྒྱལ་སྲས།	Jang-chub-sem-pa, Gyel-se	Bodhisattva
12	སངས་རྒྱས།	Sang-gye	Buddha
13	སངས་རྒྱས་ཀྱི་རིགས།	Sang-gye-kyi-rik	Buddha nature
14	བཀའ་འགྱུར།	Kan-gyur	Buddha's teachings
15	བསྟན་འགྱུར།	Ten-gyur	Buddhist commentaries
16	ཞི་གནས།	Si-ne	calm abiding
17	དོས་གླ་	doe-la	carriage
18	ཤིང་རྟ་	shing-ta	chariot
19	བསམ་གཏན།	Sam-ten	concentration
20	རྣམ་ཤེས།	Nam-she	consciousness
21	ཐ་སྙད།ཀུན་རྫོབ།	Ta-nye, Kun-job	conventional
22	ཀུན་རྫོབ་བདེན་པ།	Kun-job-den-pa	Conventional Truth
23	འཁོར་བ།	Kor-wa	cycle of existence, Samsara
24	བརྩད་པ།	tse-pa	debate
25	སླུ་བ་	lu-wa	deceptive
26	ངེས་དོན།	Ye-don	definitive teaching
27	སྐུར་འདེབས།	Kur-deb	denigration
28	གཞན་གྱི་དབང་གི་ངོ་བོ་ཉིད	shen-gyi-wang	dependent nature
29	རྟེན་འབྲེལ་འབྱུང་བ།	Dren-drel-jung-wa	dependent origination
30	འདོད་ཆགས་	doe-chak	desire

(*continued*)

Table B5 (continued)

	Tibetan	Pronounced as in English	Translated as in English
31	འདོད་ཁམས	doe-kham	desire realm
32	རྡོ་རྗེ་ཤུགས་ལྡན།	Dor-je-shuk-den	Dharma Protector of Je Tsongkhapa
33	ཆོས་སྐྱོང་།	Choe-kyong	Dharmapala, Dharma Protector
34	སྒྲོལ་མ།	Dol-ma	Dolma, Tara
35	རྨི་ལམ་འདྲ་བ་	mi-lam-dra-wa	dream-like
36	རྣ་བའི་རྣམ་ཤེས།	Na-wai-nam-she	Ear consciousness
37	བརྩོན་འགྲུས།	Jon-drue	effort
38	ལུས་ཅན།	Lue-chen	embodied beings
39	སྟོང་པ་ཉིད།	Tong-pa-nyi	emptiness
40	མིག་གྱི་རྣམ་ཤེས།	Mik-gyi-nam-she	eye consciousness
41	བརྫུན་པ་	juen-pa	falsity
42	ཚོར་བ།	Chor-wa	feeling
43	ཕུང་པོ་ལྔ།	Pung-po-a	five aggregates
44	གཟུགས།	Sook	form
45	གཟུགས་ཁམས	sook-kham	form realm
46	གཟུགས་མེད་ཁམས	sook-me-kham	formless realm
47	འཕགས་པ་བདེན་པ་བཞི།	Pak-pa-den-si	Four Noble Truths
48	རྩ་བའི་རྣམ་ཤེས།	Za-wae-nam-she	fundamental consciousness
49	དྲི་ཟར།རོལ་མོ།	Di-sa, Rol-mo	Gandharva
50	སྦྱིན་པ།	Chin-pa	giving
51	ཞེ་སྡང་།	she-dang	hatred
52	སེམས་ཅན་དམྱལ་བ་	sem-chen-nyel-wa	hell beings
53	ཐེག་དམན།	Tek-men	Hinayana
54	ལྟེ་བ་	tae-wa	hub
55	ཡི་དགས་	yi-dak	hungry ghost
56	མ་རིག་པ།གཏི་མུག།	Ma-rik, Ti-muk	ignorance
57	གཏི་མུག	ti-muk	ignorance
58	སྒྱུ་མ་འདྲར།	Gyur-ma-dar	illusion-like
59	ཀུན་དུ་བརྟགས་པའི་ངོ་བོ་ཉིད	kun-du-tak-pa	imputed nature
60	དབང་པོ།བརྒྱ་བྱིན།	Wang-po, Gya-jin	Indra

(*continued*)

Table B5 (continued)

	Tibetan	Pronounced as in English	Translated as in English
61	བརྒྱ་བྱིན་གྱི་དྲ་བ།མིག་འཕྲུལ་ཅན།	Gya-jin-gyi-da-wa	Indra's Net
62	བརྗོད་མེད།	Joi-me	inexpressible
63	དྲང་དོན།	Drang-don	interpretable teaching
64	རང་བཞིན་གྱིས་གྲུབ་པ།	Rang-shin-gyi-drup-pa	intrinsic existence
65	ལས།ཕྲིན་ལས	le, Tin-le	karma
66	དལ་འབྱོར།	del-jor	leisure and opportunity (wealth)
67	རྣམ་ཐར་	nam-tar	liberation
68	དབུ་མ་པ།	Woo-ma-pa	Madhyamaka
69	ནག་པོ་ཆེན་པོ།	Nak-po-chen-po	Mahakala
70	ཐེག་ཆེན།	Tek-chen	Mahayana
71	འདུ་བྱེད།	Du-je	mental construction
72	སྤྲོས་པ	toe-pa	mental fabrication
73	ཐབས་ཤེས།	Tap-she	method and wisdom
74	སེམས།	Sem	mind
75	སེམས་བསྐྱེས།	Sem-kae	mind generation
76	སེམས་ཙམ།	Sem-zam	Mind-only, Cittamatra
77	སྨིག་རྒྱུ།	Mig-gyur	mirage
78	ཚུལ་ཁྲིམས།	Chool-tim	morality
79	ཀླུ།	Lu	Naga
80	ཀླུ་མོ།	Lu-mo	Nagini
81	དགག་བྱ།	Gak-ja	negatee
82	མྱ་ངན་འདས།	Nya-en-de	Nirvana
83	གཉིས་མེད།	Nyi-me	nondual
84	ཀུན་མཁྱེན	Kun-kyen	Omnisicent One
85	དཔལ་ལྡན་ལྷ་མོ།	Pel-den-ha-mo	Palden Hamo
86	རིགས་ལམ།	Rik-lam	path of reasoning
87	བཟོད་པ།	Soi-pa	patience
88	འདུ་ཤེས།	Du-she	perception
89	ཤེས་རབ་ཀྱི་ཕ་རོལ་ཏུ་ཕྱིན་པ།	She-rab-kyi-pa-rol-tu-chin-|	Perfection of Wisdom
90	ཡིད་དམ།	Yi-dam	personal sacred deity

(*continued*)

Table B5 (continued)

	Tibetan	Pronounced as in English	Translated as in English
91	དབུ་མ་ཐལ་འགྱུར་བ་	woo-ma-tel-gyu-wa	Prasangika Madhyamaka
92	བསླབ་བྱ།	Lab-ja	precepts
93	ཟབ་མོའི་ཐེག།	Tek-pa-sap-mo	Profound Vehicle
94	སྐྱེ་བ།	Kae-wa	rebirth
95	སྒྲོ་འདོགས།	Dro-dok	reification
96	སྤྲུལ་སྐུ།	Tuk-ku	reincarnated lama
97	ལྷག་བསམ།	Hak-sam	resolute intention
98	ཐུགས་དམ།	Took-dam	Samaya, spiritual pledge, meditation
99	དགེ་འདུན།	Ge-duen	Sangha
100	བདག་མེད།	Dak-me	selflessness
101	སེམས་ཅན།	Sem-chen	sentient beings
102	དབྱུག་མདའ་	jook-da	shaft
103	ཕ་རོལ་ཕྱིན་དྲུག།	Pa-rol-chin-duk	six paramitas
104	གྲོ་བ་རིགས་དྲུག།	Do-wa-rik-druk	six realms of existence
105	དབང་པོ་དྲུག།	Wang-po-druk	six senses
106	ཐབས་མཁས།	Tap-ke	skillful means
107	ལྷག་མཐོང་།	Hak-tong	special insight
108	རྩིབས་ཤིང་	chip-shing	spoke
109	དེ་ཉིད་	de-nyi	suchness, reality
110	དབུ་མ་རང་རྒྱུད་པ་	woo-ma-rang-gyue-pa	Svatantrika Madhyamaka
111	སྐྱབས་སུ་འགྲོ་བ།	Kyab-su-do-wa	taking refuge
112	དགེ་རྒན།	Ge-gen	Teacher
113	ཚུ་རོལ།	Choo-rol	This side (cyclic existence)
114	དཀོན་མཆོག་གསུམ།	Kon-chok-sum	Three Jewels
115	ངོ་བོ་ཉིད་གསུམ་	o-o-nyi-sum	three natures
116	དུག་གསུམ།	duk-sum	three poisonous minds
117	ཁམས་གསུམ་	kham-sum	three realms
118	ཐེག་པ་གསུམ།	Tek-pa-sum	three vehicles
119	ལེགས་བཤད་ཉིང་པོ།	Lek-she-ning-po	true Eloquence
120	བདེན་པ་	den-pa	truth

(continued)

Table B5 (continued)

	Tibetan	Pronounced as in English	Translated as in English
121	འགོག་བདེན།	Gok-den	Truth of cessation
122	སྡུག་བསྔལ་བདེན་པ།	Duk-yel-den-pa	Truth of suffering
123	ཡོངས་སུ་གྲུབ་པའི་ངོ་བོ་ཉིད	yong-su-drub-pa	ultimate nature
124	དོན་དམ་བདེན་པ།	Don-dam-den-pa	Ultimate Truth
125	ཟུང་འབྲེལ།	Sung-del	union
126	རྡོ་རྗེ་ཐེག་པ།	Dor-je-tek-pa	Vajrayana
127	ཚད་མ།	Che-ma	valid cognition
128	རྣམ་སྣང་།	Nam-nang	Virochana
129	འཁོར་ལོ་	kor-lo	wheel
130	འཁོར་བའི་འཁོར་ལོ	kor-wai-kor-lo	wheel of cyclic existence
131	ཆོས་ཀྱི་འཁོར་ལོ།	Choe-kyi-kor-lo	Wheel of Dharma
132	ཤེས་རབ།	She-rab	wisdom
133	ཡིད་བཞིན་ནོར་བུ།	Yi-shin-nor-bu	wish-fulfilling Jewel
134	གཤིན་རྗེ་གཤེད།	Sin-je-she	Yamantaka, VajraBhairava
135	རྣལ་འབྱོར།	Nel-jor	Yoga; Yogi
136	རྣལ་འབྱོར་སྤྱོད་པ།	Nel-jor-joi-pa	Yogacara
137	རྣལ་འབྱོར་མ།	Nel-jor-ma	Yogini
138	གཉའ་ཤིང་	nya-shing	yoke

Index[1]

[1] Note: Page numbers followed by 'n' refer to notes.

S. N. Seo, *The Economics of Singularities of Science Elucidated with Buddhist Thoughts*,
https://doi.org/10.1007/978-3-031-69118-8

J

K

L

M

N

The manufacturer's authorised representative in the EU is Springer Nature Customer Service Centre GmbH, Europaplatz 3, 69115 Heidelberg, Germany. If you have any concerns regarding our products, please contact ProductSafety@springernature.com

Printed and bound by CPI Group (UK) Ltd, Croydon, CR0 4YY
01/10/2026
02225912-0003